ut until the
IVE

The Protestant Dilemma

OTHER BOOKS BY

DR. CARL F. H. HENRY

Remaking the Modern Mind
The Uneasy Conscience of Modern Fundamentalism
Notes on the Doctrine of God

The Protestant Dilemma

An Analysis of the Current Impasse
in Theology

by

Carl F. H. Henry, M. A., Th.D.

Professor of Philosophy of Religion,
Fuller Theological Seminary, Pasadena, California

WM. B. EERDMANS PUBLISHING COMPANY
Grand Rapids   1949   Michigan

TO THE MEMORY

of one of my teachers

DR. HENRY C. THIESSEN

in the year of whose departure
these pages were commenced

Foreword

The works of Professor Carl F. H. Henry are too well known for this one to need an introduction. It is a pleasure, however, to testify that one has tasted this vintage and found it good. In the last generation Western thinking has changed from confidence in, to despair of, man. Nowhere else have we found this remarkable change so vigorously focussed. The kaleidoscopic world of current theology is here delineated and the path of Biblical truth marked with wisdom and sobriety.

Standing at the cross-roads of the twentieth century, Dr. Henry gives a clear picture of the changing estimates of man, of sin, of the Bible, and of Jesus Christ. These studies reveal the author's familiarity with current theological thought and provide a sound basis for evaluating this thought, namely the Biblical faith. I know of no other such comprehensive presentation of the current theological situation. Among the treasures that linger in the memory are the New Testament study on the Word of God and the insight that the Christian pathway of faith has always pursued a "Christological course."

Martin Niemoeller has said that no two theologians agree in every detail, and much less can exact accord be expected in every judgment made. In a situation changing as rapidly as this, it is easy to take a man's earlier statements as his present views and easier still to differ in our respective evaluations of these views. In an earnest endeavor to represent fully and fairly those whom he cites, Dr. Henry has given large space to direct quotations, and has sought carefully to give the true laminations of their several writings.

The thoughtful reader finds here rich food for his meditation, for his classroom discussion, and for his pulpit ministrations.

WILLIAM CHILDS ROBINSON

Professor of Historical Theology, Columbia Theological Seminary.

Decatur, Georgia

Preface

With a fervor almost religious, modern man pursued the naturalistic pathway, suddenly to discover that the great convictions which shaped the culture of the western world could not long survive on such a trek.

Our generation has been one of philosophical no less than of sociological upset. Both modern empires and ideological shrines have fallen; totalitarianisms political and conceptual have capitulated.

Much that is distinctive in western culture, as it goes down in death, has its indestructible roots in the Hebrew-Christian tradition. The culture perishes, but an organism of unique convictions and values survives. This residual organism, however, is not nurtured so as to guarantee a vigorous continuance. For, just as contemporary man saw quite instinctively that supernaturalistic metaphysics was an incompatible companion for Naturalism, so he has come to discern that supernaturalistic ideals cannot be wedded to naturalistic dogmas. Hence, sooner or later the divorce and ruin now conspicuous in the disintegration of the Occidental outlook will rise up to haunt the cultivation of such blind romance.

But precisely what is worthy of retention in our heritage, and how can it be retained? These are the momentous problems of this critical hour, and to them are given different answers by such imperialisms as Roman Catholicism, Russian Communism, and Islamism, as well as by competitive traditions, such as religious Humanism, classical Liberalism, and Neo-supernaturalism.

9

The higher mood is tracing its steps back to the factors which lifted the world out of paganism, and which accounted for the vast difference between the Occidental and the Oriental worlds. At the center of those factors stands Jesus Christ. And He stands at the center of a great redemptive movement, the Hebrew-Christian tradition. Cherished by that movement is a written record with a unique view of God, of man, of the world, of history.

Are the modern compromises of the historic Christian convictions adequate to nurture the ideals drawn from Biblical sources? Furthermore, are not those ideals, themselves so often compromised or recast by contemporary man, a clarion call to restudy the original context of our inheritance? Certain it is that, without a sufficient source of vitality, the higher ideals of the western world are bound to wither and die, for all the moral and spiritual optimism of the philosophic traditions.

So then, it is not so much Christianity, as we ourselves, at the cross-roads. Christianity is at a cross-roads only in an accommodated sense. What vigor it possesses in our generation and the coming era may well depend upon the decisions which grow out of the present interlude of uncertainty. Ultimately, it goes without saying for those who stand within the Christian movement, the triumph of the Man of Galilee is assured; the final chapter of history is not in human hands.

Yet, whether history retains meaning and whether life retains significance in our day may well depend upon the momentous times through which we are now passing. The view which the mid-twentieth century man takes of God, of man, and of sin and redemption, will in the last analysis color his view of everything else. That is what makes the questions of revelation, and of sin, and of Christology, so remarkably contemporary. And that is precisely what creates of the present cultural stalemate an opportunity for a vigorous proclamation of the

Biblical *good tidings,* an opportunity unrivaled in church history even by the Reformation.

In the preparation of the manuscript, the author has had the helpful suggestions of numerous scholars to whom he wishes to acknowledge a debt, although the conclusions are his own. Among those who read the manuscript in whole or part, and offered comments of which a liberal use was made, were the author's brother-in-law, Dr. Thorwald Bender, of North American Baptist Seminary; Dr. Loraine Boettner of Washington, D. C.; Dr. Edgar Sheffield Brightman, of Boston University; Dr. Edward J. Carnell of Fuller Theological Seminary; Dr. Nels F. S. Ferré of Andover-Newton Theological Seminary; Dr. William Meuller of Southern Baptist Theological Seminary; Professor Bernard Ramm of the Bible Institute of Los Angeles; Dr. William Childs Robinson of Columbia Theological Seminary, who graciously consented to write the foreword; and Dr. Cornelius Van Til, of Westminster Theological Seminary.

Appreciation for permission to use the rather extended quotations by which the volume has been documented, is expressed to the publishers indicated in the footnote references.

CARL F. H. HENRY

Pasadena, California
Sept. 1, 1948

CONTENTS

THE MID-TWENTIETH CENTURY IMPASSE

I

The Mid-Twentieth Century Impasse

THE reversals which have befallen man in his tedious march through the vast uncertainties of human history have been many. None, however, has come with such a sense of unmitigated shock as the ideological upset of the past generation. Unlike the cultural upheavals of ancient and medieval times, which made their way by the gradual leavening of great multitudes, the contemporary crisis has set upon modern man with the quickness of apocalyptic doom. Our generation of two world wars has witnessed a reversal of ideas unprecedented in human history for suddenness, and surpassed on few occasions for significance.*

When Christianity appeared beneath oriental skies, it won converts by great numbers from the very first, but not until three whole centuries later, at the fall of Rome, which is usually regarded as the midnight of ancient Graeco-Roman civilization, could Christianity be referred to as the dominant ideology.

When the Renaissance mood arose on the European continent, many centuries intervened before the populace made decisions in a context other than that of the previous medieval Supernaturalism. While the twelfth century reveals a humanistic interest in the classics and an increasing concentration on the physical sciences, not until the beginning of the seventeenth century does modern philosophy actually get under way with its efforts to answer, on non-Biblical premises, the per-

---

*The first section of this chapter appeared in *The Philosophical Forum* (Boston University), Spring, 1948.

sistent problem of existence. The empirico-naturalistic approach
did not win the commitment of the masses until the nineteenth
century, and even then both Reformation Protestantism and
Roman Catholicism continued as vigorous competitors.

A. The Striking Modern Reversal of Ideas.

But the years 1914-1946 mark the midnight of modern culture,
compressed into a single generation. Almost in an hour—when
one thinks in terms of the history of cultures—modern man
has abandoned his accepted premises regarding man and the
totality of existence. Just as the sack and fall of Rome wrote
a bloody picture finish to ancient civilization, so it is apparent
that the plunder of Berlin and the atom-bombing of Hiroshima
are gigantic visual aids disclosing the corruption and judgment
of modern culture. Contemporary humanity, as a result of the
generation of two global wars, is involved in an unprecedentedly
swift and far-reaching reversal of ideology. The sun has set on
the distinctive premises of modern thought.

1. The Optimistic Tenets of the Past Generation.

Unbounded optimism ushered in the generation of two world
wars. Come the mid-twentieth century and surely its ideals
—an imminent Utopia, a world of health and peace and plenty—
would already be actual. Was not existence, as Spencer had
said, put together according to developmental laws whereby
ever higher and higher patterns *must* be realized?

a. The Inevitability of Progress.

The inevitability of progress charged the air. Those who
stressed some supercosmic *sine qua non* were dismissed good-
naturedly as antiquarians who had been unable to make a satisfactory adjustment to the thought-environment of evolutionary
science. True, once, in pre-scientific medievalism, men thought
that only spiritual alertness to the supernatural purpose of God
in history could guarantee a meaningful future, but mankind
in those distant days, mused the contemporary enthusiast, lacked
two cherished modern insights: that nature is an automatic

enigma-solving machine on the inside, and that scientifically enlightened humanity can direct nature from the outside. Modern man presupposed a cosmic guarantee of an imminent golden age. And where nature lagged behind, mankind could facilitate its advances.

b. *The Natural Perfectibility of Man.*

The perfectibility of man also was thought to be a necessary implication of evolutionary philosophy. The Biblical idea that man's nature includes a radical defect which inevitably undercuts the realization of his ideals and distorts his moral insights, was dismissed as unrealistic. Naturalistic evolutionists[1] countenanced no *super*-natural redemption, and most theistic evolutionists felt that the heightened divine immanentism of post-Hegelian, post-Darwinian thought implied not only a closer kinship between the human and the divine than the traditional theology[2] had done, but also discouraged the notion of a miraculous reversal of the natural self. Already at the turn of the century, William James reported the inroads which Liberalism was making into the traditional view of man:

> "The advance of liberalism, so-called, in Christianity, during the past fifty years, may fairly be called a victory of healthy-mindedness within the church over the morbidness with which the old hell-fire theology was more harmoniously related. We have now whole congregations whose preachers, far from magnifying our consciousness of sin, seem devoted rather to making little of it. They ignore, or even deny, eternal punishment, and insist on the dignity rather than on the depravity

1. Here, too, Herbert Spencer had encouraged the mood: "From the laws of life it must be concluded that unceasing social discipline will so mould human nature, that eventually sympathetic pleasures will be spontaneously pursued to the fullest extent advantageous to each and all. The scope of altruistic activities will not exceed the desire for altruistic satisfactions" (*Data of Ethics*, p. 250. New York: P. F. Collier and Son, 1905).

2. New England Transcendentalism on its neo-Hegelian flight, soared in climate uninfested by sin. Wrote Ralph Waldo Emerson: "Our young people are diseased with the theological problems of original sin, origin of evil, predestination and the like. These never presented a practical difficulty to any man — never darkened across any man's road, who did not go out of his way to seek them. These are the soul's mumps, and measles, and whooping-coughs" ("Spiritual Laws").

of man. They look at the continual preoccupation of the old-fashioned Christian with the salvation of his soul as something sickly and reprehensible rather than admirable; and a sanguine and 'muscular' attitude, which to our forefathers would have seemed purely heathen, has become in their eyes an ideal element of Christian character."[3]

Man was innately perfectible—the rise from barbarous brute to enlightened ethicist unquestionably foreshadowed his unilinear progression to the role of unerring messiah. Men were separated from Christ only by degree. A perfect society seemed obviously latent in the evolutionary process. Never in all history, it appeared, was there such a healthy-minded society, within reach of perfection, as that at the beginning of our generation.

c. *The All-Sufficiency of the Scientific Method.*

The scientific method was considered the main asset of modern man in outworking his temporary problems while a utopia-unwinding universe raised him to ever higher social status. No longer was man at the mercy of a universe which could frustrate his desires, for man was learning progressively to control nature. The Greek mood may have brooded over the resistance of matter, and the medieval mind may have fled for consolation to the miraculous, but the modern man had the empirical method and the scientific laboratory. The methodology of experiment and verification was to provide the solution for all pressing problems; it held forth the hope of freedom from the cruel mercy of nature.

The enthronement of scientific method involved numerous implications. For one thing, it struck vigorously at the notion of the miraculous, and fixed upon repeatable and experimentally verifiable events as the most important happenings; all else was identified with the disorderly, the disteleological, the

---

3. William James. *The Varieties of Religious Experience,* p. 89. New York: Longmans, Green and Co., 1902. Used by permission of Paul R. Reynolds and Son.

unmeaningful. Furthermore, the scientific method encouraged the conviction that nature is the ultimate real; the supernatural came to be viewed either as a projection of the emotional or irrational element in man, or as some mysterious fringe of the natural world which had not yet been brought within the scope of science. The major problems were assumed to be phenomenal, that is, of the sort which fall within the province of sensatio-inductive inquiry.[4]

Inevitable progress, human perfectibility, scientific method—these were the watchwords at the dawn of this generation, which in its own estimate, throbbed to Renaissance ideals which were presumed to be just within reach in a healthy-minded and healthy-bodied world.

2. The Reversing Effect of Global Warfare.

The came the two world wars, bringing with them a new appraisal of human affairs. The first war, to end war, was but the preliminary phase of the second. Were the entire population of the United States destroyed, the deaths would not be as numerous as those who perished by the violence, starvation, or disease which accompanied the wars of the past fifty years. Remarks one commentator,

> "The history of mankind for the last half century has been a history of deepening horror. . . . Ours is a sick age. . . . Western man has preoccupied himself with war as a continuing occupation."[5]

---

4. The mood of Naturalism is voiced for us by James Bissett Pratt: "The crystalline spheres, revolving in the one perfect motion, each presided over by a pure and mighty spirit, and all animated by love for God — was it not a noble and inspiring conception? . . . The music is gone now; so are the spheres; so is the comfort of the limited and shapely universe. So are the dominating spirits moving through their love for God. Instead, the uninhabited, purely material masses of matter, the crushingly unpicturable distances, the silence and the cold of the interstellar spaces. And the Kind Heavenly Father who created the world . . . for man to live in, who always answers the prayer of faith, and whose loving Providence intervenes miraculously to care for each of His children — where is He?" (*Naturalism*, pp. 44f. New Haven: Yale University Press, 1939).

5. Howard Mumford Jones, *Education and World Tragedy*, pp. 3, 5, 79. Cambridge, Massachusetts: Harvard University Press, 1946.

a. *The Inevitability of Disaster.*

Who today believes in the inevitability of progress? *The inevitability of disaster,* unless we travel a different road,—this expresses the mood of modern man at his mid-twentieth century crossroads.[6] We are told that the next ten or fifteen years are crucial, not for utopia but for survival. "The direction taken by western man in this period," writes Harvard's Dr. Howard Mumford Jones, "will probably determine his existence or disappearance within a century."[7] A turn in the road, or *the inevitability of disaster!*

b. *The Ineradicable Evil of Man.*

Who today believes in the essential goodness of man? It is "man in revolt", contemporary man in a desperate "predicament", modern man "always and inevitably a sinner", of whom we now read. The inescapable, *ineradicable evil of man!*—that is the thesis of up-to-date anthropology, which views the generation of two world wars as linked to antecedents continuous with all human history.

c. *The Need for Super-Scientific Method.*

Who today believes in the adequacy of the scientific method to answer all our problems?[8] It is no longer invading armies

---

6. Almost a decade before the second World War, Reinhold Niebuhr saw the handwriting on the wall, when he wrote that man's concern "for some centuries to come is not the creation of an ideal society in which there will be uncoerced and perfect peace and justice, but a society in which there will be enough justice, and in which coercion will be sufficiently nonviolent to prevent his common enterprise from issuing into complete disaster" (*Moral Man and Immoral Society*, p. 22, New York: Charles Scribner's Sons, 1932).

7. Jones, *op. cit.,* p. 41.

8. It is not a sufficient reply to say, *the humanists!* For the proposition that the scientific method is adequate to answer all of our problems is itself not derived from the scientific method and, if accepted, transcends that method at the very outset. There are, it is true, prominent philosophers and scientists who still trust implicitly that the scientific method will rid modern man of the menace of the atom bomb, but the prevailing mood appears now to involve an appeal to moral and spiritual factors which a naturalistic framework can hardly accomodate. Most alert thinkers are no longer certain that the scientific method is enough. Edmund W. Sinnot, director of the Sheffield Scientific School of Yale University declared in 1947 at its centennial celebration: "My plea is to push on in science with the utmost vigor and enthusiasm we possess but also to admit that there are many aspects of reality with which it evidently cannot deal, matters of the utmost moment to mankind if he is to build that Good Society which all of us in these dark days so ardently desire . . . I urge the recognition of this (other) avenue of truth and its diligent exploration" ("Science and the Whole Man," in *Mechanical Engineering,* Vol. 70, No. 2, Feb., 1948, p. 117).

which we fear, but a device of our own invention, a product of our much-vaunted method for discovery, an offspring of our laboratory technique: the atom bomb. Its use once more in warfare will revert vast reaches of the globe to the dark ages, and millions will perish before the world knows the device has been employed. The very method to which modern man looked for deliverance into utopia now has delivered him over to dire insecurity. If there be a next war, it shall *begin* with the atom bomb, and who can dream with what it shall end? Ours is a frightened age.

> "So far as the western world is concerned, it is possible to assume either that our culture is breaking up around us or that we are experiencing the pangs of a global revolution so vast, so profound, and perhaps so incomprehensible that men—even educated men—do not want to face it and to try to estimate its causes, its direction and its possible end. . . . Even in prosperous America men are afraid."[9]

Who today does not see that *the scientific method now has given us a monster so terrible that we all need to be saved from it?* No promise of deliverance lies in a weapon worse than the atomic bomb, for that can only multiply our predicament.[10] Who does not sense that the yearning heart of man today reaches for some power beyond nature, some method beyond the scientific, to govern the fickle human temper, lest in the conviction that nature alone speaks the last word, it be to atomic might that men tomorrow will resort in defining what is good and what is true?

The sun has set on the distinctive premises of modern thought. We stand today amidst the spiritual, moral and phi-

---

9. Jones, *op. cit.*, p. 41.

10. The Nagasaki and Hiroshima bombs were already obsolete when they were dropped; bombs fifty times as powerful are now in production. But they are not regarded as devastating as are chemical, biological and climatological weapons also in production — and not by Americans only — such as the highly infectious psittacosis virus, which can be manufactured cheaply in bulk in small laboratories, and a single milliter of which contains enough respiratory doses to kill twenty million men (see the article "Absolute Weapons," Nov., 1947, issue of *UN World*, in which is stated the only secure defense against such weapons: "There is no defense against absolute war, except to make itself obsolete.")

losophical collapse of western civilization—amidst a people aware
that "the darkness deepens" but without a spontaneous "Lord,
with me abide." There are those, assuredly, for whom the
present world events token little or no significant change in
viewpoint, as witness *An Unrepentant Liberal* and *Religious
Liberals Reply*. But the virtue of impenitence remains to be
judged on broader issues than that of human resolve, and the
defensive note in the liberal mood is in curious contrast to its
haughty lordship of yester-year. The five-letter word is as significant in today's "we are liberals *still*" as it was in a different
context during the first world war, when Rudolph Eucken asked,
Can We Still Be Christians?

Perhaps one may be forgiven for injecting a reference to a
philosophically-famous chicken (the mental projection of a
much-discussed philosopher) contrived to demonstrate that a
consistent Empiricism makes it impossible to predict the future
with any high degree of probability. The life of a chicken,
as a result of its accumulated experience, contains few memory
images so vivid as the periodic appearance of its master with
a generous handful of scratch feed or some of the other satisfy-
ing things of a fowl's existence. But when, on the basis of its
accumulated experience, the fowl has the most reason to expect
its caretaker to come with a hearty breakfast, on that very
morning he comes with a hatchet to perform a somewhat
indelicate operation on the chicken's neck. It may be suggested, if crudely, that to many a modern who at the beginning of this generation shared the distinctive Enlightenment
premises—automatic progress, human goodness, scientific uto-
pianism—it now seems almost as though in the war years 1914-
1946 the Master of history appeared with the axe of judgment,
to lay bare the perversion of overoptimistic modern man. Many
who looked yesterday for a bountiful millennium are concerned
mainly that tomorrow we shall avoid the lake of fire.

The sun has descended on the Renaissance ideals of the
Occidental world.

B. The Alternatives Competing for
Mid-Century Commitment:

The sun will rise tomorrow on a new set of premises. The fact that the pre-World War I ideology is now in discard is not in itself an occasion for rejoicing. Those now-abandoned premises were poor, but it is possible to replace them with something worse. The tensions which will result in the birth of a new world mind are now in action, but the mere exchange of one set of controlling ideas for another is hardly a justification for optimism.[11]

What alternatives are competing for commitment in this desperate hour when the survival of humanity and the meaningfulness of existence are at stake?

May it be that tomorrow's alternative to the inevitability of progress will be the impossibility of progress (in the form of a revival of the cycle theory of history, perhaps), or are we ready to affirm that progress rests upon specific spiritual conditions? Are we prepared to say that history is the lengthened shadow of what happens in a man's encounters with God? If so, are we willing to become intelligibly explicit about what we mean?

Or, as to the essential goodness of man, is tomorrow's option the essential animality of man? or the neo-supernaturalist notion of man being "always and inevitably" a sinner? or a saner anthropology, which refuses to make sin an inevitability of normal human nature, but nonetheless deals realistically with it, in contrast with smug and unrepentant Liberalism?

Or what will tomorrow's mood affirm about the scientific method, great in glory and awesome in power? Does its inadequacy mean the inadequacy of all method? Or does the new

11. In this connection, I recall an interesting note from Eugen Rosenstock-Huessy, commenting on my *Remaking the Modern Mind* (Grand Rapids: William B. Eerdmans Publishing Company, 1946), in which reference was made to Ralph Barton Perry's statement between the wars, that our so-called modern premises may "soon cease to be modern." Dr. Rosenstock-Huessy detects in Dr. Perry's mood "a light-heartedness which betrays the horrifying ease with which this kind of philosopher elopes to a next and next philosophy. The *meta-noia* of our mental institutions obviously will not come as long as the minds think that they can move as fast as weather vanes, simply by observing the signs of the times."

metaphysical thirst suggest the need for supplementing Empiricism? If so, by what? Philosophical methods are not better merely because they transcend the scientific. Even philosophic idealisms are legion, and have tensions all their own. Is it the revelational method, to which dialectical Neo-supernaturalism is now giving an irrationalistic turn, that will point the way? Or is the Hebrew-Christian tradition still, for all the modern tendency to reduce it to something else, the lamp unto our feet?

Tomorrow's sun will rise on another "definitive" modern view of reality. The movement to a new set of premises need not be an occasion for optimism.

1. *Implications of the Inadequacy of Scientific Method.*

The conviction of the inadequacy of scientific method might be differentiated in several directions,[12] in its implications for the rationale of the space-time universe.

A modification of the notion that only repeatable and experientially verifiable events exist within a pattern of the total uniformity of nature, has issued from Heisenberg's principle of indeterminacy, with its alertness to the unpredictable behaviour of nuclear phenomena. Physical science can no longer say *as science* that nature is absolutely uniform in its present behavior, any more than it could ever properly declare *as science* (even before Heisenberg's studies) that nature will be absolutely uniform in its future behavior, or that it must have been absolutely uniform in its past behavior. Such judgments about the course of nature are not scientific but philosophical; they reflect what the scientist *thinks* and not what he *sees*, and if they happen to be correct they are so not because they have been formulated by a scientist, but because a scien-

---

12. The topics of the inevitability of progress and the essential goodness of man are treated at length in *Remaking the Modern Mind*. Erich Frank has neatly summarized the contemporary predicament: "The development of modern philosophy i. e., empiricism) has led to the paradoxical result that in terms of his own philosophy modern man no longer understands himself" (*Philosophical Understanding and Religious Truth*, p. 152, New York: Oxford University Press, 1945).

tist, in stepping beyond the limits of scientific knowledge, has pronounced a judgment which conforms to super-scientific fact.

Once it is said that nature may not be totally uniform, several competing notions press into view. Perhaps nature is totally arbitrary and meaningless, so that the so-called laws of science are merely a humanly-imposed rationale. Or again, perhaps nature is to some extent a mathematical machine, and to some extent unpredictable, and irrational.

The compromise of the total-uniformity concept does not involve a necessary declaration, that is, for a Biblical view of nature. Or again, perhaps nature is a purposive realm, with both a moral and a rational reference, so that a supernatural God works out His ends, whether by uniformity or by miracle.

a. *Nature as Totally Incoherent.*

In point of fact, one of the most serious concerns is that some modern thinkers are flirting with the nihilistic alternative. As A. E. Taylor wrote,

> "I find it hard, and I am not alone in this, to avoid the conclusion that whether intentionally or not, some eminent exponents of the 'new physics' explain the 'principle of indeterminacy' in a way which distinctly implies that they mean by indeterminacy pure freakish haphazard and are in effect saying that the pattern of events is at bottom *incoherent*."[13]

Those who are caught up in this mood were often in the ranks of the opponents of a Biblical Supernaturalism on the ground that it involves an irruptive, order-upsetting notion of the universe. It now becomes evident that what they really objected to was not an incoherent nature so much as a coherent God.

It is true, of course, that the "laws of science" are not "discovered" so much as "chosen"; the scientist himself decides where, within the margin of variability, to settle for a formula. But that this means that science *imposes* whatever rationality

13. A. E. Taylor, *Does God Exist?*, p. 6, New York: The Macmillan Co., 1947.

there is in nature, rather than approximates it, cannot be sustained from an *a priori* insistence that nature is meaningless.

When we are confronted by an incoherent universe, in which man appears as a cosmic trick, a morality-concerned creature in a morality-indifferent context, we have an invitation to Skepticism and Nihilism. Such a view is a preface to an immoral existence.

b. *Nature as Partially Predictable, Partially Unpredictable.*
Another course—that of nature partially predictable and nature partially unpredictable—is taken by the emergent evolutionists, with their stress on both repetition and novelty. Here not a meaningless universe, but a natural world with an immanent purpose, is urged by naturalists like Samuel Alexander and Roy Wood Sellars. The concept of emergence, without any reference to a precedent Mind,[14] constitutes a baffling enigma, especially since it is precisely the appearance of new levels which is decisive for the upward movement of events. Actually, the emergent evolutionists have modified the total uniformity pattern by introducing once-for-all, unpredictable events, which is nothing other than a miracle[15] notion which cannot be identified in those terms because of the arbitrary rejection of an initial God. The theory, in an effort to find a non-theistic alternative to the total uniformity dogma, makes the total of reality—both predictable and unpredictable elements—doubly the subjects of confusion. In principle, this theory, by the introduction of genuine novelties at the strategic levels of the origin of life and of mind, is separated from a purposive Supernaturalism only by its naturalistic bias. What did the Hebrew-Christian tradition mean by miracle other

---

14. C. Lloyd Morgan is the classic representative of those who insisted that emergent evolution demands a divine mover, and who consequently formulated his system in terms of idealistic pantheism, rather than naturalism.

15. This is, of course, an oversimplification of the miraculous — which is never in Biblical theology reducible to sheer wonder or novelty or mutation, but involves the notion of "sign" or revelation.

From a certain standpoint, emergent evolution is theistic evolution working itself free of theism (the theory that from simple causes there arise complex effects was not at peace with the theory that from an initial infinite cause there arose less complex effects), and retaining the idea of miraculous gaps without the miracle-working God, so that the notion of emergent novelties, without a precedent Mind, appears.

than significant but unpredictable events in nature, except that here such events occurred in a divine purposive context rather than as order-upsetting enigmas.

c. *Nature as Providentially Ordered.*

The Biblical alternative, the view of a universe in which a deity works out His purposes both in the regularity of nature and in the miraculous, was the predominant view before science uncritically committed itself to the uniformity dogma. Early scientists saw no conflict between a detailed knowledge of the mathematical behavior of nature and the possibility of purposive novelty at strategic points. They did not regard total irregularity as the only logical alternative to total regularity, as did scientists at the beginning of our generation. Christian scientists subjected the mathematical to the moral.[16]

(1) *Philosophical Idealism and the Miraculous.*

In contemporary philosophy, however, the supernaturalists, or teleological idealists, are almost wholly precommitted to the anti-miraculous. This antipathy for the miraculous roots in the interaction of modern philosophies with dogmatic science, and also in the notion that, since on idealist premises the world is simply the externalization of the divine thoughts, it would be a reflection upon rather than a tribute to the divine ability to make room for miracles, or divine "after-thoughts"— for surely deity would comprehend all significant events in an original plan.[17] But is it not somewhat presumptuous for

16. The reader is referred to Taylor, *op. cit.*, pp. 1-7, for lucid suggestions along this line. Although he suggests that Christian thinkers learned from Greek philosophy "to think of God as supreme and perfect *intelligence*, and from the Hebrew Scriptures to conceive of Him as a supreme and wholly righteous *will*," Taylor concedes that the contrast "is in the main one of emphasis. The God of the Hebrews, of course, has knowledge, and a Greek deity has will. But for the Greek thinker the emphasis falls on knowledge . . . For the Hebrew it would be impossible to think of God apart from some 'mighty work' in the world of nature and history without a complete rupture with the national traditions" (pp. 1f.).

17. It has always seemed to me that Personalistic Idealists who follow Edgar Sheffield Brightman in his view of a finite God inconsistently rest their case against miracles on this ground. They set out with the notion of a finite, good God, in whose nature exists a "Given" over which He is progressively gaining control. Now, is it not conceivable that such a God should at some time after creation gain such a significant control over the Given that He *must*, if benevolent, work out new and previously impossible events in the world of nature? The finite God concept, in my opinion, undercuts the foundation for a dogmatic anti-miraculous approach.

modern philosophy to dictate what manner of plan deity, assuming there be such, shall adopt? Granted that if God were a twentieth-century scientist trained at Columbia University or the University of Chicago or California Institute of Technology, He would avoid the miraculous like the black plague, and declare rather for the irrational. But suppose God is God? Need one who swallows the camel and declares for supernatural *being* strain at a gnat by hesitating to affirm the *possibility* of supernatural *activity*? It is only in the modern supernaturalisms, in which God is granted either an inadequate transcendence or no transcendence at all, that one need be enmeshed in this difficulty.

(2) *Biblical Supernaturalism and the Miraculous.*

It is apparent, of course, that irregularities within the order of nature *as constituted,* such as the phenomena occupying the attention of the indeterminacy students, are not the equivalent of Biblical miracles. The Biblical miraculous involved the notion of a special exercise of purposive divine power,[18] without which the previously ordained order of nature was inviolate (though of course sustained by the divine immanence). But what the Heisenberg discoveries have done is to soften the modern dogma of absolute uniformity, and to bring once again to the horizon of visible alternates the Christian view,[19] the

---

18. The connection between miracles and revelation is coming in for renewed treatment in contemporary apologetics; cf. C. S. Lewis' *Miracles* (New York: The Macmillan Co., 1947); and Edward John Carnell's *An Introduction to Christian Apologetics* (Grand Rapids, William B. Eerdmans Publishing Co., 1948). Lewis claims that "Christian miracles have a much greater intrinsic probability in virtue of their organic connection with one another and with the whole structure of the religion which they exhibit" (*op cit.*, p. 160). Carnell defines miracle as "an extraordinary visible act of divine power, wrought through the efficient agency of the will of God, through secondary means, accompanied by valid covenantal revelation, and having as its final cause the vindication of the righteousness of the Triune God."

19. Even a dogmatic scientist ought to admit that, if there are irregularities in nature conceived non - theistically, there may be irregularities in nature conceived theistically. But the extent to which the uniformity dogma has permeated the old-line scientist is shown by his tendency to explain Heisenberg's phenomena as establishing not irregularity, but the inability of our instruments to measure the *regularity* presumed to be there. Such a view proves not the regularity of nature, but the fact that the old-line scientist unscientifically presupposes that nature *must* be wholly regular whether the scientific method validates this or not.

main features of which, such as the supernatural resurrection of Jesus Christ, were automatically dismissed at the turn of the century as holding only a mythological interest.[20] The contemporary mood reaches out for some view which, while not doing violence to the regularity of nature, offers some alternative to the dogma of absolute uniformity. It had better not dismiss too lightly that view to which modern science was committed, before it turned aside to follow the dangerous roadway of inviolable regularity.

2. The Breakdown of Empiricisms.

The stumbling-block for modern science was that the Christian view was dogmatic about a reality beyond nature, whereas modern empirical science came more and more reconciled to the notion that nature alone is real, that beyond nature there is simply more unidentified nature. The modern gods were simply some aspect of the space-time universe, no more. The atmosphere today, however, is surcharged with modifications of this insistence.

The decline of the Empiricisms is indicated, as Paul Schubert notes, by the appearance of various types of philosophical metaphysics:[21] Wieman's naturalistic Theism, Whitehead's Realism, Husserl's and Heidegger's existential philosophy, Barth's, Brunner's, and Niebuhr's variation of existential theology, the humanistic and Christian Neo-Thomisms. Side by side with these one may list personalistic Idealism, and also the new apologetic thrust by evangelical Protestantism.

a. The Option of Sensationalistic Pessimism.

Naturalism has conceded since ancient times, of course, that there is more to nature than is perceptible to the senses. Nature is a system, and deep within is composed of invisible things or events, as even Democritus knew. In principle, the door was

---

20. And, of course, still are, by those who hold to an antiquated Naturalism. Cf. Shirley Jackson Case, *The Origins of Christian Supernaturalism* (Chicago: The University of Chicago Press, 1946).

21. Paul Schubert, *The Journal of Bible and Religion*, "The Synoptic Gospels and Eschatology", August, 1946, p. 152.

here opened to a supersensible spiritual realm no less than to
a supersensible rational realm. But Naturalism characteristic-
ally has insisted that reality, however much more there may be
to it than is disclosed to the senses, is reducible to matter, or
rather in our times to non-mental and non-moral events. In
the world of scientific preoccupation, the supernatural seemed
only a projection, man being complex product of nature only,
and morals being simply a humanly-sanctioned device to guarantee survival.

The pessimistic group of Sensationalistic thinkers are prone
to declare, in view of the widely acknowledged inadequacy of
empirical methodology, that there is no method broad enough
to cover reality and man had better be reconciled as soon as
possible to his predicament as a freak monstrosity in a hostile
space-time environment. Within limits, doubtless, we can predict and even control nature, but let there be no doubt about
the limitations—for nature always gets the last word, and none
can be sure what it will be. To echo the much quoted words
from Bertrand Russell:

> "The life of Man is a long march through the night,
> surrounded by invisible foes, tortured by weariness and
> pain, towards a goal that few can hope to reach, and
> where none may tarry long."[22]

Doubtless this is sharper thinking than the speculative luxury
of many of the Rationalisms which, simply by the device of
philosophical projection, interweave their phenomenal uncertainty with postulated optimism, only to be rudely awakened
from such artful dodges by the stern demands of empirical
reality. Here too, without a sure ground of faith, the admission of the inadequacy of scientific method may be a broad
invitation to pessimism.

But, face to face with the destruction of our generation,
modern man cringes before the notion that morals have no

22, From "The Free Man's Worship,"

firmer rooting than this. The German war guilt trials were conducted with the inarticulated conviction that the Nazi leaders had committed crimes against humanity which were wrong from something more than a naturalistic standpoint. And, *confronted by the atom bomb, contemporary man does not want to believe that morals are merely servants of the self-preservation impulse,* that actions need no further justification than that they are necessary to survival. Modern man is restless to find a beyond-nature reference for the use of the atom missile. It is simply the vague conviction that such a reference exists which prevents the bomb from being used again at once except as men parry for a more opportune moment to use it. It is the metaphysical upreach alone which prevents modern man from the descent to despair.

The quest for solution, then, leads inevitably to the problem of a substitute for, or a supplement to, the scientific method, in formulating an adequate interpretation of reality. The eschatological hopes of the modern Empiricisms are now in collapse; it is all too evident that sensational Empiricism in rejecting Christianity made the fatal mistake of illegitimately retaining Biblical optimism about a future kingdom in which righteousness would prevail. The Hebrew-Christian certainty about the triumph of right was not simply an ingredient that would mix with any philosophy of human making. On almost every hand today we are being reminded of the inadequacy of the *scientific method* to cover the whole of reality.[23]

---

23. Doubtless there are still unrepentant empiricists who have not matured to the significance of 1914-46. Edwin McNeill Poteat in *Last Reprieve?* declares that the survival of Western civilization depends upon the discovery of objective and pragmatic moral laws under which man must come to live. He asserts that these laws should be discovered not by philosophers or theologians but by scientists: "Call together historian, anthropologist, sociologist, endocrinologist, psychiatrist, psychologist and physicist and commit to them the quest for a universal moral law" (p. 30. New York: Harper and Brothers, 1946). But this was precisely what precipitated the modern moral crisis, and hence is precisely the wrong course if contemporary man is to find deliverance. See Mortimer J. Adler's lucid address, "God and the Professors", in *Science, Philosophy and Religion, A Symposium,* pp. 120ff. (New York: Conference on Science, Philosophy and Religion, 1941).

b. *The Option of Philosophic Idealism.*

Even at the turn of the century before naturalistic Optimism had come to its judgment day, the absolute idealists (Josiah Royce, W. E. Hocking) and the personalistic idealists (Borden P. Bowne, succeeded by Edgar S. Brightman) were arguing from the existence of values to a spiritual, moral realm in terms of which the natural realm must be understood.[24] The shadow of Immanuel Kant, who had contended that human knowledge has no content beyond sense phenomena, hovered over the modern Idealisms, so that the argument for a superphysical realm customarily followed the postulation path; the existence of a personal God was held to be a necessary demand of the conscious moral nature of man. The Idealisms appealed also to the evidences of design and purpose, but everywhere the edge of the argument was blunted by the naturalists, who overexercised Occam's razor by whittling away every point of reference for design and purpose other than evolutionary process.

The modern upreach toward the world of supernature is now being differentiated in many directions. One hears of naturalistic Theisms which, simply because they are not genuine Theisms, obscure their naturalistic genealogy. But one hears also of Pantheisms, Panpsychisms, personalistic Idealisms, Existentialisms. There is, assuredly, a metaphysical urge in the latest philosophy: it is increasingly fashionable to reach beyond the natural realm. Not every Theism, however, will save significance for human existence; and a stopgap on the road to Nihilism, when once its inadequacy is exposed, will hurtle man twice-frustrated to the pit of meaninglessness. If the bias that nature alone is real proved the stumbling-block of modern philosophy, let us not forget that the bias that a supernatural realm also is real—if it distorts the supernatural—may be a delusion no less serious.

---

24. Cf. Edgar S. Brightman's famous essay on "An Empirical Approach to God," reprinted in Muelder and Sears' *The Development of American Philosophy*, pp. 510ff. (Boston: Houghton Mifflin Co., 1940).

The history of philosophy discloses many alternatives to Empiricism. The philosophic method, rather than the scientific method, is hurriedly offered as a general panacea for our crisis. Here, it is urged, is a method to deal with the supernatural as well as the natural realm, a means for doing justice to the spiritual and moral no less than to the physical.

Here one thinks spontaneously of Kant and Hegel, and before them of Plato and Aristotle.

But Kant and Hegel, for all their use of philosophic methodology, are in one way or another contributory sources to the irresolvable tensions of modern thought. Kant's major fault lay in the fact that his theory of knowledge gave the palm of victory to Empiricism, whereas Hegel's failure was involved in notion that man and the universe are parts of deity.

Plato and Aristotle avoided those fallacies, but they were not on that account free from other serious errors. By both thinkers, man's reason was viewed as part of the divine reason, so that the competency of man to solve his problems by education alone was assumed; as in much modern thought, the bridge between cognized values and volitional commitment is not carefully delineated.[25] Granted that classic Greek Idealism championed relatively high moral ideals, the truth remains that the multitudes were unable to realize them experientially; Greek civilization, and later Roman, crumbled with the dissipation of ancient moral fiber. By contrast, with even higher ethical norms insisting upon Godlikeness rather than a "golden mean", the early Christian community found in its spiritual reference the dynamic for achievement. The growing Christian churches towered head and shoulders above the moral level of the ancient pagan world. Biblical Theism proclaimed a higher moral demand than the non-Biblical religions and philosophies, for all their preoccupation with works, and nurtured the works which the "works religions" themselves were unable to effect.

---

25. This is a failure also of the Harvard report on *Education in a Free Society*.

The philosophic Idealisms, of whatever stamp, all must stand in reverence here. For Christianity offered itself not only as a resolution of the philosophic dilemma, but also as a solution of the moral dilemma of ancient times.

What the mid-twentieth century crisis demands most is a method with implications for both the philosophic and the moral failure of our age, a message with more self-evidence about it than the problematic postulations of the recent mind, a message with an authoritarian self-authentication not found in merely speculative gropings. Even when the rationalistic formulas appear inviting, the present world is weary of the human babel and cannot forget the similarly appealing alternatives have proved a pilgrimage to disillusionment. What modern man longs for in his deepest moments is some voice from beyond, some self-disclosure of the spiritual-moral sphere, some initiative which God—if there be a deity—shall take in the present plight of humanity's lostness.

A similar longing is found at a high point in Plato's *Republic*. The great Greek thinker, foreseeing that the prevailing moral instability would lead to the downfall of the nation, urges his contemporaries to become explicit about the spiritual-moral universe. Plato then proposes his outline for an ideal state, which will function with reference to an eternal good, and eternal truth, an eternal beauty. At this point a very practical question arises: how are the multitudes to be prevailed upon to undertake the change from the old order to the new? What compelling sanction can be appealed to, that the people will dedicate themselves to their proper roles?

Plato's answer is the "one royal lie."

> "Well then, I will speak, although I really know not how to look you in the face, or in what words to utter the audacious fiction, which I propose to communicate gradually, first to the rulers, then to the soldiers, and lastly to the people. They are to be told that their youth was a dream, and the education and training

which they received from us, an appearance only; in reality all that time they were being formed and fed in the womb of the earth, where they themselves and their arms and appurtenances were manufactured; when they were completed, the earth, their mother, sent them up; and so, their country being their mother and also their nurse, they are bound to advise her for good, and to defend her against attacks, and her citizens they are to regard as children of the earth and their own brothers. . . . There is more coming; I have only told you half. Citizens, we shall say to them in our tale, you are brothers, yet God has framed you differently. Some of you have the power to command . . . others . . . to be auxiliaries . . . others . . . to be husbandmen and craftsmen. . . . And God proclaims as a first principle to the rulers, and above all else, that there is nothing which they should so anxiously guard, or of which they are to be such good guardians, as of the purity of the race. . . .

"Such is the tale; is there any possibility of making our citizens believe in it?"[26]

For all its brilliance there is no more pathetic moment in Plato's *Republic*. For here Plato, who would have been the last to concede that an eternal spiritual-moral realm was merely a postulation of his own mind, would nonetheless ride the conviction into the hearts of the multitudes by anchoring it to mythology.

c. *The Option of Biblical Theism.*

The contrast with the Hebrew-Christian emphasis on God's self-disclosure to man could hardly be more poignant. For while formally agreeing in the great convictions that nature is not alone real, that man is not merely an animal, that morals are not merely artificial conventions—here are two great interpretations of reality—in two remarkably contrastive moods. And

---

26. Plato. *The Republic*, Bk. II, 415, (Jowett's translation).

the Platonic mood is the modern mood, unsure of some special self-disclosure by the supernatural to the natural world.

That is what makes so timely the Hebrew-Christian message offered to mankind as God's "one royal truth." One frequently finds in Fundamentalist literature the notation that the Old Testament contains 3,808 variations of the expression "Thus saith the Lord", and this fact has indeed a curious statistical interest. But the fact that God spoke uniquely at all—*even once*— that is the emphasis for which one looks in vain outside the Biblical tradition. It is never God over against man in the non-Biblical religions and philosophies, but rather it is God nowhere or everywhere. Never is room made for a *special* revelation, for a once-for-all divine disclosure—and that for the sufficient reason that God reserved His redemptive revelation for the Hebrews, among whom it culminated in Jesus Christ. It is the revelation method, the proclamation of God's self-disclosure in the written Word and in the living Word Christ Jesus, that alone can resolve the corrosive uncertainty of the confused mid-twentieth century mind. Not Hume and Comte, but Jesus. Not Kant and Hegel, but Jesus. Not Plato and Aristotle, but Jesus. For here is found at once the answer to the philosophic quest and the answer to the spiritual and moral quest; here straightway, as Justin Martyr suggested, a flame can be lit within men's souls.

It was at this point that the Neo-Supernaturalist movement, by a strategic attack, cut across the modern mood somewhat in the spirit of the Biblical tradition. Kant had dominated the modern philosophies—idealistic as well as naturalistic—by the insistence that man cannot know the superphenomenal because of the limits of human reason. The Neo-Supernaturalists declared that Kant was wrong. God speaks to man; He does not leave man to search Him out, nor abandon humanity to postulation. As Kierkegaard put it, God cracks the master whip in special revelation. The supernatural realm centers in a personal, holy God who discloses Himself and demands moral and spiritual decision.[27] Karl Barth and Emil Brunner drove home this insistence to liberal theologians, first on the European continent, and then in America. The war is a divine judgment, they shouted. But Naturalism has no categories of judgment when it measures history, the empiricists seemed to say. And Barth and Brunner shouted back, That is what is wrong; the sense of divine confrontation and judgment has gone out of modern history.

Here the Neo-Orthodox protest against both Neo-Thomism and liberal Protestantism formally took its stand, with Barth and Brunner carrying the banner for the cause of revelational priority. Etienne Gilson, the famed Thomist, wrote of *Reason and Revelation in the Middle Ages,* and Brunner penned his *Revelation and Reason.* As against Thomism, Brunner makes a conclusive case; the emphasis on natural theology tended to make Biblical revelation irrelevant rather than relevant. As against Protestant Liberalism, the case is also decisive; the modernist god was simply a composite of modern philosophers shouting in a loud if pious voice. But the Neo-Supernaturalist case for revelational priority is offered also as an alternative to the classic evangelical view, and this raises the question whether Barth and Brunner have fully escaped the influence of Rationalism in their return to revelation.

The theological tensions in the mid-twentieth century concern the whole gamut of world thought. But the pivot point of these tensions is the question of revelation. Still, if the relation of revelation and reason is a crucial concern, it is only because we are anxious that we escape error in our definition of man, for it the salvation of ourselves with which we

---

27. As W. P. Paterson remarked, "It is inconceivable that Isaiah or Paul, even if they could have studied the *Critique of Pure Reason,* would have admitted that they had been mistaken in supposing that their faculties could reach so far as the Divine Being, and could know His purposes of judgment and mercy" (*The Nature of Religion,* p. 163. New York: George H. Doran Co., n.d.).

are so eagerly occupied. And just as there is a new view of revelation, so, too, there is a new anthropology, identified in America for these past two decades with the name of Reinhold Niebuhr. How does this newer anthropology appear, when appraised from the Biblical viewpoint, and how effective does its revolt against the optimistic liberal view of man promise to be? Moreover, just as the subject of revelation has immediate implications for anthropology, so, too, it brings to renewed centrality the Man of Galilee, Jesus Christ. What is the place of Christology in the mid-century theological movement, which has effectively rescinded the modernist moratorium on the discussion of the central Figure of Christianity? How satisfactory is the appraisal, with which the higher strands of contemporary religious thought are coming to rest? And assuredly, the convictions reached in these areas—the central areas of theological interest, for they carry with them the answers to practically every other sphere of theology—will finally affect the role of evangelical Christianity in this perilous moment of world opportunity.

Such then are questions which press into view along with our modern recognition of the inadequacy of the scientific method. The alternatives, though they may not yet be apparent to thinking moderns, will come in the end to either a wholly irrational world or a purposive world embracing both regularity and miracle; to either a postulate superworld or a personal, ethical God who discloses Himself to man; to either some variety of the philosophic method, with its inability to give either certainty or moral dynamic, or the revelational message of God's redemptive provision for men in Jesus Christ. Basically, when once all the illegitimate halting-places are exhausted, the choice is between Nihilism and Revelationism.

THE MID-TWENTIETH CENTURY VIEW
OF REVELATION

II

The Mid-Twentieth Century View
of Revelation

THAT human knowledge of God is interlocked with the very notion of divine revelation has been an insistence of liberal no less than of the unreservedly evangelical theology of the past century. The whole theological impulse has shared a common interest in revelation. But the center of controversy is over the content of revelation—whether what matters is simply the natural data which theologians lump together in the field of "general revelation", or whether also a *special* divine disclosure is involved. If so, what is the precise nature thereof?

The theological pendulum in the mid-twentieth century has swung to a renewed insistence on the reality of special revelation, which is somehow to be marked off from general or universal revelation, and which is found in the Hebrew-Christian tradition. The tendency now is to seek not points of approximation between the Biblical and the non-Biblical religions, in terms of which both movements are to be explained, but rather to discern points of dissimilarity between the two movements, in terms of which the superiority of the Hebrew-Christian mood is seen.

The decline of western culture, signaled by the disintegration of Renaissance ideals, has placed in a more conspicuous

light the non-Renaissance roots[1] of the loftier cultural convictions of the Occidental world. Although western culture
could not by any means be identified as a Christian culture,
nonetheless it was inexplicable in its higher moods apart from
a reference to the Hebrew-Christian movement—to that unique
view of God which among the Hebrew peoples culminated in
the Christian conviction of the divine incarnation in Jesus
Christ. The historical events of the past generation have put
in new relief the series of "revelational acts" out of which issued
this distinctive view of God, of man, and of the world.

A. Supernatural Disclosure Precluded by Past-
Generation Bias of Evolutionary Naturalism.

The contemporary mood, then, is in revolt against the continuity patterns according to which all religious concepts were
explained in terms merely of human insight. There is little
favor, in the vocal and productive theological quarters, for
Julian Huxley's *Religion Without Revelation*,[2] or for Shirley
Jackson Case's *The Origins of Christian Supernaturalism*,[3] but
after all, such leftist views of revelational Theism were already
vigorously combatted by the higher liberals of the past genera-

---

1. "The awakening interest in theology represents one of the most heartening signs
of life in the field of Old Testament research and augurs well for the future. It
gives us real reason to believe that Biblical studies are actually far from coming to a
standstill. It is particularly re-assuring in an age when our Hebrew-Christian ideals
and beliefs are being attacked with ever growing bitterness, for only by such vitality
can we hope to maintain ourselves in the ideological struggles into which man now
appears to be descending" (Frederick C. Prussner, "Problems in Old Testament Research," in *The Study of the Bible Today and Tomorrow*, p. 189. Chicago: Univ. of
Chicago Press, 1947).

2. Julian Huxley, *Religion Without Revelation*, suggests that religion may exist
without God, as well as without revelation, and should be treated as an aesthetic value
even though explicable as a product of man's natural environment. Writes Huxley:
"Is it perhaps the fact that Religion firmly based in actuality of emotion and experience, but feeling the absolute need of some intellectual explanation, has invented an *ad hoc* explanation, satisfactory enough as provisional hypothesis, but which
she has afterwards made the grave mistake of setting up as immutable truth? . . .
If that be true — and the rest of this book will be largely an attempt to prove it
so — then the chief task of religion in helping to build up the unified thought of the
future is to abandon the intellectual arrogance of its theology and to take a leaf out
of the book of science as to the methods by which truth may best be pursued . . ."
(pp. 97f. New York: Harper and Bros., 1927). Cf. C. C. J. Webb's lengthy criticism
in *Religion and Theism* (New York: Charles Scribner's Sons, 1934).

3. Shirley Jackson Case, *The Origins of Christian Supernaturalism*, Chicago: University of Chicago Press, 1946.

tion, especially by the absolutistic and personalistic idealists. Now it is the liberal mood, in both the higher and lower expressions voiced in the half-century just closing, which is under heavy fire. Whether men questioned the supernatural, or whether they combined the supernatural with indifference to special revelation, they had capitulated to a naturalistic mood. For we read now of the demise of a viewpoint, expressed however competently by Harry Emerson Fosdick's *A Guide to Understanding the Bible*.[4] The shadow of Naturalism, rather than of Biblical Supernaturalism, is seen to have hovered over representative liberal statements of revelation in the recent past.

1. *Uniqueness of Biblical View Explained Away.*

The classic Liberalism of the past generation so evaluated Biblical religion in terms of similarities, that it mainly divided the Hebrew-Christian movement into (1) a heightened expression, at best, of elements in other religions; (2) mythological superstitions not found in other religions. The evolutionary interpretation of religion so dominated the approach to the Biblical manuscripts that, as Norman H. Snaith has noted, "it has taken two generations for the Graf-Wellhausen theory of the literary structure of the Pentateuch to settle down into a moderately fluid mellowness"[5] and theologians are still trying to dig Biblical criticism out from the ruins of always stressing the similarities and slurring over the differences.

In the classic liberal pattern, the rise of ethical monotheism on Israelitish ground was viewed as the culmination of a slow process that could not be disentangled from roots in a primitive, polytheistic, history of religions, above which the eighth century prophets raised their peoples because of their peculiar religious insights. The whole structure of Old Testament literature was recast in the interests of this presupposition. On this pattern, the development of religion was traced from the human

---

4. Harry Emerson Fosdick, *A Guide to Understanding the Bible.* New York: Harper and Bros., 1938.
5. Norman C. Snaith, *The Distinctive Ideas of the Old Testament,* p. 14. Philadelphia: The Westminster Press, 1946.

side, being a movement from man toward God, rather than from the conviction of a special divine disclosure in which Israelitish Monotheism has its foundations. Hence the emphasis fell on the divine immanence, on the continuity of religious experience, on the psychology of religion rather than on theology proper. Almost all the definitive theological treatments of the past generation, which molded the thought of the "accredited" liberal divinity schools, were shaped by such convictions.

The classic liberal view tended to reduce revelation to merely a functional activity of the divine energy, not necessarily conceived in personal terms,[6] which aims at a higher spiritual adjustment on man's part. The notion of divine revelation was emptied of all doctrinal significance, and Christianity was treated as the preferable way of life, but not also as a creed. Doctrines were dismissed as secondary accretions; Liberalism was caught up with the modern retreat of the importance of reason in religious experience. And the divine activity, defined in functional terms, was overcast with philosophic assumptions of divine immanence and continuity, so that even in its highest statements, the doctrine of revelation included little of the nature of "divine encounter", scant appreciation of the "divine otherness", and a concentration on man's moral and spiritual continuity with the divine rather than on man as sinner in rebellion against the divine holiness. Indeed, the evolutionary assumption of man's harmonious relationship to his environment, physical and spiritual, was so dominant that divine revelation could be looked upon as merely another manner of viewing human insight; they were two sides of one and the same process, for the interaction of the natural and the supernatural come within a seamless garment of reality in which words like "unique" require quotation marks or mental reservation. The differences, at most, could be in degree, but never in kind.

---

6. Although personalistic Idealism vigorously championed the personality of God against those who took impersonalistic ground, and not all liberals parted with a unipersonal god.

Fosdick wrote of "the varied causes and occasions which led to the gradual enlargement and elevation of the Hebrew idea of deity[7], but the "process of enlargement" seems never to involve a specific divine disclosure; the development of the deity concept proceeds, in principle, along the same lines as Shailer Mathews' *The Growth of the Idea of God.*[8] One can say that the "ultimate outcome" of the "development of Israel's idea of God" is ethical Monotheism, without a reference to special revelation,[9] only if one believes the final result is latent in the process itself. The notion of a divine covenant or election is never more than a *prophetic idea.* Elijah, for example, "is notably important as a *creative* influence";[10] there is an eighth century "*emergence* of practical monotheism";[11] and the "even more astonishing *development* of moral ideas" throws us back "in wonder upon the *'abysmal depths of personality'* in the great prophets";[12] "Yahweh, *in their thought, became...* a moral judge who would throw into the discard even his chosen people if they violated his ethical standards";[13] Hosea *"went beyond* the *idea* of God as judge to the *idea* of God as savior."*[14]

The whole empirical theology movement arose, of course, as the conviction of a special divine revelation lessened. How

---

7. *Op. cit.*, p. 17.

8. Mathews' volume (New York: The Macmillan Co., 1931) begins with an idea of God which originates in the religious quest (p. 6. where Mathews never touches the question whether the idea has an ontic reference). It then proceeds to show how man's social environment colors the idea of God, furnishing "the patterns for religious ideas and teachings" (p. 9). Curiously, the Old Testament prophets give as an internal criticism the fact that religion is environmentally conditioned, but Mathews does not grapple with the problem latent here. The word God is shown by its history to stand for more than the idea of God (pp. 26ff.), but Mathews nowhere rises above a functional significance. The word God represents certain cosmic activities, which one may symbolically regard as personal (p. 232), and with which we are organically one. But when we are all through with Mathews' history of the growth of the idea of God, we are left with the shaky doubt that it may be, after all, nothing but a subjective imaginative flight — a romanticizing of hard nature — for that the idea has a history nobody would question, but that it is justified by objective being is what we hunger to know. Mathews told us, in effect, that there is no God who *discloses Himself;* the history of the idea has its manward initiative only. The emphasis on "personality-producing forces" was, after all, a reading back.

9. Fosdick, *op. cit.*, p. 21.　　　10. *Ibid.*, p. 22.

11. *Ibid.*, p. 23.　　　12. *Ibid.*, p. 23f.

13. *Ibid.*, p. 25.　　　14. *Ibid.*, p. 26.

the abandonment of transcendent, supernatural revelation resulted in the growth of countless varieties of epistemological Dualism—in which man's knowledge of God was always overcast with probability and uncertainty—is abundantly demonstrated by D. C. Macintosh's comprehensive survey in *The Problem of Religious Knowledge*.[15] Macintosh himself had served as Timothy Dwight professor of systematic theology at Yale, and his volume, which has many excellencies, has no defect worse than its refusal even to take *special* revelation as a possible option.[16] Here, of course, Empiricism labors under the handicap of unempirical prejudices. But the point of interest is that Macintosh was so convinced that the case for Theism is to be constructed without any necessary reference to the Hebrew-Christian tradition, nor to the events in which it had its rise, that he declares that "the essentially Christian type of religion and theology is logically defensible, apart from any dependence upon the outcome of historical investigation of the historicity of the Jesus of Christian tradition."[17] Here the miraculous is equated with the undependable, the Biblical ideal of election is dismissed as arbitrary; the whole notion of a *special* revelation is precluded in advance by assumptions which limit intelligibility to the universal, the repeatable. The result is precisely what would have been a matter of no surprise to Biblical prophets and apostles; Macintosh tells us that his empirical methodology does not afford a knowledge of a personal God, but that one is justified in postulating, on grounds of imaginal intuition, a personal deity. What the empirical theologians never seemed to comprehend, when thus giving a positive turn to the ambiguity of their quest, is that the initial insistence of Empiricism that an acceptable faith must not transcend its basis in *knowledge,* here meets itself walking backward.

---

15. Douglas Clyde Macintosh, *The Problem of Religious Knowledge*. New York: Harper and Bros., 1940.

16. Macintosh deals at length with Kierkegaard, Barth and Brunner, affording keen criticisms of what he terms "reactionary irrationalism", but he dismisses with hardly a wave of the hand the religious epistemology of the Reformers and contemporary evangelicals, and regards them as epistemological dualists at that.

17. Macintosh, *op. cit.*, p. 365.

2. Contemporary Mood Stresses Divine Initiative.

But it is precisely against some phases of this viewpoint on the doctrine of revelation that the current theological revolt is aimed, for the contemporary mood emphasizes the *divine initiative* as the only intelligible key to the uniqueness of the Hebrew-Christian movement. Hence it is that Walter Eichrodt, one of Germany's active Old Testament scholars, comments in his review of Fosdick's volume that it "gives the stamp of a period of intellectual investigation come to an end while a new epoch of Biblical knowledge is coming to the fore... In truth, we cannot evade the impression that here to a certain degree a stroke of finality is dealt to an intellectual movement and its method of procedure."[18] Doubtless the tension at this point justifies the translation of a rather extended comment in Eichrodt's review, because of its insistence on the divine initiative for a proper understanding for the Biblical message. For Eichrodt declares that

"... one cannot gloss over the explanation of the central conviction concerning the special relationship of God to His people, which has been expressed in the words 'covenant' and 'election.' This relationship to God, however, is grounded in and is always designated by, certain acts of God which penetrate with ordering power into the life of the people, and demand obedience. The Old Testament sources serve as the proclamation of these deeds; from them, the deeds derive their authority with which they proclaim their message to the hearers. For they know that thereby something new and absolutely compelling has been introduced into earthly history, something which seeks to penetrate in all directions and seeks to establish new relationships... And thus the message of the prophets is determined by the certainty of a new inbreaking of the reality of God which through the Law proceeds

18. *Journal of Biblical Literature*, vol. LXV, part II, June, 1946, p. 209, where appears Eichrodt's review in German, a section of which is here translated, although the review is accompanied by a summary in English by William F. Albright.

to salvation and to completion of the covenant. All attempts to understand them as ingenious thinkers who present a new religious or social ideal, or who develop a new concept of God, make of their announcement of God's will, demanding decision and practically directed, a *teaching,* an *idea,* and from the union of the spiritual with the earthly world viewed by them, fabricate a religious moral system which crystallizes in the abstraction of moral monotheism."[19]

The line of demarcation between the classic liberal and the more recent interpretation of revelation thus comes into clear focus. The older liberal treatment, it is now seen, obscured the inner genius of the Scriptures by imposing upon them an artificial unilinear evolution, propped up by an arbitrary selection of texts frequently torn from context. It came to frustration by its inability to show how ethical Monotheism ever emerged from "primitive Polytheism" on a continuity pattern.* Here the tension with revelation was pushed to the breaking-point; Wellhausen had no explanation for the "radical change" in Israel's religion. Worse yet, the very presence of the prophets was not a *result,* but rather presupposed the Israelitish belief in the divine holiness, mercy, and gracious purpose in the calling out of the Hebrews.

This was, in fact, a fatal weakness in the classic liberal view at which competent evangelical scholarship had pointed a finger

---

19. *Ibid.,* pp. 215f.

*The main stumbling-blocks in the way of regarding the Hebrew-Christian tradition as essentially unique are two-fold: (1) the working principles of modern science, which assume universal causality; (2) the assumption that an exclusive supernatural-ism reflects upon the love and justice of God. Although the closed structure of modern science is disclosing more and more crevices and making increasing room for discon-tinuity (cf. the author's *Remaking the Modern Mind*), the second objection is pressed both by empirical and philosophical theologians. Declaring that any once-for-all revela-tion is an "obvious contradiction of the Christian faith in the impartiality and reason-ableness of God," D. C. Macintosh added: "It is not that the ideas of divine grace and divine creativity are objectionable, either religiously or philosophically or even from a sufficiently self-critical point of view. What is objectionable from all three points of view is what Troeltsch called an *exclusive* supernaturalism, according to which God, purely of his own arbitrary will, works miracles of revelation and faith for some and not for others" (*op. cit.,* pp. 342 ff.). The use of such adjectives as "arbitrary" hardly conceals the more elemental presuppositions of such reasoning—the denial of the seriousness of human sin, and the consequent assumption that God is under some antecedent obligation or debt to all mankind which the newer views of revelation vig-orously attack.

of warning throughout the whole development of the modern view of the Scriptures. In his famous Kerr lectures, James Orr had proclaimed: "Date your books when you will, this religion is not explicable save on the hypothesis of Revelation."[20]

But, now, the newer insistence on the divine initiative in revelation, while it marks the reintroduction of the transcendent supernatural, does not by any means mark a return to the classic evangelical doctrine of revelation. In fact, one of the most delicate tasks of contemporary theology is that of finding the elements which unite and divide recent thinkers in revolt against the classic liberal view. The current trend has not issued in anything more than a broad movement of thinkers having significant individual differences, but who nevertheless stand midway between the classic Liberalism of yester-year, and the orthodox theology of the Reformation still current in evangelical circles.

There is, for example, J. Y. MacKinnon's *The Protestant Doctrine of Revelation*,[21] which insists upon divine initiative but refuses to go as far as Barth and Brunner, preferring rather to single out the view of John Oman as an acceptable contemporary statement of revelation.[22] At the other sweep of the pendulum one finds the conservative and evangelical works,

---

20. James Orr, *The Christian View of God and the World*, p. 15. New York: Charles Scribner's Sons, 1893. (Reprinted 1947 by William B. Eerdmans, Grand Rapids). Orr was not, of course, indifferent to the dating of the books, as witness his *The Problem of the Old Testament*, but he saw that the liberal redating did not escape the basic necessity of accounting for the uniqueness of the Hebrew view of God and the world.

21. J. Y. MacKinnon, *The Protestant Doctrine of Revelation*. Toronto: The Ryerson Press, 1946.

22. Cf. Oman's *Grace and Personality* (Cambridge: University Press, 1925); *Vision and Authority* (London: Hodder and Stoughton, 1929); *The Natural and the Supernatural* (Cambridge: University Press, 1931). Oman's view hardly marks a significant break with that of the older Liberalism, for man's insight or capability for discovering divine truth remains as the key to spiritual advance. We are told that a prophet is "a conscience ruled alone by insight into God's will" (*The Natural and the Supernatural*, p. 451. New York: The Macmillan Co., 1931). The whole story of the evolution of living creatures, we are informed, is that of reconciliation to and revelation of environment; revelation comes as the discerning of the eternal in the changing. "If reconciliation to the evanescent is revelation of the eternal, and revelation of the eternal a higher reconciliation to the evanescent, that is only as we know all environment, which is by living in accord with it . . . Religion must be a large experience in which we grow in knowledge as we grow in humility and courage, in which we deal with life and not abstractions, and with God as the environment in which we live and move and have our being . . ." (*ibid.*, p. 471). Not without reason did H. R. Mackintosh

in the general spirit and mood of Benjamin B. Warfield's *Revelation and Inspiration*,[23] which would include, though lacking some of the comprehensiveness of Warfield's work, such efforts as *The Infallible Word*, by John Murray and others;[24] and *Scripture Cannot Be Broken*, by Theodore Engelder,[25] volumes which speak for vigorous conservative Presbyterian and Lutheran circles in America, as well as the fuller statements in the recent comprehensive theologies of Berkhof and Chafer.[26]

But between these two viewpoints comes by far the largest bulk of recent literature on the problem of revelation. In a real sense, Karl Barth is the spearhead of this movement, though he is as much a product of earlier tensions as a prophet, for the influences of Hegel, Schleiermacher and Ritschl upon subsequent theology contained already the seeds of their own undoing. And yet, it is an over-simplification thus to assign the literary stirrings to a single camp, for within that camp serious differences exist, as between Barth[27] and his former student, Emil Brunner[28] through whom Neo-Supernaturalism is most

---

23. Benjamin B. Warfield, *Revelation and Inspiration*. New York: Oxford University Press, 1927. (Reprinted by Presbyterian and Reformed Pub. Co., 1948). Despite differences, one would include with this school — in broad contrast with the Neo-Supernaturalists — such older writers as L. Gaussen's *The Plenary Inspiration of the Holy Scriptures* (Chicago: B. I. C. A., n. d.) and James Orr's *Revelation and Inspiration* (London: Duckworth & Co., 1919).

24. John Murray, et. al., *The Infallible Word* (a compilation of essays by members of the Westminster Theological Seminary faculty). Philadelphia: Presbyterian Guardian Pub. Co., 1946.

25. Theodore Engelder, *Scripture Cannot Be Broken*. St. Louis: Concordia Publishing Co., 1944.

26. Louis Berkhof, *Reformed Dogmatics: Introduction*. (Grand Rapids: Wm. B. Eerdmans Pub. Co., 1932); Lewis Sperry Chafer, *Systematic Theology* (Dallas: Dallas Seminary Press, 1948).

27. Barth's most definitive, revised work in the area of religious epistemology is his *The Doctrine of the Word of God* (translated by G. T. Thomson). New York: Charles Scribner's Sons, 1936.

28. The detailed statements differentiating general revelation from natural theology, on Brunner's part, will do much to remove the differences in this area, though other differences remain. Barth's horror of natural theology was placated at too high a price —his denial of general revelation.

---

reply, in reviewing Oman's effort, that "The Hebrew prophets, if we can trust themselves, did not rise from a view they had gained of the meaning and purpose of the Natural to believe that God was such and such; God invaded their life, and spoke to them. To their minds God is not waiting to be discovered; He comes in upon their souls, and they cannot shun the hand that has been laid upon them" (*The British Weekly*, Oct. 29, 1931).

widely known in America because of his translated writings and
his lecture engagements. But also between these two and others
who stand in a general way with the movement, as against
classic Liberalism and historic Evangelicalism there are differences. It would be a task quite impossible, within the campass
of a single essay, to deal competently with significant literature
such as John Baillie's *Our Knowledge of God*,[29] F. W. Camfield's *Revelation and the Holy Spirit*,[30] E. P. Dickie's *Revelation and Response*,[31] the compilation on *Revelation* edited by
Baillie,[32] Nels F. S. Ferre's *Faith and Reason*,[33] Edwin Lewis'
A Philosophy of the Christian Revelation,[34] H. Richard
Niebuhr's *The Meaning of Revelation*,[35] and other related[36]
but not specifically neo-orthodox literature such as H. Wheeler
Robinson's *Redemption and Revelation*.[37]

The elements contributory to the neo-supernaturalist thrust,
however, are quite clear. The holdover of liberal ideas includes
an evolutionary view of origins, a higher critical view of the
Scriptures, and a reluctance to define revelation in propositional terms. But there is an insistence on God's special intrusions in history: His unique revelation in the divine acts out
of which issued the Hebrew nation, with its conviction of a
divine covenant and election, and consummated in the divine
incarnation in Jesus Christ. God discloses Himself in special

---

29. John Baillie, *Our Knowledge of God.* New York: Charles Scribner's Sons, 1939.
30. F. W. Camfield, *Revelation and the Holy Spirit.* New York: Charles Scribner's Sons, 1934.
31. E. P. Dickie, *Revelation and Response.* New York: Charles Scribner's Sons.
32. John Baillie and Hugh Martin, editors, *Revelation.* New York: The Macmillan Co., 1937. This contains essays in behalf of almost all but the traditional Protestant view.
33. Nels F. S. Ferre, *Faith and Reason.* New York: Harper and Bros., 1946.
34. Edwin Lewis, *A Philosophy of the Christian Revelation.* New York Harper and Bros., 1940.
35. H. Richard Niebuhr, *The Meaning of Revelation.* New York: The Macmillan Co., 1940.
36. Mention should be made, of course, of volumes in the Neo-Thomist fold, as Etienne Gilson's *Reason and Revelation in the Middle Ages* (New York: Charles Scribner's Sons, 1938) and Jacques Maritain's *The Degrees of Knowledge* (New York: Charles Scribner's Sons, 1938), though Maritain's views do not necessarily express the prevailing Catholic position with a precise finality. In its broadest outlines, the mid-twentieth century interest in special revelation comes, of course, directly in opposition to the Thomistic exaltation of natural theology.
37. H. Wheeler Robinson, *Redemption and Revelation.* New York: Harper and Bros., 1940.

redemptive deeds, and finally in Person. In this movement God makes Himself known as a God of holy love, taking sin with a high seriousness, yet mercifully providing redemption. The Scriptures are a necessary and normative record in the divine self-disclosure, but are not to be identified, contrary to the older evangelical theology, with the revelation itself, rather, revelation is a dynamic event consummated to the responsive heart, by a union which involves the Scriptures, the preaching of the Word, and the illumination of the hearer by the testimony of the Spirit. These are the ingredients for the mid-twentieth century discussion of the vital problem of divine revelation.

3. *Unrelieved Tensions in the Newer View of Revelation.*

The differences from the evangelical formulation of special revelation[38] are quite apparent; indeed, neo-supernaturalist spokesmen are usually as eager to differentiate their perspective from Fundamentalism[39] as much as from Liberalism.

A major dissimilarity is one on which all orthodox communions stand in concert, against recent vigorous expositions of the neo-supernaturalist position. That God's self-disclosure

---

38. A disturbing factor, which can hardly infuse clarity into the already complicated theological terminological confusion, is the eagerness with which recent writers climb aboard the "special revelation" bandwagon, all the while affirming some species of higher general revelation which is precisely what the Biblical and traditional view of general revelation is not. S. Paul Schilling argues vigorously, for example, for the "validity of both general and special revelation", only to tell us that "special revelation serves much the same function in the sphere of religion as that fulfilled by the intuitions of musical and poetic genius" (*Journal of Bible and Religion*; "Revelation and Reason", Vol. 16, No. 1, Jan. 1948, p. 16). And this sort of revelation, he concedes, never affords complete coherence, hence does not get beyond probability (p. 19) — that is, we have a species of special revelation which is still in need of special revelation! That the assumption of continuity of religions precludes any adequate view of special revelation in the writer's approach is apparent from such echoes as: "God is manifested most adequately in particular events . . . for the Christian, in the events centering in the coming of Christ", and "For Christian believers the Bible inevitably holds a highly significant place in all thought concerning revelation" (p. 14). Here the plea for special revelation conceals the denial of it.

39. It may appear unjustifiable to equate the older evangelical theology with Fundamentalism, and that from two vantage points. Liberalism often points out that there are many systems of Fundamentalism — Plymouth Brethren, Missouri Lutherans, Wesleyan Methodists, Orthodox Presbyterians, and Northern Baptists, for example. What is meant is that one finds here competing viewpoints not only with reference to eschatology, the place of ritual and creed, and ecumenical ideals, but also deep-rooted theological differences which separate Arminians and Calvinists. Again, from the side of Fundamentalism, the equation with the older evangelical theology is sometimes protested; the new *Systematic Theology* by Lewis Sperry Chafer, for example, has been commended as expressing the pre-millennial Scofield view which is

is in terms not only of events or saving acts, but also in terms of doctrine—in other words, that He gives a propositional revelation of Himself—is an insistence common to the Greek Orthodox,* Roman Catholic, and Protestant Reformation movements, despite their differences as to the significance of church fathers, councils and popes. Here divine revelation involves more than divine activity or events, but presses beyond the divine acts in history to a divine impartation of knowledge about God. Revelation is not merely dynamic, but is propositional, and consequently involves revealed truth. Out of this conviction grows the evangelical insistence that the Scriptures are to be viewed as an organ of revelation. From this point of view, a question which Dr. E. G. Homrighausen of Princeton Theological Seminary asks (with whatever reserve) in view of Brunner's minimizing of the importance of doctrine and magnifying of personal encounter with God, may in the next decade come to express one central point of tension as the mid-twentieth century grapples with the problem of special revelation. Says Dr. Homrighausen,

> "Whether the Christian revelation is only personal and not to some extent propositional is another question, for if God reveals Himself adequately, man's mind must also be satisfied."[40]

A second dissimilarity is the lesser centrality given the Scriptures in the neo-supernaturalist approach, with unavoidable consequences for the problem of authority. It remains to be

*Even out of this tradition, however, have come echoes to the newer view. Nicolas Berdyaev wrote: "Divinity cannot be rationally determined and remains outside the scope of logical concepts . . . All the dogmas of Christianity giving expression to the facts and events of spiritual experience have a supra-logical and supra-rational character and are above the law of identity and contradiction" (*Freedom and the Spirit*, pp. 64f. London: Geoffrey Bles: The Centenary Press, 1944).

40. In Homrighausen's review of Brunner's *The Divine-Human Encounter*, in *Theology Today*, Vol. I, No. 1, April, 1944, pp. 135f.

then called the system of thought characteristic of Fundamentalism. But the latter identification is too narrow; the title Fundamentalism takes its rise from the insistence on the part of evangelicals, against the liberals, on certain doctrinal fundamentals held to be essential to the revelational position, including the deity, virgin birth, substitutionary atonement, bodily resurrection, and second coming of Christ, — all of which were unquestioned by the older evangelical theology. The divisions between Fundamentalists likewise are acknowledged to be secondary to these primary affirmations.

seen whether Neo-Supernaturalism, despite its protest against Roman Catholicism in the name of the Reformation, does not take a view of revelation which, in a sense, merely varies the unbiblical Roman formula, except that the authority of councils is replaced by an even less objective authority, in which the testimony of the Spirit is subdued in a personalistic Mysticism. Thus a second focus of the mid-twentieth century problem of revelation, is that of an adequate objective authority.* The plight of Liberalism of the generation past, with reference to the loss of objective authority, was eloquently voiced by Gordon Poteat, in his volume, *We Preach Not Ourselves*:

> "The deficiencies of modern topical preaching are becoming widely recognized even among those who have followed the method... The weakness of tradition-detached, non-Biblical preaching is felt by many. The lack of *a message* is confessed... Aware of this situation, a liberally trained minister will occasionally express a nostalgia for the assurance of the fundamentalist which makes it possible for that brother to use the Bible as the Word of God. The so-called neo-orthodox movement is in large measure a back-to-the-Bible movement among preachers and theologians who have been trained in the Higher Criticism. But back to the Bible for such men cannot signify a repudiation of what they have learned from their historical studies. They cannot revert to the old authoritarianism of an infallible, inerrant Bible. . . . But can he ever find his authority in the Bible? He must not dissemble; he must not affirm as truth what his mind has long since rejected. If he is to make a fresh start at Biblical preaching, how is it to be done? This remains

---

* The search is on, of course, for a *via media* which will retain both orthodoxy's allegiance to the Scriptures and liberalism's sacrifice to higher critical methodology. Continental scholars like Franz Leenhardt are groping for a doctrine of Biblical authority which will retain both emphases (cf. his *Pour une orthodoxie liberale*. Lausanne: 1944). What sort of "Biblical authority" will issue from such orthodox-liberalism is apparent from Leenhardt's protest against the dialectical theologians, on the ground that they have restored an orthodox "biblicism," and that "while the traditional doctrine of inspiration is rejected, in practice its over-simplifications are pursued" by the Neo-Supernaturalists. In the end, the mood of orthodox-liberalism can only issue in an unauthoritative non-biblicism.

an unanswered question in the minds of many ministers.[41]

It is too early, but not much too early, to hear some representative neo-supernaturalist inquire realistically whether the movement which is inheriting Liberalism's vigor,[42] is not also inheriting its unsolved problems. Central among these is the risk of losing a sure word of God.

B. Biblical Infallibility Precluded by Brunner's Statement of Special Revelation.

Few contemporary theologians with whom conservative Christianity is in vital disagreement can teach the critical evangelical reader so much, by interaction and reaction, as Emil

---

41. Gordon Poteat, *We Preach Not Ourselves*, pp. 5f., New York: Harper and Bros., 1944.

42. The naturalistic approach, however, has still its ardent champions, as William A. Irwin in his essay on "Revelation in the Old Testament" (*The Study of the Bible Today and Tomorrow*, Harold R. Willoughby, editor, pp. 247ff. Chicago: University of Chicago Press, 1947). Irwin will "make concession to those who seek for a 'special revelation' in Israel" only in the sense that "the Bible stands supreme in the exaltation of its knowledge of God, in the nobility of its vision of human duty, and in its power to seize and quicken the imagination with a vision of possibilities that lie open to the human spirit" (p. 266). Revelation is viewed ultimately as a social process (p. 265), is identified with God's working "in the hearts of men everywhere, calling, persuading, insistently urging and imploring them to higher things" (p. 263). Irwin thinks it "apparent that the source and origin of the prophets' knowledge of God lay in their own human endowment of thought and feeling. They pondered deeply, devoutly, and long on the issues of their days, and they were profoundly concerned about them; out of such activity there came to them the convictions which they have set down for us as revelations of the will of God" (p. 258). But he insists that this is not "a denial of the reality of divine revelation — a view to which, indeed, the critical movement came close at one point in its development but from which it has happily turned away" (p. 259). For we are to understand divine revelation, although fully human and natural, in terms of universal divine process. (pp. 259ff). But in the same volume Otto J. Baab, in his essay on "Old Testament Theology: Its Possibility," issues the appropriate reminder that: "The Old Testament's 'Thus saith the Lord' or 'The Word of the Lord is like a burning fire in my bones' and scores of similar statements demonstrate conclusively the orientation of its prophets and saints toward the God who spoke to and through them. The critic may declare that these men were mistaken and confused a personal ethical urge with divine revelation, but he must acknowledge the existence of these passages and offer an explanation of their prominence . . . Any effort to explain away this experience of God or the supernatural in the Old Testament betrays an unscientific bias which is unfriendly both to biblical religion and to truth. For example, an interpretation of the phrase, 'The Word of the Lord came to . . .' as signifying simply the figurative language of the Hebrew prophets or editors, whereby they indicated the importance of what they had to say, reveals a serious misunderstanding of prophetic psychology and religion. Such an interpretation is a polite way of reducing God to a figure of speech. Surely the language which the prophets themselves used nowhere justifies this attitude . . . Their courageous defiance of the status quo and stern criticism of powerful rulers in the name of God would be inexplicable apart from their personal experience of a living God who was far more than the verbal symbols used to describe him" (*op. cit.*, pp. 413f.).

Brunner of Zurich. Brunner champions revelation before reason. Whereas the neo-Thomist Etienne Gilson captioned his apologia for natural theology *Reason and Revelation in the Middle Ages,* Brunner's treatment of faith and knowledge inverts the order to the Augustinian *Revelation and Reason* (440 pages translated by Olive Wyon and published by Westminster Press in 1946), upholds general revelation (as against Karl Barth's notion that the image of God is destroyed), insists that the incarnation is crucial for Theism (against philosophic Idealisms). But Brunner is not on that account a champion of Protestant orthodoxy; indeed, orthodoxy he singles out as an arch-foe. The Zurich theologian declares war on convictions which have long been championed by large segments of the evangelical camp.[43]

1. *Verbal Inspiration Equated with Idolatry.*

In past generations, some evangelicals have at times been reluctant to subscribe to verbal inspiration because of the easy confusion of this view with a theory of mechanical dictation which, as Hodge carefully pointed out, was never the prevailing view of the Christian church.[44] Hence some scholars declared only for plenary inspiration, while yet defending infallibility, although the evangelical camp, since the rise of modern higher criticism, at times included men like James Orr, who made limited concessions to the critics but championed the authority of the Bible nonetheless.

Brunner's attack on Biblical infallibility—under whatever garb—takes a rather different line. He is in revolt against

43. Brunner's adverse criticism of American Fundamentalism, as well as of the Lutheran High Orthodoxy of the 16th and 17th centuries on the Continent, goes far beyond the self-examination currently going on in alert fundamentalist circles (cf. the author's *The Uneasy Conscience of Modern Fundamentalism,* Grand Rapids: William B. Eerdmans Pub. Co., 1947), and involves, as we shall see, a direct attack on basic convictions championed in common by the whole evangelical movement. Brunner has emphasized the "sickness" of Fundamentalism almost as much as the "sickness" of Liberalism, indicating his essential revolt against both camps.

44. Brunner himself tends to equate verbal inspiration and dictation (pp. 127f.), but his attack is far wider than this; he is hostile to the plenary idea, and to a doctrinaire view of revelation. Hence the objection to "verbal inspiration" comes from some who fear the phrase will be confused with a mechanical view; and from others who reject plenary inspiration; and from still others who reject propositional revelation of any kind.

idolatrous Bibliolatry, he declares. The doctrine of verbal inspiration he handles with uncompromised hostility. It rests upon a mistranslation, he avers, of II Tim. 3:16, which text he affirms to be the *locus classicus* of the doctrine (p. 9, footnote).*

The view has saddled Protestantism with a "paper-Pope", we are told. But God is not a "Book God"; what matters is the Person, not the Book (p. 143). Fundamentalism deifies the "letter" of the Bible, "as if the Spirit of God were imprisoned within the covers of the written word" (p. 145); it "makes the Bible an idol, and me its slave", binding one to the letter which killeth (p. 181). Hence the Fundamentalist is in "bondage to the Biblical text" (p. 182). The word of God is not reducible, he contends, to the Bible. The Helvetic confessional formula—*praedicatio verbi divini est verbum divinum*—"proceeds from an unwarranted identification of the doctrinally established word of the Bible with the Word of God," protests Brunner, "whereas authoritative preaching, not severed from the basis of the word of the Bible, has as much right to be called the Word of God as the word of the Bible" (p. 144).

If Brunner castigates Roman Catholicism for putting natural theology in place of special revelation, he finds Protestant Christians "scarcely less" blameworthy for the orthodox emphasis on the Bible. Orthodoxy even gets blamed for obscuring the Mediator!

> "Orthodoxy... confused the fact of revelation with the witness to the fact. It was necessary that both should be connected, but orthodoxy made them identical. All the passionate interest which belonged to the unique event, to the Mediator and His act, was thus diverted from its true object and directed towards the scriptural testimony to it. *Hence the destruction of the dogma*

---

* Page references not otherwise identified are to Brunner's *Revelation and Reason*. On II Tim. 3:16, Brunner contends that *didaskalia* should be translated "is profitable for *teaching*" (not *doctrine*). Admittedly, the Greek word *didache* suggests concrete, systematized teaching more than *didaskalia*, but the latter can hardly be fully denuded of doctrinal significance. The Latin word *doctrina* has in view both teaching and doctrine; nor ought the two meanings to be opposed in translating II Tim. 3:16. Even the translation of "teaching" can hardly be made to mean that the teaching value of the Scriptures is restricted to spiritual (as against cosmological or historical) truths.

> *of Verbal Inspiration, with its emphasis upon an Infallible Book, by the modern process of research in natural and historical science inevitably carried away with it the whole Christian faith in revelation, the faith in the Mediator.* For in traditional Christian doctrine these two great forces, the infallibility of the Bible and the revelation of God in Christ, had been coupled together too closely. The fall of the one led inevitably to the fall of the other."[45]

Brunner concedes that Old Testament prophetic utterances—"even if we do not accept the view of Philo: 'a prophet says nothing of his own' "—furnish the closest analogy to the meaning of the theory of verbal inspiration, and hence "the words of God which the Prophets proclaim as those which they have received directly from God, and have been commissioned to repeat, as they have received them, constitute a special problem" on his viewpoint. But this, we are told, is an "Old Testament level of revelation, where the Word of God is not yet a personal reality and the testimony to a personal reality" (p. 122, footnote). Again, "it is the peculiarity of the apocalyptic writings," Brunner suggests, with a note of disparagement, "that they claim for themselves the authority of divine dictation" (p. 125, footnote, where Brunner refers to Dan. 12:4, II Pet. 1:20, Rev. 1:2f., 11).

2. *Concessions to Higher Criticism and Evolutionary Science.*
Higher criticism has made impossible the dogma of infallibility, Brunner contends. The Old Testament "may contain" magical elements derived from contemporary religious thought of the Near East (p. 88); the theophanies are "a relic of popular mythology" (p. 90);[46] the Old Testament writings disclose "impressive and far-reaching differences" both in the historical

---

45. Brunner, *The Mediator*, p. 34 (italics supplied). Philadelphia: The Westminster Press, 1947.

46. This is one of the points at which Barth's less critical view of the Scriptures discloses itself; in discussing the doctrine of the Trinity, he comments: "We must already in the Old Testament point to the remarkable figure of the angel of the Lord who at certain points comes into action in a way identical with *Yahwe* . . ." (*The Doctrine of the Word of God*, I, p. 342). But Barth is as hostile as Brunner to verbal-plenary inspiration.

books and in doctrinal matters which are "devastating to the claims of the theory of verbal inspiration" (p.133) ; the whole primal history of the early chapters of Genesis is lost "in the sense of a credible record of events"; "all that the Old Testament... records of the story of the Patriarchs has ceased to be part of our scientific picture of history" (p. 286) , but the denial of the historicity of the primal history of the Old Testament, or of the stories of the patriarchs, does not mean the ruin of the Christian faith (p. 282) . Brunner scores apologists who think they must cling to the Mosaic historical picture of the beginnings of mankind to save the faith in the witness to Christ in the Old Testament, because this attitude reintroduces the orthodox dilemma: either a Biblical faith or scientific criticism (p. 286, footnote) . He commends the Anglo-Catholic theologians who in *Lux Mundi* combined evolutionary anthropology and historical criticism with an apostolic Christology as early as 1889. Also, historical criticism since Wellhausen, whose view Brunner says remains on the whole victorious,[47] has greatly altered our notion of the history of Israel, so much so that the traditional view of the unity of the Biblical record, and our belief in the trustworthiness of the harmony of Biblical history, must be questioned (p. 287) . Scientific historical critics have given us the prophets anew. Likewise the Psalms, largely unintelligible on the supposed Davidic authorship, reveal new depths of meaning when severed from this pseudonymous authorship (p. 287) , as with second Isaiah (p. 58) .

The Johannine *ego eimis,* while stating explicitly what the historical Jesus is, are not His actual words (p. 112) . Actually, we may have no authentic writing of any of the original twelve apostles (p. 126) . Attack upon the Pauline or Johannine authorship of certain New Testament books, was not an attack upon an

---

47. Such broad concession does not go undisputed in many liberal circles today. J. Coppens' *The Old Testament and the Critics,* (translated from the French by Ryan and Tribbe; Paterson, N. J.: St. Anthony Guild Press, 1942) traces much of the revolt against Wellhausen's strictures. Some forceful objections to the Wellhausen theory are set forth in *The New Bible Handbook,* G. T. Manley, editor, pp. 117ff. (Chicago: Inter-Varsity Christian Fellowship, 1947). See also the capable analysis by A. Noordtzy, "The Old Testament Problem" (translated by Miner B. Stearns) in *Bibliotheca Sacra,* Vol. 97, No. 388, Oct.-Dec., 1940, and the two subsequent issues.

essential point of the faith (p. 282). John's Gospel is excluded
as a record (p. 285, footnote). Jesus gave his teaching as
Matthew, Mark and Luke record it, not as John gives it; the
most important result of Biblical criticism is the radical difference it has uncovered between the Synoptic Gospels and the
Fourth Gospel, between the teaching of Jesus and that of the
apostles, but this has no negative effect on faith, for the true
humanity of Jesus demands a difference (pp. 288f).

Brunner disparages further the ideal of Biblical infallibility.*
Human research, admitted by Luke's introduction, "does not
exclude inspiration, but it does exclude automatic dictation
and verbal inspiration, with its claim to an oracular divine
infallibility" (p. 128). The element of human research and
selection, in the tradition of historical facts in the Gospels,
Acts, and Epistles, precludes verbal inspiration. To deny "certain errors and inconsistencies" in this tradition one must shut
his eyes to the facts; only an ignorant or insincere person can
produce a complete Gospel harmony or reconcile all contradictions in the reports of Luke and Paul (p. 129). The Apostles
who strove with each other in the Jerusalem council were not,
in their written accounts, free from inconsistency and error
(p. 129). Historical criticism has corrected the story of the
apostles and first Christians, pointing out various contradictions

---

* Barth's view of Scripture is less radical than Brunner's, though both men in their
movement "toward" Biblical authority reject verbal-plenary inspiration. Barth's first
edition of *Roemerbrief* indicated he would prefer the old doctrine of inspiration to the
historical-critical study of the Bible if the choice were necessary, and many critics
felt that *Roemerbrief* itself quite snubbed higher critical demands. But his rupture
with plenary inspiration has been quite clear for two decades. The emphasis of his
1925 article on "Das Schriftprinzip der reformierten Kirchen" (*Zwischen den Zeiten,*
III, pp. 215ff.) is retained in his *Dogmatik.* Yet Barth appears at times to appeal to
Biblical authority alone; the latest volume of his *Dogmatik* is an extended work on the
Genesis creation narrative, quite indifferent to modern science as in any way relevant
to the subject. Barth may not go the length of Brunner's declaration that the Bible
has no significance in cosmological and historical matters, but he has not drawn fire
for a return to verbal inspiration (a charge made against some of his followers, e.g.,
Hellbarth, Wilhelm Vischer and Arthur Frey) but for leaning "so heavily upon
minute exegesis of scriptural verbiage" that he "implicitly suggests" such a return
"by the attention he gives to the *ipsissima verba*" (cf. Walter M. Horton, "Neo-
Orthodox Conceptions of Biblical Authority," *The Journal of Religious Thought,* Vol.
V, No. 1 (Autumn-Winter, 1948), p. 55). Barth denies as vigorously as Brunner that
revelation is inscripturated.

in the book of Acts, and various inconsistencies in the assignment of certain writings to well-known apostles (p. 285).[48]

Contemporary science, too, has overthrown Biblical infallibility. Brunner heralds "the breakdown of the doctrine of verbal inspiration as the result of modern scientific knowledge" (p. 11). *Both natural science and historical science, we are told, have collapsed the "whole edifice of orthodox doctrine." On the verbal inspiration theory, "even the smallest concession to 'Biblical criticism', whether from the side of natural science or from that of historical science, was a catastrophe for the whole fabric of the doctrine of the Church,"* Brunner notes (p. 274, italics supplied). "If the Bible is an infallible book, written down under the dictation of the Holy Spirit, then no Biblical criticism could exist—no admission of any inconsistencies, errors, or mistakes in the Bible. Here the slogan was, 'Everything must be believed or nothing will be believed.' " (p. 274). But Brunner disparages the assumption that "I must believe that the sun stood still in the Vale of Ajalon, because it says so in the Book, just as much as I must believe that God in Christ forgives me my sin and gives me His love."[49]

a. *Supposed Errors in Biblical History and Cosmology Show That Testimony of the Spirit is Restricted.*

The way to come to terms with science, declares Brunner, is to acknowledge frankly that "the Holy Scriptures contain no divine oracles about all kinds of possible cosmological facts" (p. 280). "The Christian faith does not presuppose any definite

---

48. The dogma of the canon is not final and infallible, remarks Brunner, but it is possible and right continually to re-examine, test and revise it. Although the present canon differs so greatly from other books that one who admits the necessity for a canon will continually return to the currently received books, we are forced to recognize a peripheral area to the canon, including II Peter, Jude, James and the Apocalypse (p. 132). Brunner favorably contrasts Luther's touchstone for canonicity — does the writing honor Christ? — with the "purely historical and authoritarian conception" — the question of authorship — championed by Protestant orthodoxy and "even Calvin and Bullinger" (p. 131, footnote). The key question on Brunner's approach becomes: what Christ?

49. *Op. cit.*, p. 174. Brunner states the theory of verbal inspiration in a most extreme mood; not all Fundamentalists, by any means, interpret the "sun standing still" literally, in view of similar poetic passages in Joshua, though they have no anti-miraculous bias which would preclude even such a possibility. But Brunner revolts against a miracle-apologetics; even the miracle of the resurrection is not the basis of belief in Christ (p. 305).

view of the world as preferable to another" (p. 281). The theology of the church conflicted with science, we are told, because the Bible was understood in a Judaistic, rabbinical way, instead of in a prophetic and apostolic manner, and the Reformers failed to eliminate completely the leaven of Judaism and legalism, because they still looked to it for authoritative teaching on cosmology and history. "Hence the structure of orthodoxy had to be rudely shaken," declares Brunner, "in order to compel Protestant theology to rethink her own classic doctrine of Scripture" (p. 280).[50]

The Holy Spirit, declares Brunner, "does not guarantee the truth of world facts, whether historical or cosmological. The *testimonium spiritus sancti* is strictly limited to its own sphere of reference. The Spirit testifies to the Father and the Son, but not to all kinds of other matters."[51] Brunner remarks that the Spirit "binds us to the Scripture, in so far as it witnesses to Christ, in so far as it discloses the will of God and His nature, but not in so far as it teaches us ordinary facts about the world" (p. 181).

Brunner sometimes makes it appear—in his eagerness to impute as much obscurantism to the position from which he wants his Neo-Supernaturalism clearly distinguished—that fundamentalists take the view that the Bible answers all questions of every kind, and that fundamentalists therefore are unlettered emotionalists of but one book.[52] Elsewhere, however, he strikes

---

50. Brunner does not go on to point out how it is, since on his assumptions the Word is not the Bible but Jesus Christ, that nowhere in his ministry does Jesus repudiate the significance of doctrine for the Old Testament, nor the doctrinal significance of Jesus' own teaching.

51. *Op. cit.*, p. 175. If this is so. is not Brunner entirely dependent for his knowledge that there is a Spirit, not identifiable with the Father or Son, upon the Bible and tradition — which testimony he elsewhere regards as inadequate? And, if the Bible is not trustworthy in historical matters, how can Brunner appeal to its record of "God's self-manifestation within history," of the saving event? And is it self-evident that the historical or cosmological spheres might have no bearing on a witness to Christ, on the will of God and His nature?

52. It is true, of course, that to the Puritans the Bible was a book on *all* questions. On first approach, this seems ridiculous to the modern mind. But may it not be less ridiculous than the contemporary bias of secular education, which militates exclusively against the Bible in the public schools, and thus takes the attitude that the Bible is a book on *none?* A hasty visit to the campuses of Christian colleges which receive the unqualified endorsement of American Fundamentalists will make it plain that fundamentalists are often persons with as many books as liberals, but that they accept some other book than that which the liberals accept (whether by Kant, or Hegel, or

a more objective note: "Can anyone seriously maintain that all questions in mathematics, physics, biology, and astronomy are 'answered in the Word of God'?...Not even that school of theology which regarded the geological, astronomical, and archaeological statements of the Bible as infallible ever held this view; for they admitted, at least along-side of faith, that the reason was a source of knowledge for the knowledge of the world and the formation of judgment in secular matters" (p. 378).

At three points, Brunner contends, modern thought has decided against the champions of the authority of the Bible ("but not against the Bible itself", he adds, in view of the insistence that the Bible has no specific ultimate teaching in these areas): the Biblical view of space, the Biblical view of time, the Biblical view of the earliest history of mankind (p. 277).

In all fairness, it must be said that Brunner rightly lays to the charge of proponents of verbal inspiration a certain inconsistency in dealing with scientists. It cannot be denied that, in the name of verbal inspiration, war has been waged upon proponents of scientific views which fundamentalists today champion as involving no conflict at all with the Scriptures— as for example, the geocentric view of the world, and the vastly widened notion of planetary space, which is nowhere challenged today; the antiquity of the world, in view of geologic findings, which has encouraged the interpretation of the Genesis creation accounts along the line of successive ages, rather than literal days. Without doubt, a certain unreadiness to admit the possibilities of serious misinterpretation which are latent even within a view of verbal inspiration is involved in the superficial way in which it is now often said that there is

James, or Dewey) as authoritative, and do so with a conviction of divine revelation. The Commission on the Christian Philosophy of Education sponsored by the National Association of Evangelicals has pointed out, and rightly so, that the ruling of the Supreme Court — that the teaching of religious education in the public schools is an illegal infraction of the separation of church and state — has opened the door for a vigorous attack against Naturalism as an anti-supernaturalist religious philosophy. Apparently the only legal academic treatment of moral and spiritual subjects in the public schools is an endorsement of accepted values, coupled with the maximum amount of obscurity about any metaphysics which justifies them.

no conflict between the Scriptures and science if one holds a viewpoint, for devotion to which equally sincere believers not many generations ago were vigorously opposed. An age theory of Genesis, or a view of the antiquity of creation, has not always been readily allowed in evangelical circles. Obviously, even within a view of verbal inspiration, not all problems of exegesis are settled, and science has some rights.

But the fundamentalist will continue to insist that the scientist's dogmatisms in the area of origins are as pre-scientific or super-scientific as philosophy proper. Hence, many fundamentalists still champion a fiat creation in six literal days, seeking to do justice to the facts of geology in terms of a world-wide flood and by a reminder that while the geologic principle of uniformitarianism holds good for laboratory time, it can hardly be legislated upon miracle time.[53] But again, it is certainly not true that the age-theory of Genesis is a modern fundamentalist device to save those chapters from a reddened countenance in view of modern science, for church history discloses champions of an age-theory of Genesis long before the rise of modern science. Biblical exegesis, in fundamentalist as well as in liberal circles, demands that the Bible and the assured results of science be reconciled, and among these assured results Fundamentalism reckons the Copernican view of the world, in its main outlines, and the possibility if not probability of geologic antiquity. And it views the dogmatic opposition of Biblicists to science at these points as an unjustifiable dogmatism not Biblically sanctioned, and no more commendable than the dogmatism of scientists who, from an observation of the present world in operation, declare dogmatically how and when the world came into being, although indisputably outside the scientist's range of experience.

Modern Fundamentalism hardly grants that modern science has overturned the Biblical view of the earliest history of man-

---

53. Brunner is hardly right in his remark that "the literal words of the Bible leave us in no doubt . . . that according to the view of the Bible the world is six thousand years old" (p. 278). The Usher chronology should not be so easily confused with the Mosaic.

kind, despite Brunner's conviction that man must be regarded as forming part of the evolutionary series. This position, contends Brunner, "has for a long while past left the stage of plausible hypotheses behind, and like the teaching of Copernicus, Kepler, and Newton, has become scientific truth, with which all honest theology has to come to terms" (p. 279).

The terms are clear: "a large part of Christian traditional doctrine has been annihilated by historical criticism" (p. 286). But there is no need for alarm: *"all that historical criticism has 'destroyed' does not belong to the central object of faith, but only to the cosmological way in which it is conceived; thus we ought not to speak of the 'destruction' of faith, or even of an 'injury' to it, but merely of a necessity to express its content in other terms"* (p. 286, italics supplied). In fact, this statement is a great victory for the Christian faith: "the idea of a historical primitive state in paradise, and of a visibly continuous 'covenant' narrative from paradise to Moses, can no longer be an essential part of Christian doctrine, as it was for some fifteen hundred years; but these changes of view have not affected the vital truths contained in the concepts of Creation, original revelation, the Fall, the Covenant. On the contrary, with the elimination of the historical element from the story of the 'primitive state' a certain deterministic burden of dogmatic conceptions has been removed, which since the Augustinian formulation of the doctrine of original sin has made the understanding of the Biblical message increasingly difficult. Here too *the 'reduction' has proved to be simply a purification"* (pp. 286f., italics supplied).

b. *The Word of God Not Identified With The Words of the Bible.*

Brunner's final verdict is that, despite all dislocations and gaps in the text, the history of Israel and the substratum of divine revelation and of the Covenant has not become essentially different, for the conviction of the divine saving event within Israel remains (pp. 287f.). Even if we are obliged to take our picture of the life and actions of Jesus solely from the

Synoptics, and to eliminate what the most radical critics (e.g., Wellhausen, Bultmann) demand from the Synoptic narratives, remarks Brunner, the picture of the life and person of our Lord remains essentially the same as the tradition before the rise of higher criticism (pp. 284f.).

(1) *Brunner's Appeal to the Reformers Unconvincing.*

We may now, in the shadow of this rather extreme critical view of the Bible, inquire as to the view of revelation which Brunner feels to be necessitated by modern criticism. We are told first, as Brunner grapples for historical rootage for his position, that two views are latent in the Reformers, and that orthodoxy pursued the least promising of the alternatives. Brunner remarks that the leaders of the Reformation differed on their attitude toward the Scriptures not so much according to confessional position as by generations: "The Reformers of the first generation, Luther and Zwingli, are not favorable to the doctrine of verbal inspiration, whereas Melanchthon, Calvin and Bullinger are" (pp. 127f., footnote). Elsewhere Brunner declares that "the difference between Luther and the first genera- tion of Reformers as a whole, and the orthodoxy which began even with Melanchthon, cannot be exaggerated. For Luther the 'Word of God' is the event of the divine self-communication through the Scriptures and through the preaching; for the orthodox Reformers the 'Word of God' is the Bible as a Book which has been given, and correct doctrine" (p. 145, footnote).

If this is so, might it not suggest that the self-testimony of the Scriptures at this point made itself heard increasingly as the Reformers were removed temporally from the legislation of doctrine by the illusory authority of the Roman Catholic church? Brunner notes Calvin's fondness for the notions of the "oracula Dei" and of "divine dictation." "We cannot imagine him making critical statements about the documents of the Old and the New Testament such as Luther used to make," concedes Brunner, while yet admitting that as a student of the Bible text Calvin "did not in any way ignore the human aspect of the Scriptures" (p. 128, footnote) Calvin, in the dogmatic formulation of the authority of the Bible, "was already entirely under the sway of the orthodox view of literal divine inspiration" (p. 275).[54] The Reformers, we are told, were "not fully aware of the significance of their new knowledge" of the Living Word in the Scriptures, "and of its incompatibility with the traditional view" (p. 275). Their successors concealed the new knowledge, and, in their views of the Bible, became "more Papist than the Pope" (p. 276).

But is Luther's position clearly one of opposition to verbal inspiration? Brunner concedes that Luther "on the one hand expressed himself with amazing freedom about certain books in the Old Testament, and in the New Testament; then suddenly, when engaged in controversy, he would appeal to the letter of the Scripture as infallible because it was wholly and literally inspired by God" (p. 275).[55]

True Biblical faith, declares Brunner, is wholly different from the "ethically neutral 'faith' that everything which is written in this Book is true" (p.176). But that is hardly an argument against verbal inspiration, any more than against Brunner's view. True Biblical faith is not Brunner's view of the Scriptures; it is a relationship to God. But that this relationship can be safeguarded in a context other than one of Biblical authority, Brunner fails to establish. False faith, declares Brunner, is satisfied with a *sacrificium intellectus* to dogma or the Bible as an infallible Book, and this legalistic obedience involves an ethically neutral faith "because it is applied equally to all parts of Scripture alike—the cosmological and the historical parts as well as the theological." But is there nothing dogmatic about Brunner's view, and is it impossible to combine Bible belief and true faith? Surely the Reformers did not think so!

But the Reformation principle of the Scripture—*Christus dominus et rex Scripturae*—solves in principle, we are told,

---

54. See Appendix Note A: "Calvin on the Word and the Spirit."
55. See Appendix Note B: "Luther on the Word and the Spirit."

the problem of Bible faith and Bible criticism (p. 276) : "The Bible is the human, and therefore not the infallible witness to the divine revelation" (p. 276) .[56]

The view of Brunner, despite his claim to return to the inner spirit of the Reformation, is not continuous with the views of Luther and Calvin—nor even of Zwingli—in the matter of revelation and inspiration. It is a view which gives more emphasis to the divine initiative than did the Liberalism of a generation and two ago, and which also claimed the inner spirit of the Reformation movement. But it hardly gives to the Scriptures that centrality and authority which the Reformers championed, and the compromise of which they would not tolerate.[57]

The neo-supernaturalists fasten upon Luther's reluctance to view James, Hebrews, Jude and Revelation as capital books, as if this involved a loose view of inspiration. This is hardly so. Luther viewed them as inferior so far as lighting up his one absorbing interest: justification by faith without works. Perhaps his criterion of superiority was hardly wide enough! May it not have been his very conviction of the authority of the Scriptures which gave Luther trouble with certain books, which seemed on his presuppositions to teach doctrinal novelties? And surely even those who reject a doctrine of degrees of inspiration, do not deny that different books and sections are

---

56. *Op. cit.*, p. 128, footnote. Brunner's suggestion, that the church must develop its doctrine of the Scriptures, along the same lines as its doctrine of the two natures (p. 278), raises the question of the fallibility of the God-man in view of the implication that humanity necessitates fallibility.

57. The appeal to the Reformers, by both the neo-supernaturalists and the fundamentalists, often overlooks the fact that the Reformers were hardly infallible. Curiously, both competing moods — denying the authority of the fathers — struggle to find the Reformation on their side, and claim precedent for opposed viewpoints on the crucial issue of revelation and inspiration. The three main Reformers did not agree on all matters among themselves and further, Luther appears the least consistent and systematic. But, granting the fact that the view of the Reformers are not the touchstone by which Biblical teaching is to be tested, there is no need to concede the Reformation mood needlessly to the newer theology. On this point, Barth is more ready than Brunner to grant that the Reformers appealed to the letter. It is also curious how eager Brunner is to find in the New Testament some teaching which opposes verbal inspiration — yet in this very procedure the appeal presupposes verbal inspiration (even if unconsciously) in an effort to disprove the theory.

more profitable than others for different purposes.[58] There are "right strawy" passages for many purposes, but that is hardly a disproof of canonicity nor of verbal inspiration.

It is incontrovertible as one reads all standard accounts of the Reformation, that the Reformers summoned the Church to hear the testimony of the written word, as against the proclamation of the church. The Reformation was a "to-the-Bible" movement; it was not a "Spirit rather than the Bible" movement. Hence, the Waldensians as also the followers of Wycliffe, who had insisted on the authority of the Bible, are often called "reformers before the Reformation."

The attitude of the Reformation toward the testimony of the Spirit apart from, or in priority to the written word, is disclosed by the vigorous opposition of Luther to the Anabaptists,[59] who presumably held that, having the Spirit of Christ to teach them, they had no need of the Scriptures. As against the priority of the testimony of the Spirit (Anabaptists) or of the church (Catholicism), Luther appealed to the Bible.[60] Luther opposed lifeless dogmas, but he saw also that the Christian life is anchored in the written word as firmly as in the testimony of the Spirit. Luther declares: "I will not... waste a word in arguing with one who does not consider that the Scriptures are the Word of God: we ought not to dispute with

---

58. For all this, however, Luther's refusal to number James, Hebrew, Jude and Revelation among the canonical books in his New Testament translation of 1522 cannot be justified. The conviction of verbal inspiration, when already subordinated to other presuppositions, can lead to far-reaching error. But, for all this, there remains in the acknowledgement of a genuinely objective authority hope for its rectification. Indeed, in view of the modern cultural crisis, the problem of canonicity has once again taken an apostolic turn. Instead of a preoccupation with the secondary question — however important — of whether this or that "marginal" book belongs in the canon, the higher theological mind is discerning the importance of the fact that the apostolic and post-apostolic age was convinced that here is a literature — to be separated from all other literatures except the Old Testament which it carries to fulfillment — in which God speaks as nowhere else to man.

59. Yet the moderate Swiss Brethren never put the Spirit over the Word or ignored the Word. It is unfortunate how the excesses of some of the mystical Anabaptist groups have colored the attitude towards the entire movement, especially in view of the sweeping indictments hurled by Luther and Bullinger. Cf. W. J. McGlothlin's *Baptist Confessions of Faith*, pp. 1ff., for representative Anabaptist confessions (Philadelphia: American Baptist Publication Society, 1911).

60. W. P. Paterson remarks, in *The Rule of Faith* that "the presupposition of Luther's theological thinking was that the Bible is the Word of God given by revelation of the Holy Spirit, and that it alone transmits and proves the truths of revelation" (p. 405. New York: Hodder and Stoughton, 1912).

a man who thus rejects first principles,"[61] and "It is impossible that the Scriptures should contradict themselves, save only that the unintelligent, coarse, and hardened hypocrites imagine it."[62] Elsewhere Luther affirms: "He has resolved to give no man the internal things except through the external, and He will give no one the Spirit or faith without the external Word and sign which He has appointed."[63]

The same attitude pervades Calvin's utterances, whose view is set forth in the sixth chapter of the *Institutes,* where we are told that the written word is not fully acknowledged until sealed by the testimony of the Spirit to the inquiring heart; the Spirit convinces of the truth of the prophetic and apostolic word.[64]

(2) *Nor is the Fundamentalist Appeal to an Infallible Original an Escape Mechanism.*

Brunner speaks with biting sarcasm against the appeal to an "infallible original" and away from the present text. "The critics who pointed out all kinds of inconsistencies of contradictions in the Bible were confronted with a hypothetically faultless and consistent text. The Bible 'at present' was not free from errors, it was true, but the 'original' text was perfect"

---

61. Cited from Koestlin in *The Evangelical Quarterly,* April, 1947.

62. Dorner, *History of Protestant Theology,* Vol. I., pp. 244f. Contrast Brunner's comment in his *The Philosophy of Religion,* where he summarizes his rather radical critical view — myths and legends in the New as well as the Old Testament, inaccuracies and contradictions. See also his *The Theology of Crisis:* "The words of the Scriptures are human; that is, God makes use of human and therefore, frail and fallible words of men who are liable to err . . . who identifies the letters and words of the Scriptures with the word of God — does not know what constitutes revelation." (p. 19).

63. Luther, *Against the Heavenly Prophets* (Works, Erlangen Edition), Vol. 29, p. 208. There is no need here to raise the question of the Lutheran view of ordinances (signs).

64. Barth writes that Calvin "approximated revelation and Scripture much more closely than did Augustine" (op. cit., p. 128) and, after finding in Luther the "three forms of the Word of God", the revealed, written and proclaimed word, yet he is "painfully aware of the absence, in all the utterances of this transition period, of the Reformers' insight into the dynamics of the mutual relationships between the three forms. This is shown in the doctrine of inspiration, which so to speak signifies a freezing up of the connection between Scripture and revelation" (*ibid.,* p. 139). Barth is so sure of the untenability of Biblical infallibility (in view of his concessions to higher criticism) that it does not seem to occur to him how much the necessity for disjunction of revelation and Scripture grows out of his desire to "save face" for revelation in view of a compromised Bible. What is to Barth an absence of insight on the part of the Reformers may well have been to them an avoidance of error.

(p. 274), a view which Brunner identifies with the orthodox Hodge-Warfield view at Princeton in earlier days. *There arose, Brunner remarks, "an infallible Bible-X, of which two things only were known: first, that it was the infallible word of God; and, secondly, that although it was very different from the present one, yet it was still the same Bible"* (pp. 274f., italics supplied). Thus an "honorable orthodox view" of Biblical authority was "forced to descend to apologetic artifices" as a result of which the theology of the Church "rightly" became the "butt of scientific criticism." In the long run the appeal to an infallible original was untenable; today, Brunner remarks, "it only continues to drag out an unhappy existence in certain Fundamentalist circles" (p. 275).

Brunner's statement is highly prejudicial to the whole case, conveying the impression that the fundamentalist contends for an original of which he knows nothing, but to which he assigns infallibility. For, in point of fact, there is a question over only one in a thousand words, as to the text of the New Testament, on the word of Westcott and Hort,[65] so that the original is not even overcast, as a whole, with 999/1000 probability, but is about 999/1000 continuous with the present text. Surely the Fundamentalist claims that the present text is much more continuous with the unseen original, than the consistent structure of liberal destructive criticism has contended that the present manuscripts are continuous with the unseen supposed original sources from which the Bible was supposedly edited, redacted, interpolated, etc., and the nature of which has been variously conceived a hundred times over since the days of Wellhausen. What the liberal theologian clearly objects to, whether this is overtly expressed or not, is not the illegitimacy of the leap to an unseen original, but rather a notion of revelation which necessitates a personal break with the non-

---

65. Westcott and Hort remarked: "If comparative trivialities, such as changes of order, the insertion or omission of the article with proper names, and the like, are set aside, the words in our opinion still subject to doubt can hardly amount to more than a thousandth part of the whole New Testament" (*Greek New Testament*, pp. 564f). This is hardly more than a half page of a standard Greek New Testament.

Biblical assumptions of contemporary evolutionary science, except to a limited degree.

That the theory of verbal inspiration presents difficulties, in view of the present record, no sincere evangelical scholar will dispute. The problems are of various kinds. The narrative of the woman taken in adultery—if the best available manuscript evidence is trustworthy—is not a part of the Fourth Gospel, but incorporates a tradition, which may nonetheless be trustworthy. The manuscript evidence is against the ending of Mark's Gospel. If one tends here to view the manuscript evidence as incomplete, he still faces parallel accounts in the Synoptics in which the evangelists, recording the words of Jesus, report them differently, not differently in substance to be sure, but verbally different. Here the evangelical tends to say that the occasions may not have been the same, or that Jesus may have expressed the same idea in numerous ways on the same occasion. Or he will say that verbal inspiration must not be defined so narrowly as to preclude the use of different words on the part of the evangelists in reporting the precise sense of the Master's remarks, for inspiration did not preclude vocabulary differences. Immediately this is said, the advocate of verbal inspiration recoils, to differentiate his position from a mere thought or concept-inspiration, for, after all, how is one to fix thoughts precisely except in words? And, doubtless, the appeal to an infallible original is sometimes an immediate cure-all for such disturbing moods.

(a) *The Importance of a Trustworthy Text.*

But the ideal of an infallible original had, for Evangelicalism, a pragmatic value (though that is not its only justification) to be found in no theory outside of verbal inspiration. The liberalist theology, which accepted no Biblical authority but professed to trust only those parts of the Bible which could be underwritten by scientific Empiricism, soon overcast the Bible with a non-Biblical mist that finally saturated the whole with a non-miraculous Secularism. Fundamentalism saw that, if one thinker could appeal to non-Biblical doctrine X as against Biblical doctrine Y, in principle the whole notion of objective authority had broken down, and there was no reason why non-Biblical doctrines A-Z could not be enthroned and the whole Hebrew-Christian doctrinal system dispelled. Hence Fundamentalism challenged the cardinal dogmas of Liberalism against which Neo-Supernaturalism is belatedly in revolt, and others as well. In a certain sense, Brunner agrees with Fundamentalism, and sees much more deeply at this point than the shallow classic Liberalism of a half century ago, that higher criticism and scientific dogmatism, if pitted against the inner claims of the Bible, makes impossible the notion of a consistency of doctrine which ties together the Hebrew-Christian view. But, whereas Evangelicalism accepts the testimony of Scripture as authoritative, and thus retains the conviction of a progressive revelation involving doctrinal unity, Brunner declares for higher criticism and evolutionary science, and abandons entirely the idea of the doctrinal unity of the Bible in his view of special revelation. Thus in Brunner the revolt against verbal inspiration takes the form also of revolt against the doctrinal consistency of the Scriptures.

Was it not the assault on the trustworthiness of the Bible, motivated often by biases derived from scientific Naturalism, which drove some evangelicals to extreme statements of the inspiration of the Scriptures—as the dictation view—by which the integrity of the Hebrew-Christian revelational view was defended? The Fundamentalist saw clearly that the destruction of the integrity of the text meant the downfall of a genuinely objective formulation of Christian Theism.[66]

Now, sometimes uncritical fundamentalists have made it appear that the case for Theism rests upon the existence of an infallible Bible; that if God exists, the Scriptures must be iner-

---

66. A. E. Taylor referred to "the dwindling number of educated Christians who continue to assert the inerrancy of Scripture in all respects" (*op. cit.*, p. 11). But the same might be said about other Biblical convictions. And, after all, the moderns are "educated" to disbelieve Biblical infallibility; proud Modernism regarded believers in an infallible Book as uneducated. Now Modernists are being educated to some errors of Modernism.

rant. But it is not even possible, if the Protestant view be true, to derive from the proposition that God exists, the further proposition that the Bible must be an infallible book. If God exists, there need not even be a Book; rather, God's special revelation is a matter of grace, and does not come from God as something which sinful man has a right to expect. Apart from God's special revelation there is no antecedent probability that there will be a special revelation. The nature of the revelation, when God has communicated such, can be determined only from the revelation itself. To say that the revelation claims to be divine and inerrant, for example, is not to say that it *might not* have been communicated through fallible instruments. Surely there was a revelational case for Theism before the canon was complete, before the New Testament was written, before Isaiah was written, in fact, before any Old Testament book was written. The existence of God does not depend upon the Bible (though indeed a *proper knowledge* of His existence and nature may be conditioned for us upon the written revelation). If the God of the Hebrew-Christian revelation exists, His existence is not conditioned upon anything external to Himself, not even the sacred Scriptures.

The truth of Christian Theism is not impossible of establishment, on historical grounds, even if the Scriptures were not inerrant. For the inspiration of the writings is not established prior to an examination of the evidence for their authenticity, historical credibility, and general trustworthiness. Nor are the writings the ground of Christian faith, but rather a means, and the divinely ordained means. But the writings are not on that account less important. By them we are able to certify the historic doctrines; by them we are directly related to the divine revelation consummated in the incarnation; by them we possess that literature of the early church the rejection of the authority of which involves us consistently in the rejection of every distinctively Christian doctrine. Hence the problem becomes the retention of Biblical authority, once inerrancy is modified, however slightly. It is this problem which drove

Christian apologists to such theories as the verbal inspiration of the text. What was *given,* in Biblical data and church precedent, was the final and complete—or plenary—inspiration of the Bible; the extent of inspiration was clearly outlined. But as to depth—whether a safe-guarding from error in thought or word, or divine superintendence in the choice of words, or dictation, or varied combinations of these and other possibilities—no over-all *modus operandi* was set forth in the Bible. All Scripture is God-breathed *(theopneustia)*; that much was an apostolic certainty. Where apostles afforded no certainty as to the mechanics of inspiration, later expositors created problems for themselves by identifying Biblical authority with a specific theory designed to cover all the facts. A true view of Biblical authority can champion inerrancy without being freighted with unnecessary dogmas about the mechanics of inspiration. But if a theory must be chosen, verbal inspiration as differentiated from both dictation and mere concept inspiration, is the most satisfactory conservative formulation.

b. *Verbal Inspiration Does Not Imply Idolatry.*

But even a dictation theory of inspiration was hardly Bibliolatry; no fundamentalist ever held that God became a book, nor have fundamentalists worshiped the Bible, as the Sikhs of India worship the Granth. Nor have they, contrary to Brunner, made the Bible an idol. It might be countered that the Roman Catholic Church distinguished at the Council of Trent between worship of God and reverence for idols, but that masses of communicants do not make the distinction, and so fundamentalists often do not distinguish the living word from the letter of the Bible.[67] The reply is, if there are Bibliolatrists, who worship the Bible, then *amen* to Brunner; they have added an impersonal deity to the Godhead, and Evangelicalism has no part

---

67. The late Dr. Henry C. Thiessen, author of *Introduction to the New Testament* (Eerdmans, 1943), thought that the original manuscripts were providentially permitted to disappear, lest they be worshipped as idols. This suggests, on the one hand, a danger of bibliolatry on the Fundamentalist approach, but on the other hand, disclaims it. On II Tim. 3:16, Calvin wrote: "that the same reverence is due to Scripture which we pay to God, because it flows from Him alone, and has no admixture of what is human."

with them. But where is such a fundamentalist, save in the fertile imagination of the Zurich scholar? Even one who affirms a dictation theory of the Bible need not on that account worship the Book, however much he may cherish it.[68]

The crucial problem, in the matter of inspiration, is after all not that of minor variations in the Synoptic reportings, which involve vocabulary rather than content differences; or which invariably suggest some possibility of reconciliation. Rather, verbal inspiration is precluded today, in the eyes of Neo-Supernaturalists and Modernists alike, because the evolutionary view of origins—cosmology, anthropology, the development of religions—is held to be in hopeless conflict with the Biblical pattern. Here men worship at the shrine of evolutionary philosophy.[69] Once this view is taken, is seems like idle futility to try to reconcile passages of lesser import; one will tend to look for *the one unique* element in the Bible which can be salvaged from this house of ruins. The fundamentalist, rejecting all but cultural evolution, does not have a patchwork Bible, redated to derive its doctrinal elements from the earliest-known non-Biblical sources; for him, the ideal option is a pattern of progressive revelation. For Brunner, the Bible is not a divine instrument molded specifically for revelation—for the Bible is not regarded as revelation, but as a fallible record—waiting on a subjective oft-repeated act. But for the evangelical, the Bible is an objectively true revelation, fashioned as such, whether the modern man receives it thus or not. At this point of interaction with Fundamentalism, Brunner does not establish his case for the scientific evolutionary view, but merely assumes it. The fact that Brunner says that Evolution is now beyond dispute, does not prove that it is now beyond dispute, but only that Brunner thinks it is.

---

68. Evangelical theologians often distinguish between the Bible as the *ratio cognoscendi* and Jesus Christ as the *ratio essendi* of faith.

69. The evolutionary theologians have their "unseen original" also — an original man who was not, as the Biblical Adam, created in the image of God and holy in character, but rather one whose rise to morality came against the background of a brute ancestry. It is quite a leap to reconcile this anthropology with the present Biblical text for which the Neo-Supernaturalists would retain a high, even if sub-evangelical, significance.

c. *Dangers of a Mechanical View of Revelation.*

Some fundamentalists have preached the Bible at times with a certain artificiality and a lack of divine contemporaneousness, as though God's really significant interventions in history ended when the back cover was placed on the New Testament. Wherever doctrinal belief was made a substitute for a Christian experience which enlists the total man, emotions and will no less than intellect, the doctrine of present divine confrontation, by the Holy Spirit of conviction and illumination, did not receive its proper emphasis.[70]

But Neo-Supernaturalism opens the door far too wide in the liberal direction. Its doctrine of revelation does not do justice to the centrality of the Scriptures* in God's self-disclosure to man. According to this view revelation does not take place until the written Word is preached to an enlightened hearer, that is, until it becomes the appropriated Word. Revelation is said to presuppose three elements: the Bible, preaching, and

---

70. Lutheran orthodox theologians like A. Quenstedt and D. Hollaz argued that the preached and written Word has a power apart from any effect on hearer or reader, so that there is a divine *actus primus* whether or not the *actus secundus* follows in human hearts. Karl Barth concedes the claim that "the Bible and preaching are the Word of God, in their full compass, as independent of subjective experience and superior to it" (*op. cit.*, p. 124; cf. p. 175). But Barth denies that efficacy is inherent in the Bible apart from the accompanying testimony of the Spirit. The direct identification of revelation and the Scriptures "takes place as an event when and where the word of the Bible becomes God's Word . . . Where the Word of God is an event, revelation and the Bible are one in fact" (*ibid.*, p. 127). Therefore "revelation is to be regarded primarily as the superior, the Bible primarily as the subordinate principle" (*ibid.*, p. 128). The Bible is real attestation only as related to the past revelation which it attests (*ibid.*, p. 132). But this then becomes for Barth prolegomenon for an attack on a "fatal doctrine of inspiration" (p. 128, footnote). The Word of God "is not to be regarded primarily as history, and then, and as such, as a decision also, but first and fundamentally as a decision and then, and as such, as history also" (*ibid.*, p. 178; cf. p. 244). Though we are told that "It is the letter of proclamation and the Bible that conveys the Spirit but it is the Spirit that will also bring us back every time to the letter" (*ibid.*, p. 205), yet in the twilight of neo-orthodox dialectic the Bible loses its infallibility and its objective authority.

*Brunner tells us that the Bible has normative authority—but that its authority is incomplete (does not extend beyond spiritual to cosmological and historical data) and relative (the New Testament data about Christ are conflicting and contradictory, and the Old Testament data reveal an even greater disunity). The Bible, for Brunner, is the unconditional *source* or *ground* of our teaching, but only conditionally its *norm;* the Living Christ beyond the witnesses is the norm. It would be curious to learn where Brunner found this separation of the Living Christ and the Christ of the New Testament in his acknowledged source of Christian teaching.

the responsive hearer.[71] But is there not a revelation, a divine self-disclosure, if prophets and apostles enter into the secret of God, wholly apart from the question of whether the written record is subsequently believed or not? True, the Spirit in contemporary energizing personalizes the Biblical knowledge-content, but does that mean that revelation—defined as the disclosure by God to humanity of that which man by his unaided effort could not attain—takes place anew each time it is believed? The tension between the Word and the Spirit can be retained by a proper restudy of the evangelical emphasis on a Biblical revelation which the Holy Spirit illuminates to the succession of believers.

The basic trouble with the neo-supernaturalist mood is its loose attitude toward the Scriptures, in which it refuses to "freeze" revelation.

The element of truth in Brunner's view of the Word is that the Living Word is not *merely* the written word. A danger in evangelical circles is a mechanical view of revelation and inspiration, which crystallizes in a dictation theory and which, by a relapse to a Catholic ritualistic dogmatism, involves no genuine faith. It is possible to make a mental transference of the same authority which the medieval Catholic ascribed to the church, to the Book, and merely to accept a set of lifeless dogmas. This danger, in which the testimony of the written Word is ritualistically appropiated in a speculative, credal way, without a genuine experience of saving faith, is less present in communions which practise exclusively believer's baptism, but it can hardly be said to be absent even there. It is possible to receive the testimony of the written Word without receiving the testimony of the Holy Spirit in an act of faith, but

---

71. Perhaps I have not clearly understood Dr. Brunner, but I cannot see how, in view of his declaration that there is no revelation until it "gets through" to the believer, he can so dogmatically insist on general revelation (as against Karl Barth) and yet deny natural theology (as against the Thomists). Does not the insistence that there is no natural theology drive him, on his own premises, to a denial of a general revelation?

the Spirit always testifies in and through the written Word.[72] Historical faith is not the equivalent of saving faith, but saving faith involves historical faith. There is a vital, as well as a mechanical view of verbal inspiration. Revelation has in view communion with God, as well as knowledge of God.

d. *Testimony of Spirit Does Not Dispense With Need for Authoritative Bible.*

The element of error comes by an over-separation of the written and Living Word. It is true that, for the glorified believer, the Living Word will be known without the instrument of a written word; "we shall know even as we are known." But the sin principle runs too deeply through the believer's life—even that of the sanctified believer—to relate him to the Living Word in over-divorce from the written word. True, the Living Word is Jesus Christ; to Him, the Holy Spirit testifies, and this testimony makes the written word "quick and powerful." But the Scriptures themselves do not hesitate to affirm of the writings that they are "the Word". The prophetic and apostolic teachings and writings communicated the Living Word as men responded in faith, and were themselves linked to the Living Word in a manner more intimate that Brunner concedes.[73] The Holy Spirit makes subjectively true to me the objectively true written revelation by revealing Christ through the Book. The knowledge content of revelation is in the writ-

---

72. G. W. Bromiley remarks that the Barthian movement is seeking to solve "the central relationship of revelation to history on the one side, to the individual believer on the other." Bromiley asks pointedly: "Ought we to think that the Bible is trustworthy merely because we can demonstrate its historical accuracy? Ought we to think it authoritative merely because we have come to know the truth of its message through the Holy Spirit, and irrespective of the historical reliability or otherwise? Ought we not to seek the authority of the Bible in the balanced relationship of a perfect form (the objective Word) and a perfect content (the Word applied subjectively by the Holy Ghost) — the form holding the content, the content not applied except in and through the form?" (*The Evangelical Quarterly*, Vol. XIX, No. 2, April, 1947, p. 136).

73. See Appendix Note C: The New Testament on the Word of God. For a long series of New Testament quotations showing that the content of faith is not Christ alone, as Brunner contends, but also a unity of revealed truths about Christ, God, and other spiritual entities, see Lorenz Volken's *Der Glaube Bei Emil Brunner* (Freiburg in der Schweiz: Paulusverlag, 1947). Volken argues that, according to Catholic theology, justifying faith is not mere intellectual assent to doctrines, but surrender of the whole man to the self-revealing God who speaks, as Catholicism contends, through His inspired Bible and His infallible Church. The problem of objective authority remains, in a different way, for Catholicism.

ten word, but the communion content waits on the Holy Spirit.[74] But the Spirit affords no propositional knowledge of God over and above what the Scriptures provide. Without the Bible the communion would be a mystical confusion; without the Spirit, the Scriptures would afford no life. We are born of the word, and for us this word is never only the Living Christ—for Jesus Christ himself declared of the Scriptures that "they testify of Me," as if the testimony of the letter and of the Spirit go together. The Incarnate Word did not disparage the written word: "Scripture cannot be broken" and "not one jot or tittle shall perish." The Scriptures themselves declare, "thus saith the Lord", and it is not an adequate treatment of this repeated conviction—expressed more than 3,800 times in the Old Testament—to say that such claims constitute a special difficulty in one's view of inspiration. Dismissed thus, the suspicion mounts that the special difficulty is the fault of the theory of inspiration, rather than with the Scriptures.*

The question is not whether one's theory of inspiration is a saving truth; it is not. In salvation, the Holy Spirit makes real to the sinner the truth of the written word in its witness to the mercy of God in Christ. The Spirit reveals the Christ of the Book through the Book; there is no revelation of Christ apart from the Scriptures (how does Brunner know the Holy Spirit testifies to the historic Christ?) All we know of Christ is conveyed to us through the Scriptures which interpret to us the Living Christ whom the Spirit discloses; we know nothing

---

74. The passages in Augustine's *On the Spirit and the Letter* are not particularly helpful on this problem. It is true that Augustine clearly contrasts the Old Testament law and the work of grace by such words as: ". . . Without His assisting grace, the law is 'the letter which killeth;' but when the Life-giving spirit is present, the law causes that to be loved as written without" (ch. 32); and "What then is God's presence of the Holy Spirit, who is, 'the finger of God,' and by whose presence is shed abroad in our hearts the love which is the fulfilling of the law, and the end of the commandment" (ch. 36, *The Nicene and Post-Nicene Fathers*, V. New York: The Christian Literature Co., 1888). But Augustine is dealing here with the contrast of the law and the Gospel, of the external demand for and the internal impulsion to holiness, and not with the problem of the relationship between the written word of revelation and the testimony of the Spirit.

* American liberals like Walter M. Horton are relieved over Brunner's compromise of Barth's approaches to Biblical authority. "If Barth pays lip-service to biblical criticism—while actually handling the Scriptures pretty arbitrarily—Brunner really honors its principles and obeys its laws," wrote Horton (*op. cit.*, p. 55).

about Christ beyond the written word except the living experience of Him, and our conviction that it is He depends not alone upon the testimony of the Spirit, but also the witness of the written word which the Spirit enlivens.[75] The Spirit persuades us of the truthfulness of Scripture, but it does not replace the objective authority of the written word. The Scripture is the source from which theology is drawn.[76]

Brunner's insistence on a fallible Scripture, coupled with the Reformation rupture with the notion of an infallible Church, leaves him without infallibility of any kind for, however much one may insist upon a subjective certainty in view of the testimony of the Spirit, there is no objective criterion by which this testimony may be tested, and this exposes the Protestant theological movement anew to the charge of Roman Catholicism that, since the Reformation, Protestantism has been a movement without objective authority (which Catholicism wrongly contends only the Church can provide).

The significant theological differences between neo-supernaturalistic spokesmen who appeal to the testimony of the Spirit in conjunction with a fallible Bible, should serve to underscore the inescapable subjectivism in such an endeavor.* That those who on the one hand profess a return to Biblical theology, at the same time delight to indict Fundamentalism for its Biblicism, provides a curious theological study.

---

75. Berkhof has a pointed statement on the testimony of the Spirit, which he says is "not so much the final ground as the means of faith. The final ground of faith is Scripture and Scripture only, or, better still, the authority of God which comes to the believer in the testimony of Scripture. The ground of faith is identical with its contents, and cannot be separated from it. But the testimony of the Holy Spirit is the moving cause of faith. We believe Scripture not because of, but through the testimony of the Spirit" (*op. cit.*, p. 201).

76. A. G. Honig remarks: "The question is not on what ground we confess that the Holy Scripture is the Word of God and therefore the Christian religion the true one, but rather how we, who by nature are not in condition and not inclined to recognize the divinity of Scripture, are led to believe that this Holy Scripture is God's Word?" (Translated from *Handboek van de Gereformeerde Dogmatiek*, p. 126. Kampen: Kok, 1938).

* There is Barth with his denial of general revelation, Brunner with his denial of the virgin birth, Bultmann with his denial that Jesus ever claimed to be the Messiah, and Edwin Lewis with his recent adoption of dualism (cf. *The Creator and the Adversary*. Nashville: Abingdon-Cokesbury Press, 1948). Nor has Barth successfully laid the ghost of suspicion that he believes in universal salvation, in contrast with the Biblical doctrine. D. C. Macintosh remarks that "it is even rumored that Barth's neo-Calvinism is taken by himself with a generous grain of the liberal salt of universalism" (*op. cit.*, p. 344) and Van Til has given the rumor some rather firm support (*The New Modernism*).

How, if the written word is necessary but fallible, the Spirit conveys an infallible testimony, is hardly clear. Can there be, in this pattern, a way back to an authoritative faith?[77]

The Neo-Supernaturalist movement, precommitted to an evolutionary view of origins and to many negativisms of higher criticism, is seeking an objective revelation without the "embarrassment"—in view of its opposition to Biblical infallibility and its insistence on considerable Biblical fallibility — of "freezing" that revelation in the already compromised Scriptures. What better appeal than to the testimony of the Spirit— without which, the tradition had conceded, the written word does not beget faith.[78] But how differentiate the testimony of the Spirit and that of the written word? Simple! Wherever Barth and Brunner find higher critical and scientific objections to the Bible the Spirit will be silent. And thus the suspicion grows that we are to accept the Scriptures not where they are consistent with an ultimate revelational rationale of the universe, so much as where they are consistent with the presuppositions of the Neo-Supernaturalists.

True, Brunner declares that the apostolic word is "absolutely essential" and "shares in the uniqueness and historical exclusiveness of the historical revelation of Christ" (*Revelation and Reason*, p. 123); that the written Scriptures are "the medium in which the word of God comes to us" and are not to be reduced to the same level as tradition (p. 126); that the apostolic testimony to Christ is both the foundation and norm of the later witness of the Church to Him (p. 127); that the apostolic writings are inspired and hand on revelation (p. 128); that the Bible is not merely a record of revelation but "a special form of divine revelation" in which God reveals to us the meaning of His self-disclosure (p. 135); that "no one can come to the Son save through the Holy Scriptures" (p. 136); that "we have no Christ apart from the Bible, is true for the Church as a whole" (p. 143); that "we possess the historical revelation of

---

77. See Appendix Note D: Subjective and Objective Authority.
78. That verbal-plenary inspiration is the historic position of the Christian church is effectively argued by Gaussen, *The Inspiration of the Scriptures*, pp. 139ff.

God in the Old Covenant, and in Jesus Christ, in the Holy Scriptures alone" (p. 273) ; that even the most radical views of the Synoptics do not do away with a picture of the life and person of Jesus" in essentials the same as it was prior to the rise of historical criticism (pp. 284f.) ; that "nothing of vital consequence to faith has been in any way affected by historical criticism" (p. 285).

But the revolt against Biblical sufficiency ends not only in an attack on infallibility; it runs on in Brunner, to a discard of the whole evangelical insistence on the doctrinal unity of the Bible. Not only does he over-differentiate the word of God from the written Scriptures, but he distinguishes it overly from doctrine.

Brunner's insistence on the essentiality and uniqueness of the Bible does not mean its final authority, and his view of the harmlessness of higher criticism can best be evaluated when Brunner has defined for us what comprises that essential remainder which, he insists, is unimpaired. That core, it will be seen, no longer includes, for Brunner, the doctrinal unity of the Old and New Testaments. The type of Biblical authority which Brunner preserves involves a revolt against an intellectualistic view of revelation.

The one pressing problem which remains, declares Brunner, is that—denying verbal inspiration but insisting upon special revelation—one is confronted by "the difference between the theological views of the various authors of the books of the New Testament" (p. 285). Although the Hebrew-Christian tradition has found in the Bible a unity of doctrine, higher criticism has operated to minimize and to obscure this unity. How firmly Brunner stands here with the critical movement is seen in his revolt, not only against the ideal of verbal inspiration, but also the ideal of a doctrinal unity in the Scriptures.

C. Doctrinal Unity of the Scriptures Precluded by Brunner's Statement of Special Revelation.

There is a return, we are told by Brunner, to "the Biblical understanding of revelation." The new school of "historical realism" has broken with the orthodox traditional view and identifies revelation not with infallible verbal expressions, nor with the Bible, but goes behind the Scriptures "to the *facts.*"[79]

New and intensive study of the Reformers, avers Brunner, encourages a new theology of revelation. *The older theologians, he remarks, "did not understand that the inspiration of the Holy Scriptures is not the revelation, but one of the forms of revelation,* namely, the incarnation in written form of the living personal relation of the Living God in the history of revelation and salvation. The Bible itself, when it speaks of revelation, points beyond itself to an event, to which indeed it bears witness, but which is not the Bible itself. The reflection of formal theology is directed toward the *whole* of the divine revelation, including this revelation to which the Bible witnesses; *the written record is part of this revelation, but it is not the whole.*"[80]

Hence Brunner not only opposes the verbal inspiration of the Scriptures, but also the equating of "revelation" with *Biblical revelation.* He laments the fact that the Christian movement early identified the concept of revelation with a doctrine of the Scriptures, declaring that theological reflection, once entangled "with this fatal equation of revelation with the inspiration of the Scriptures, was never able to shake itself free" (p. 7). The "fundamental error which equates the revelation with revealed doctrine", although beginning with the Apologists, "has its

---

79. *Revelation and Reason,* p. 12. Brunner mentions, as influential in this shift, Schelling's *Philosophie der Offenbarung* and Jakobi's *Von der gottlichen Dingen und ihrer Offenbarung,* which "forced theology at last to place the problem of revelation on a higher plane than the problem of the Scriptures" (*Ibid.,* p. 11, footnote). While Rothe's *Doqmatics* wrestled still with the problem of the formation of the Bible, Auberlen's *Die gottliche Offenbarung* and Kaehler's *Der sogenannte historische Jesus und der geschichtliche biblische Christus,* veered from the Scriptures to Christ as crucial for revelation.

80. *Op. cit.,* p. 12. Alan Richardson parts company with both Barth and Brunner for their insistence that "saving" revelation is found only in the Hebrew-Christian tradition. All revelation, general as well as special, he contends, is saving revelation; man's sin and egocentricism, however, distorts general revelation and necessitates special revelation. But there is no simple continuity between general and special revelation for "the latter is an emergently new kind of existence; there is a saltus, a leap from the one to the other" (*Christian Apologetics,* pp. 127ff. New York: Harper and Brothers, 1947). But special revelation, he quickly adds, is not the disclosure of supernatural knowledge, but the power to apprehend the truths given in general revelation (p. 134).

beginnings even in the Pastoral Epistles and with the Apostolic Fathers".[81] Brunner concedes that the view of the orthodox Lutheran, Calovius, *forma revelationis divinae est theopneustia per quam revelatio divina est quod est,* characterizes not only Lutheran orthodoxy, but the whole of the older theology. This "grave misunderstanding of revelation," he declares, "hangs like a dark shadow over the whole history of the Christian Church" (p. 8).

It was a "false intellectualism in the concepts of revelation and of faith" (p. 10) which narrowed the idea of revelation to the doctrines of the Bible, declares Brunner. The Church, in its conflict with Gnosticism, projected the concept of divinely inspired doctrine to provide a legalistic instrument of differentiation, (p. 8) and once the Bible was viewed as the source of divine doctrinal truth the concept of infallibility became inevitable (p. 9). The Reformation, while breaking with Catholic errors about the nature of faith, retained the Catholic idea of revelation—of the Scriptures as the source of infallible doctrines—not aware that in so doing they "destroyed the real gains of the new discovery of the Reformation."[82] For the equating of revelation with the written word involves the church in creature-worship. Contemporary theology must "make a fresh beginning, at the point where the first generation of Reformers came to a standstill. Here historical Biblical criticism has opened up the way, which had been blocked by the theory of verbal inspiration" (p. 195).

---

81. *Ibid.,* p. 8, footnote, where Brunner cites the emphasis on "sound doctrine" in Titus 2:10 as an example.

82. *Ibid.,* p. 11. Brunner points out — "over against the doctrinaire views of the present day" — that Luther often preached without expounding a definite Bible text (*Ibid.,* p. 143, foonote). But did Luther preach against it? And did he, by his practise, repudiate the significance of doctrine? The intimate relationship between the word of God and doctrine is indicated by the juxtaposition of the two ideas, by express declaration, in other verses in the pastoral epistles, as I Tim. 4:6, 5:17; 2 Tim. 2:15, 4:2; and Titus 1:9. But to look for "proof texts" for the equation is to forget that the Hebrew-Christian religion involves at its very heart a teaching ministry; the doctrinal unity of Old and New Testaments is seen in Luke 24:44, and the centrality of doctrine for Christianity in Luke 1:4 — if one asks for such texts. But the whole sweep of the Hebrew-Christian tradition, in the main outlines of its letters as well as its history, shows that it places no premium on an experience of God in which clear ideas (doctrine) are not essential.

1. *Revelation Equated With Divine Acts, Not Doctrine.*

For the Biblical prophets and apostles, divine revelation "always meant the whole of the divine activity for the salvation of the world," (p. 8). meant divine saving activity, especially Jesus Christ. "Divine revelation is not a book or a doctrine" "but "is God Himself in His self-manifestation within history." (p. 8). The purely historical books of the Old Testament "constitute a better testimony to the fact of revelation than a doctrinal view of revelation" (p. 133).

Whatever errors there may be in the Scriptures raises no real difficulty with this view of revelation, for the Word of God is Jesus Christ in His loving, self-imparting activity (pp. 120, 133). "Where the main concern is with unity of doctrine, historical differences continually cause painful embarrassment; but where the main concern is the unity of the divine purpose in saving history, historical differences are not only not embarrassing; they are necessary" (p. 197). The new view of revelation, apparently, demands doctrinal flexibility and variation* as its precondition; any notion of fixed doctrine, it appears, means that history is devoided of its meaning; progressive revelation means changing doctrine but a unity of divine saving acts. Thus, while Brunner insists that the same God speaks in both testaments, he adds that "those who expound the Old Testament should know that the Old Testament does not say the same thing as the New" (p. 197). God's Word is a Person, is "the Incarnate Word, God Himself present in a human person. He Himself—not something that can be grasped in words;[83] not something that can be thought,[84] not an idea

---

* Barth and Brunner divide over the extent of variety within the unity of revelation. Barth stresses that all variety (prophets, incarnation, apostles) is a phase of the one revelation, Christ, who is found unilaterally revealed; Christ is the meaning of the O.T. (cf. Hengstenberg's *Christology of the Old Testament*, Vischer's *Christuszeugnis des Alten Testaments*). Brunner stresses the variety, protesting that Barth's "monism" conceals the historical character of revelation and tends to substitute for progressive revelation a philosophy of "eternal ideas" deducible apart from later manifestations. But Barth no less than Brunner disparages a view of doctrinal revelation. Brunner's emphasis on variety is a concomitant of the contradiction which he professes to find among prophetic and apostolic witnesses. See below, pp. 91ff.
83. Then ought not Brunner to cease writing about it?
84. Why is the reader expected to follow this thought?

in the mind—is the Truth" (p. 148). The Word of God is nothing other than Jesus Christ Himself (p. 183).[85]

Brunner's dialectical mode of statement—his "yes" and "no" —often makes interpretation difficult, for his thesis and antithesis find only partial synthesis, affording an incomplete contact with the traditional view, and yet a rupture with it. Thus he declares that "the Holy Scriptures do not teach theological doctrine" and, a short while later, "all 'doctrine' in the Bible (is) a call or summons... not doctrine in an abstract and impersonal way" (p. 149). To this latter statement all will subscribe, who stress the need for individual regeneration and who indict that type of formalism or credalism which substitutes memorization of doctrine for personal religious experience. So far Brunner is surely right. But this is not all Brunner means; he has said also that the Scriptures do not teach theological doctrine, and he means it; the ideal of a doctrinal unity of the Bible is discarded. Thus we are told that God's presence in Christ is more than any kind of theological doctrine;[86] yet He is only present through definite ideas, and thus the power of witness to Christ depends upon correct doctrinal content; but the thought-content is not the Word of God, but rather the Word is the meaning, is the self-manifestation of Christ (pp. 150f). No apostle succeeds in saying, in doctrine, in words, the one thing he wants to say, for the Word is the living Christ (p. 152), who can never be fully expressed even in infallibly 'correct' doctrine (p. 153), else formalism can replace discipleship (p. 154). Yet obedience cannot take place without correct theological doctrine (p. 154). But then Brunner declares that doctrinal emphasis minimizes

---

85. Here Barth also takes his stand. "The equation, God's Word is God's Son, makes anything doctrinaire in regarding the Word of God radically impossible. In it and only in it is a real and effective barrier raised against what can be made of proclamation according to the Roman Catholic conception or of Holy Scripture according to the theory of later Old-Protestantism, a fixed total of revealed propositions to be systematized like the sections of a *corpus* of law. The only possible system in Holy Scripture and in proclamation is revelation, i. e., Jesus Christ" (*op. cit.*, p. 156). No true evangelical would desire to remove Jesus Christ, the Living Word, from centrality in the Written Word, but that centrality need not be the oversimplified reductionistic variety of Neo-Supernaturalism.

86. And is not this itself a theological doctrine?

the personal challenge,[87] and that "in the knowledge of faith all that matters is not academic knowledge, but trust and obedience" (p. 155); theology must not be equated with the knowledge of faith (p. 155, footnote). Doctrine is a confession of faith, not an object of faith, for Jesus Christ is the object of faith,[88] the doctrine is a means to Him, and hence is never infallible (p. 156). Dogma is but a provisional attempt to express in definite formulas the doctrinal content of the Word of God, but is subject to revision in the light of better Biblical knowledge (p. 160).

a. *Modifications of the Traditional View Required by this Approach.*

That the new view of the Scriptures involves many changes from the traditional attitude becomes immediately evident.

Prophecy is no longer viewed as "foretelling" but is rather the history of revelation.[89] It is an erroneous principle of exposition, we are informed, that "the Old Testament throughout bears witness to Christ, although Christ is throughout the revealer.[90] "It is possible to ascribe to the Prophets a knowledge of Christ only by means of an artificial, non-Biblical method of allegory, which equates the Old Testament with the New" (p. 199). To project an over-anticipation into the Old

---

87. That the doctrinal emphasis *needs* to minimize the personal challenge is not demonstrated; that it sometimes does is conceded. What Brunner needs to show is that the personal challenge is of any consequence whatever when all clear ideas are absent. If their presence is insisted upon let us stop all the confusing dialectic about the interference of doctrine with adequate religious experience, and say that the trouble is not with the presence of doctrine, but with the presence of wrong doctrine. After all, the neo-supernaturalistic dialectic issues in *another doctrine*. Let us be plain then about the fact that the despite for traditional doctrine here prepares the way for novel doctrine — even if in the name of a protest against the centrality of doctrine.

88. The moment one tries intelligently to answer the question, "what Jesus?", he is on doctrinal ground. It is impossible to over-divorce knowledge and faith, and to have a specifically Christian faith. That doctrine is a means to Him — and not an end — is clear enough; that it is therefore fallible, is hardly self-evident, for if it is fallible, it is not a means. Doctrine is a means to Him precisely to the extent that it is infallible.

89. Brunner contrasts Hengstenberg's *Christologie des Alten Testaments,* as representative of the orthodox Lutheran tradition, with Hofmann's *Weissagung und Erfullung* and Eichrodt's *Theologie des Alten Testaments.* Yet Brunner concedes that the Old Testament promises of future revelation increasingly anticipate a supernatural person; Psalm 53 he interprets Messianically (*Ibid.,* p. 94).

90. Vischer's *Das Christuszeugnis des Alten Testaments* is scored for stressing unity at the expense of variety; "owing to this," remarks Brunner, "he obscures the historical character of the revelation by the orthodox view of a revealed doctrine (Christology)" (*op. cit.,* p. 82, footnote). The fact that Vischer is also a neo-supernaturalist in his overall approach indicates how much to the left Brunner veers.

Testament is to deny that the incarnation comes as something new, is to forget that God comes ever nearer in his historical revelation. This is to fall "into the old orthodox, intellectualistic, non-historical error, namely, that revelation is equated with doctrine, and that the doctrine can only be one, a mistake which has . . . blurred the distinctio temporum" (p. 83) .* The divine announcement of salvation and judgment "is not connected with any system of doctrine . . . due to the historical and personal character of the revelation" (p. 87). The orthodox view of revelation "minimized" or "ignored" the difference between prophecy and fulfillment, substituting timeless doctrine which was communicated imperfectly in one form of revelation and perfectly in another, a view which obscures the decisive element in Biblical revelation, i.e., its historical character (pp. 98f.). Brunner feels Karl Barth makes the same mistake, when he holds that The Old Covenant looks forward to the New, and the New backward to the Old, because here again "the timeless idea outweighs the historical character of our understanding of Biblical revelation."[91] This obscures the immense gap between what is foretold and what is fulfilled.[92]

The insistence of the early church on the unity between the Old and New Testaments, Brunner thinks, "has been mistaken, and has caused a great deal of confusion by undervaluing the difference between them. She has gone astray when she has made artificial attempts to harmonize the two, trying to prove . . . a unity of doctrine which is in direct opposition to God's wise and loving method of educating mankind" (p. 135).[93]

---

* The old Protestant view emphasized the unity of Biblical revelation without (1) denying that Christ is the center and source of revelation; (2) denying that Biblical revelation is progressive. in terms of promise and fulfillment; (3) denying that revelation is propositional; (4) denying that revelation is inscripturated. Brunner now makes it appear that the affirmation of (3) and (4) obscured (1) and that the orthodox doctrinal view of (2) distorted it. when all the time his dissatisfactions appear to grow out of a desire to propitiate higher criticism.

91. *Ibid.,* p. 99. Cf. Barth's *Kirchliche Dogmatik,* I, 2, par. 14.

92. It is apparent, in all of this, how Brunner's prejudice against propositional theology colors his treatment; progressive revelation is equated, not with a progressive knowledge-disclosure in which the later consistently enlarges on the earlier, but with the necessity for a non-doctrinal view of revelation.

93. One can hardly read Matthew's gospel, with its repeated "this was done that it might be fulfilled," without sensing that Brunner is here in revolt against the primitive conviction of the church; revelation was not exhausted in a continuity of act merely without a divine conveyance of its inner meaning.

The Biblical *history* of revelation—over against the "time-lessness" of the doctrinal system of orthodoxy—is caught up by Reformation thinkers from the theology of Irenaeus, Brunner remarks; Cocceius, Zwingli, Bullinger, and Calvin stressed the covenant idea, and the economy of revelation. "Far too early," complains Brunner, "the Reformation settled down into a fixed mold of sterile orthodoxy, which identified the word of God with revealed doctrine, and regarded the acts of God alongside of His Word, as subordinate to it" (p. 195).

Only where one overlooks the variety of Biblical revelation can one champion the orthodox view of a revealed doctrine; Biblical revelation is expressed by a great variety of ideas (pp. 82f.) .[94] Brunner rejects the claim that there is a "theology of the Old Testament" (p. 290). The Synoptic, Pauline and Johannine types of doctrine differ considerably from each other "and no theological art reduces them to the same common denominator" (p. 129). "The divinely present Word cannot be tied to a correct doctrine" (p. 145) .[95] All one can find in the Bible is "a convergence of certain ways of thinking, in doctrinal terms, which point to a common Center". Right doctrine means right direction, not a final system of fixed ideas, for there is no closed theological system (p. 157). "In the last resort there are not many doctrines; there is only one: that God is the holy and merciful Lord" (p. 158).

The unity of Biblical revelation is not a unity of doctrine, but "a unity of divine revealing action" (p. 195). God makes Himself known, "not in a doctrine, but in historical action"; the Bible "represents the whole of saving history as a unity, not of doctrine, but of the mighty acts of God" (p. 196). This

---

94. The older liberal theology has insisted too that one found "varieties of New Testament theology", but one New Testament religion. Here the common denominator was "religious experience", a denominator which, as religious humanism was quick to see, afforded no secure ground for distinguishing between religious traditions. For Brunner, the denominator is "Jesus Christ" — the divinely-provided Mediator, issuing from a God both holy and merciful. Now, either this is doctrine — and as such is revelational meaning of the divine activity — or it is mystical hodge-podge. And if this is the *one* Biblical doctrine, then Brunner's revolt is not against propositional revelation, but against propositional revelation not to his liking. Why should not the doctrine that Brunner settles for, be merely "an obvious consequence of" his "humanity", as he tends to dismiss apostolic doctrines? (see below).

95. Not even to the doctrine on which this sentence rests?

puts in proper perspective the different types of doctrine within the individual books of both testaments, and the difference between Old and New Testament doctrine as a whole (p. 288).

The doctrinal elements, priestly and prophetic, or the theology of ancient and post-Exilic Israel, cannot be reduced to a common denominator. For the orthodox view of the Bible "this is an absolutely hopeless state of affairs... God's revelation cannot be measured by the yardstick of theological doctrine" (p. 291). The Old Testament doctrinal contradictions "seem to mock all efforts to gain a unified view. Indeed, anyone who tried to make a scientific unity of view out of all these different and contradictory elements would only knock his head against a wall" (p. 292). "Once for all" critical research has destroyed "the unity of the doctrines of the Apostles in the New Testament and of the men of God in the Old Testament"... Indeed, "it is precisely the non-uniform doctrine of the Bible that becomes a demonstration of the divine mercy and of His education by love" (p. 293).[96] Were the Christian faith a faith in revealed truth—"as the orthodoxy of all periods thought it was"—the doctrinal differences of the apostles would be fatal for faith (pp. 289f), but for "us, who do not believe in a doctrine but in Jesus Christ Himself... the variety in the Apostolic doctrine is an obvious consequence of their humanity," although "regarded purely from the theological and intellectual point of view, is an irreconcilable contradiction" (p. 290). The various epistles contain contradictory doctrinal elements, because the truth of Christ necessarily lies beyond all these doctrines (p. 290).

"Yet our final judgment as a whole," avers Brunner, "must be this: It is only in the manifold variety... with all its con-

---

96. This is strange indeed. One wonders if the divine mercy and loving education would be impossible of demonstration except through contradictory doctrines — for then this doctrine too must get aboard the dialectical merry-go-round. Does Brunner escape a merely functional view of revelation? The functional view is defined by Brightman as testing revelation not primarily by its intellectual finality or moral absoluteness, but by its function in bringing man nearer to God. "Hence, erroneous theological, philosophical, and moral ideas may be part of the divine plan of revelation" (*The Finding of God*, pp. 41f. New York: The Abingdon Press, 1931).

tradictions—a variety which transcends all theological systems—
that the witness to Christ, in all its fulness and completeness,
is attested" (p. 130) .

b. *Criticism of Brunner's View.*

What is at the heart, we must now ask, of this distinction
between revelation as doctrine and revelation as saving activity?

For it is assuredly true that revelation is, in the first instance,
a saving event. The covenants with Noah and Abraham, the
deliverance from Egypt, the Mosaic covenant, the prophetic
disclosures, and supremely the Incarnation — with the miraculous birth, the vicarious death, the resurrection—what is all
this but *a divine working*, the entrance of God into human
history for saving ends? Rightly has it been emphasized how
the so-called Apostles' Creed throbs with narrations of what
God has done. What a contrast the Hebrew-Christian tradition
affords to the philosophic Idealisms—whether the ancient Pla-
tonic-Aristotelian varieties, or the modern post-Hegelian varieties—in which God does not enter *specifically* into history, in
which there is no notion of special historical revelation, in
which the activity of God is conceived so generally that the
philosophic Idealisms can link hands with the Naturalisms
in bitter attack against the notion of special historical revelation, against the notion of uniqueness, or once-for-all divine
acts. The Hebrew-Christian religion is a miraculous religion,
and a historical religion; it has its roots in the invasion of the
temporal and historical by the transcendent God, in a special
saving act which is anticipated in a special revelatory movement among the Israelites. Hence it can never be viewed simply
as a philosophic system, as though its right to an apologetic
is merely that of every philosopher who projects a starting
point around which he can maneuver a coherent interpretation
of reality. It is not reducible to a "system of eternal ideas,"
to a set of philosophic postulates, to a series of doctrinal or
credal statements.

(1). *Redemptive Activity Involves Divine Disclosure of Meaning Also.*

But now, if the Hebrew-Christian tradition insists that, while supernaturally grounded, it has its roots firmly entrenched in historical events of divine self-disclosure, it does not on that account depreciate the significance of doctrine.[97] For it is, after all, the meaning of the events or divine acts, upon which everything turns. And the Bible, while devoting tremendous space to narration—to setting forth the divine disclosive acts—presumes to give also the rationale or meaning of these acts. Without this rationale, the events stand as irruptive intrusions, as inexplicable and meaningless. Christ died, Christ arose — those are events; Christ died for us, Christ arose for us — that makes the events intelligible, and just because "the substitutionary death, the bodily resurrection" are doctrines, they are not on that account devoid of relationship to the historic events. Without the events, the doctrines are empty postulates; the sinfulness of man, the atonement, the bodily resurrection—what are these notions, if God has not entered specifically into history, if there is no Calvary, no empty tomb? Indeed, that same Apostles' Creed which so stresses divine acts, stresses also the forgiveness of sins, the communion of saints, the resurrection of the body, and the life everlasting, all of which presuppose the divine saving acts in history. It is not that no doctrine can be received apart from a humanly experienced installment, else the Hebrew-Christian view would have no doctrine of creation, of a consumatory judgment, of a final separation of righteous and wicked, of a glorification of the

---

97. Louis Berkhof comments that special revelation is both word and fact revelation. "Special revelation does not consist exclusively in word and doctrine, and does not merely address itself to the intellect. This is more clearly understood at present than it was formerly. The Old Testament revelation is not found in the law and the prophets only, but also in theophany of miracle. And in the New Testament Christ is not only prophet, but also priest and king. He is not merely the Word, but also the appearance and servant of God. He is the personal revelation of God's righteousness and holiness on the one hand, and of His mercy and grace on the other. And when the apostles enter the world with the message of redemption, not only their word, but also their charismatic gifts and miracles are revelations of God. The view, once prevalent, that revelation consists exclusively in a communication of doctrine, was clearly one-sided. At present, however, some go to the other extreme, equally one-sided, that revelation consists only in communication of power and life" (*op. cit.*, p. 144).

believer. But these doctrines, like those which have their fulfillments in history, are not artificial postulations, but stand organically related to the divine activity in the Hebrew-Christian movement, as part of the revealed rationale of that activity. The Scriptures give us not merely a record of the divine revelation; they are themselves a revelation, setting forth the *meaning* of the events they relate. The Christian is the first to insist that his religion is not reducible to a set of abstract notions; that, in fact, its most essential element is a divine redemptive activity from beyond, from outside himself. But Paul, in Rom. 9:9f. shows that the Christian experience of trust in God is not devoid of intellectual belief: "Confess with your mouth that Jesus is Lord, and believe in your heart that God raised him from the dead, and you will be saved." True, Paul does not here summon men to abstract philosophical doctrine. The Lordship of Christ, and His resurrection, are divine acts in history, but they are *meaningful acts,* and their interpretation is not superadded in the sense of cautious speculation, but is the divine rationale which makes the events significant.

One senses in Edwin Lewis' writings, for all his affinities with Neo-Supernaturalism, more of a readiness to see the doctrinal significance of the divine events. While embracing the refusal to identify revelation with the Bible, and yielding authority instead to the Holy Spirit, so that revelation for Him is also activistic, Lewis nonetheless thinks of revelation as "a disclosure of truth which would otherwise remain at best only a speculation."[98] The question of questions, he sees, is that of right *interpretation.* The Christian revelation is "held to be true because it issues from God himself—from God who, through the Spirit, has led men into the truth. It was not enough that God through the Word should *act*: it was also required that God should make known *that* it was his action and *what*

---

98. Lewis, *op. cit.,* p. 256: "Revelation means that God is categorically affirmed, and that he bears a certain character, and is working for certain ends, and what these ends are likewise is included in the revelation. God utters his Word, but the meaning of what is uttered is still to be conveyed, and this is the work of the Holy Spirit."

the action *signified*. This He does by the Spirit. Revelation by the Word is fundamental, but it is incomplete until it is received into a mind, and it is the Spirit which brings the mind to this apprehension and acceptance."[99]

An insistence on the necessity for intelligible revelation—for the assignment to reason of "an integral role in the revelatory process"—is voiced by S. Paul Schilling.[100] But at the same time, he decries a view of communicated truth or revealed doctrine, and pleads for a functional, dynamic, and teleological view according to which revelation seeks, "to lift man out of sin into that personal relation to God which constitutes his salvation."[101] The role of reason is to furnish a preparation for revelation, and an instrument for applying the validating test of coherence, he declares, as against neo-supernaturalist "ineffabilities" (pp. 17ff.). But now, if revelation is rational—and we not only admit but insist that it is—why must God be prohibited from propositional disclosure, or truth revelation? Does the view show too much disrespect for human personality, by minimizing the creative phase of human knowledge?[102] But then, man is a *sinner*, and special revelation in the Hebrew-Christian tradition is soteriological revelation and presupposes that man's need includes knowledge of God as well as divine power. The Biblical view is functional, dynamic and teleological, but not as divorced from propositional revelation; that is, it truly gives intellection an integral role in the revelatory process, although it does not make the human reason a seive which

---

99. *Ibid.*, p. 256. Lewis is reluctant to identify this *meaning* with the Bible as objective revelation, however. As with Brunner, so here the meaning is not delivered once-for-all to prophets and apostles, but is redelivered in individual religious experience on the testimony of the Spirit with the written word as a referential. But there is more insistence on meaning as belonging to revelation, rather than as appended to it.

100. (*Op. cit.*, p. 20). He writes: "Reason must be integrally related to revelation if the unity and integrity of personality are to be maintained. It is the whole self that receives whatever revelation is vouchsafed to man; it is the whole self that worships God; and it is the whole self that thinks about God, the world, and human destiny. A view which arbitrarily sets up a partition and says essentially, This is the sphere of revelation and that of reason, is false to the nature of the personal life."

101. *Ibid.*, p. 14.

102. Is it not curious how the personal idealists, arguing for the rationality of revelation, at the same time reject a truly unique or special revelation in the Biblical sense, while the neo-supernaturalists, arguing for a special once-for-all revelation, fall into mysticism by a failure to insist on its rational or propositional nature.

screens out transcendent ideas, but rather makes it a recipient
of divine knowledge apart from which it is futile to talk about
a meaningful revelational adjustment. On the Biblical view, the
prerequisite for genuine Christian experience is a knowledge
content—a knowledge of the nature of God, the plight of man,
and the provision of salvation. For all their stress on rationality in revelation, the modern functional theories are also
mystical, although the appeal to coherence rather than to super-
rational ineffability clouds this mysticism.

The champions of functional revelation are right, of course,
in insisting that God reveals no truth *to us;* the Hebrew-
Christian tradition has insisted firmly that prophets and apostles,
to whom revelation was given, once for all, are to be differentiated from those to whom revelation was passed on or delivered.[103] Hence it is not suprising that functional revelationalists
are unable to find propositional revelation the divine-human
encounter. But to say on that account that God is indifferent
to doctrine, or that he leaves it to man to distill the meaning
of revelation, and that his one concern is with an adjustment
which lifts man out of sin into salvation is inaccurate and is
over-simple. It is inaccurate because it is not the Biblical view
of revelation, for which the neo-supernaturalists profess to
speak, that the divine initiative embraces no "given" for the human intellect along with the "given" for the will and emotions;
in the Bible, doctrine and life go together. It is over-simple
because the notion that the salvation-experience is itself quite
obvious, apart from divine definition of it, is not borne out by

---

103. It is all too easy to ridicule the orthodox Protestant view of a closed canon
of truth by appealing to modern science and by declaring that there is no closed
canon of truth except to the mechanically and defensively minded. Nobody questions
that new scientific truth is achievable; what is insisted on by evangelicals is that nothing
can be added or taken away from the Biblical plan of redemption. The stress on the
"back cover" of the Bible means, essentially, that God's supreme and final redemptive
disclosure is complete; so far as the church is concerned, it is a *given.* God continues
to operate vitally in history, of course; there is a perpetual application of His truth
to new situations and persons; but no new soteriological truth as such. In the eschatological future there will be new truth — a progression in divine revelation — but
this side of glorification day, the church finds the knowledge-content of its faith, to be
translated into experience, in the Scriptures. Many who shouted most loudly against
the idea of a "closed canon of truth" are now slowly finding their way back to some
of the truths enclosed within that canon, and acknowledging how the so-called "truth
outside" was really a reduction or falsification of the Biblical teaching.

the facts. The champions of functional revelation almost invariably define as salvation an experience which, when appraised from the New Testament standpoint, is grossly inadequate.[104]

Now it is true, as Brunner contends, that the meaning of the divine activity, in a word, is Jesus Christ; He is the one Word which the Bible speaks. If one is led to doctrines about Him, in a merely speculative manner, without a genuinely personal relationship, the divine purpose of redemption is not effected. To substitute many words, in this sense, for the Word, is to make doctrine, or credalism, replace redemption.

But what and who is this one Word—Jesus Christ—of whom the Bible speaks? For it is not an ineffable Word, even if not fully comprehensible; it is not a Word of ultimate paradox and dialectic, but a Word of *revelation*, intelligible and coherent. Since Brunner concedes that the Word is communicated in clear ideas, the key question is whether those ideas are reconcilable or paradoxical, whether the Word can be brought within the law of contradiction—and the evidence points, in Brunner's case, to an insistence on paradox to such an extent that no doctrinal formulation can be treated with finality.[105] One may grant that

---

104. Henry P. Van Dusen provides an illustration of an insistence on divine revelational initiative, which retains a functional rather than meaningful (doctrinal) emphasis. He declares it "most important" that "discussion of the 'articulate Word' should remind itself tirelessly what is the fashion in which the Word is principally to be communicated — not through ideas, or even speech, but through life. The very term 'word' is deceptive; it suggests a 'spoken word'. The characteristic Protestant stress upon preaching aggravates the error" (*The International Review of Missions*: "The Problem of Communication", p. 500. Vol. XXXVI, No. 144; Oct., 1947). Dr. Van Dusen adds: "The successive historical theologies served an indispensable, if precarious, function in their days; they become impediments rather than instruments of true Christian Faith when they are set forth as definite formulations of Christian Faith for other days" (*ibid.*, p. 498). Here the impact of the revelational Word engenders only a doctrinally-vague adjustment to higher levels of divine-human life; there is no essential content advance on the older Liberalism, except in terms of vocabulary differences which apparently are not to be treated too seriously.

105. Here one comes upon a disjunction among the modern pleas for special revelation. Although the recent mood rejects propositional revelation (once-for-all revealed doctrine set forth in the Bible) it divides over whether revelation has a doctrinal element or not, as implicit in the subjective spiritual work of illumination. The higher mood insists upon truths of revelation as doctrinal inferences which believers make, under the guidance of the Holy Spirit, in response to the divine acts (the Bible varying in its significance from the record of the most significant of these acts to a record which contains also propositional revelation intermingled with subjective elements); the essential distinction from the traditional view is that the Scriptures are no longer the authoritative and infallible source of doctrine. The view that the divine acts or historical events are the *media* of revelation — as a protest against the location of revelation in religious experience alone — can be coupled with an insistence that (1) the interpretation of the events is a subjective and divinely unaided experience; or

the Living Word is not the same as a memorized doctrine, without granting that the Living Word is intelligible apart from
clear doctrinal affirmations which, while they are not exhaustive,
are nonetheless accurate and trustworthy as far as they go.

(2) *Bible Not Merely A Record of Revelation, Although
Illumination Is a Necessary Work of the Spirit.*

The retreat of the significance of doctrine today goes hand
in hand with the distinction, pressed by C. H. Dodd and others,
between the preaching of the "received Gospel" and the apostolic elaboration of that Gospel for the instruction of converts.
The fact that such a distinction is found in the New Testament
(I Co. 3:1-14; 2:1-7 and 15:1-3; Acts 10) is taken to imply that
doctrine should be presented with more reserve than the sheer
statement of events which characterizes the "received Gospel."
Thus the distinction arises between the basis from which faith
springs, and the concepts to which faith gives rise. But whereas
the evangelical tradition viewed the Scriptures, testified to by
the Spirit, as the basis of faith, and systematic or dogmatic
theology as a faith-motivated formulation, the neo-supernaturalists (like the Ritschlian, Wilhelm Herrmann, Barth's teacher)
distinguished between revelation and the Bible, between the
event and the written record.[106] The question is not whether
every statement in the Bible is revelational; the orthodox view,

---

106. Writes Barth: "We do the Bible a poor honour, and one unwelcome to itself,
when we directly identify it with . . . revelation itself" (*op cit.*, p. 126). The contrast of
Evangelicalism and Barthianism at this point is forcefully put by Miner B. Stearns:
"Of course, Barth is right in holding that a man may read the Bible without God's
speaking to him through it; but he is wrong in thinking that the Bible is not God's
Word in that case" (*Bibliotheca Sacra*: "Protestant Theology Since 1700", Vol. 105,
No. 417, Jan.-Mar. 1948, pp. 69f.). But when Stearns complains that "for Barth
the Word of God is Christ, not the Bible", he leaves his position too much open to
objection. Surely the Living Word, to whom the written Word ever bears witness, is
Jesus Christ; one gains nothing by identifying the written Word in such a way as to contrast Biblical revelation with Christ. But whether an objective picture of Christ is
possible without the authority of the written Word is the question. If we lose the
authority of the written Word, we lose at the same time the validity of our picture of
Christ Jesus, in any authoritative and secure sense.

---

(2) God does not give a once-for-all propositional interpretation, but guides men as
the inferences are made from the events, as William Temple held; or (3) God does
not give a propositional interpretation, but the bifurcation of event and interpretation
is artificial, and God guides in the most coherent interpretation of the facts, as Alan
Richardson appears to hold; or (4) the bifurcation of event and interpretation is artificial, and God has not only acted but spoken, giving a propositional interpretation of
the divine activity in the Scriptures, as the traditional view held.

that the Bible *is* a revelation, and not merely *contains* a revelation, has not so contended.[107] One does not need to revolt against the significance of doctrine to subscribe to Brunner's principle that "the written word is not the primary revelation, but the secondary form of revelation, even in the Old Covenant," (pp. 132f.) as expressing a valid truth. But that we today know the primary form only in terms of the secondary, and that the divine purpose secured the trustworthy inscripturation of the primary revelation by supernatural inspiration, Brunner fails to emphasize.

Orthodoxy has insisted that the interpretation as well as the event is *given* and that there is such a thing as *revealed truth* as well as *revealed action*.[108] The newer view of revelation, on the contrary, distinguishes sharply between the divine events and the apostolic teaching predicated thereon; the *kerygma*, or "received gospel", is then set off against the elementary *didache* intended for all believers, and a higher *sophia* or *gnosis* for mature minds. Dogmatic theology is then characterized as *sophia* which, as Ernest F. Scott stresses, is offered by the author of the epistle to the Hebrews, for example, "with a certain reserve... He speaks to them, not in the name of the official church, but as an individual thinker, who has arrived at this interpretation along a path of his own."*

---

107. Berkhof remarks that special revelation and Scripture are not identical, when we refer to revelation as the direct self-communication of God, for in this sense the Bible is the record of God's self-communications, which preceded their inscripturation. But "it is only through Scripture that we receive any knowledge of the direct self-communications of God. We know absolutely nothing of God's revelations among Israel through the prophets and in Christ, except from Scripture. If this is set aside, we abandon the whole of God's special revelation, including that in Christ. It is only through the word of the apostles that we can have communion with Christ . . . (Yet) we can speak of revelation in more than one sense. We can apply the name to the direct self-communications of God to prophets and apostles; and then say that some of these were not incorporated in Scripture, and that Scripture contains a great deal that cannot be regarded as a fruit of special revelation. But the term 'revelation' can also be applied to the whole complex of redemptive truths and facts that is found in Scripture . . . Scripture derives its significance exactly from the fact that it is the book or revelation. By means of Scripture God constantly carries His revelation into the world and realizes its contents in the life and thought of man" (*op. cit.*, pp. 148f.).

108. Contrast William Temple, *Nature, Man and God*: "There is no such thing as revealed truth. There are truths of revelation, that is to say, propositions which express the results of correct thinking concerning revelation; but they are not themselves directly revealed . . . What is offered to man's apprehension in any specific revelation is not truth concerning God, but God himself" (pp. 317, 322).

*Ernest F. Scott, *The Epistle to the Hebrews: Its Doctrines and Significance*, pp. 39f).

It is quite apparent how, in this anti-doctrinal mood, the original *Kerygma* is reduced to the barest minimum, as if the Old Testament preparation were devoid of doctrinal significance, as if divine activity breaks forth with a minimum of imparted meaning, as if, in the last analysis, revelation were intelligible without coming somehow within the law of contradiction.[109]

Brunner appeals repeatedly to Luther's formula, *"Christus rex et dominus scripturae"*, and to the distinction between the spirit and letter of Biblical writings, as demanding this newer view of revelation. He quotes with approval Luther's comment that "the New Testament should really be only a living Word and not a written word; that is why Christ wrote nothing." But in Luther this sentiment is opposed to the medieval tendency to stress doctrinal conformity without personal faith, whereas Brunner uses the argument to eliminate entirely any doctrinal view of revelation. If, however, one stands with a higher critical view which assigns late dates to Old Testament books and then presumes to derive their ideology from pagan sources, or which so reconstructs the New Testament that we are unsure how much, if any, of the *verba ipsissima* of Christ we possess,[110] then indeed one must seek for a view of revelation far more radical than the view which the Scriptures themselves maintain on quite different assumptions.

(3) *Brunner's View Involves Its Own Doctrinal Structure.*

---

109. James Bissett Pratt accurately observes that Fundamentalism and Catholicism, whatever their differences with regard to the relationship of revelation and reason, both oppose Neo-Supernaturalism's dialecticism which destroys the use of even enlightened reasonableness as a criterion (*Religious Liberals Reply*, pp. 103f. Boston: Beacon Press, 1947). He stresses that the content of revelation (although in some statements it appears to have no content whatever, as, e. g., Kraemer's statement in *The Christian Message in a Non-Christian World*, that revelation "is by its nature inaccessible and remains so, even when it is revealed") is that God is unknowable in our terms, and that the Eternal broke into time in Christ (p. 108). The neo-supernaturalists' contradictory predicates and snappy paradoxes he calls "firecrackers with which they celebrate their Declaration of Independence from the restrictions of reason" (p. 113).

110. E. Basil Redlich interestingly remarks: "Form Criticism by admitting that collections of sayings were made early has pointed to the possibility that the *ipsissima verba* of our Lord were treasured as oracles to guide and control the destinies of individuals and of the Church" (*Form Criticism*, pp. 79f. New York: Charles Scribner's Sons, 1939).

Brunner charges that Fundamentalism, in its identification of the word of the Bible with the Word of God, holds a non-historical, abstract Bible emphasis which makes no room for the necessary mediation between the Bible and modern man through the living voice of the church (p. 145). But, granted that the contemporary man cannot be united with God apart from an organic connection with the fellowship of the Church and its tradition, does this make impossible the believer's junction with the Scriptures? Does it not, on the other hand, presuppose just such a junction? But, Brunner protests, there is only an indirect identity between the word of the Bible and the Word of God (p. 145). On the point, that the record is only indirectly inspired, whereas the person of the writer was directly inspired, evangelical theology as a whole concurs.[111] But this is not Brunner's whole meaning, for whereas Evangelicalism found a doctrinal unity in the unfolding of the saving event, Brunner is a man in revolt against doctrinal unity, and pleads constantly for doctrinal reserve and fluidity along with an insistence upon the fact that God in Christ mercifully accomplishes our salvation. This involves a revolt against the Chalcedonian Christology combined with an insistence on the deity of Christ, an uncertainty about the virgin birth, an insistence that Christology should not transcend the soteriological emphasis and that the dogmas of the Trinity and of Christology should not be presented axiomatically. What Brunner apparently does not see is that there is here a wholly new doctrinal mood, admittedly not "systematic", admittedly vague and more mystical[112] than orthodox.

One must admit the danger, latent in any doctrinal formulation, of depersonalizing the human predicament. One may say

---

111. Orr pointed out forty years ago, and many scholars before him, that "Scripture is spoken of as 'God-inspired'; but it is important to notice that inspiration belongs primarily to the *person*, and to the *book* only as it is the product of the inspired person. There is no inspiration inhering literally in the paper, ink, or type, of the sacred volume . . . The inspiration in these cases is in the souls of the men, and only derivatively in their writings" (*Revelation and Inspiration,* pp. 162f. London: Duckworth and Company, 1919).

112. More mystical, despite the fact that Brunner's basic thrust is anti-mystical, in his opposition to Schleiermacher and the medieval mystics, whom he constantly indicts. Cf. his *Erkenntnis, Erlebnis, Glaube.*

that man is a sinner in such a way as to minimize the awful truth of man now sinning; the emphasis on the state may even obscure the present activity. But the tendency to press an activistic view of all doctrine likewise has its dangers. In avoiding a passive statement of man's condition, it may nonetheless provide a shallow statement: man as sinning is not intelligible in the total disclosure of his predicament apart from *man the sinner*. This overactivism is seen, for example, in Brunner's contention that "original revelation is never regarded as something past, but always as something which is present, but is denied" (p. 52). The Biblical affirmations about unfallen Adam clearly contradict this; nor does Brunner derive this position from the testimony of the Holy Spirit; it is forged rather, to accommodate the Biblical view of original revelation and original sin to an evolutionary anthropology.

For not only does Brunner offer an unorthodox view of special revelation, but he also breaks with the evangelical view of general revelation, and provides a substitute accommodated to his acceptance of an evolutionary view of man's origin, which opposes the notion of a primal perfection and fall of original man implicating all humanity in original sin. "The original revelation is not a historical entity," he declares; "this revelation is not something that took place long, long ago" (p. 262). "Sin no more destroys the 'primitive state' and the original revelation than it makes man no longer a creature created by God. It is obvious that our changed view of history must involve a reformulation of the doctrine of the primitive state, and also of the original revelation" (p. 262, footnote). Hence Brunner projects the view that original righteousness (not merely general revelation, but *original righteousness*) and original sin (not merely sin, but *original* sin) are joint possessions of every man, and that each man inevitably is involved in sin when he acts. The question here arises—and it is one to be treated in detail in a subsequent chapter—whether, if sin is thus ultimately inevitable, being a factor in the divinely constituted nature of man, thereby the whole notion of sin is not endangered. But an equally serious question, on Brunner's assumptions, is whether he has not here provided for contemporary theology one of these "timeless ideas", which he finds so objectionable. Might it be that, deep down, Brunner's aversion is not so much against doctrine, as against orthodox doctrine? For Brunner, the doctrine of original righteousness, means that all men have a knowledge of God; that of original sin, that all men distort this knowledge, by a selfish bent of will. "Neither this original revelation nor original sin can be placed within the historical category... Original sin... is the fundamental principle within human history as a whole, and within the life of each individual" (p. 264). If this is not doctrine—and doctrine which, at that, must square accounts with Genesis 3 and Romans 5—what can it possibly be?

Now it is evident that not all the doctrinal affirmations made within the Christian tradition can be true, for there are serious issues dividing the Protestant, Roman Catholic, and Greek Orthodox communions, and those that have branched from these bodies. But within these bounds there is still a wide doctrinal agreement—as, for example, on the first three ecumenical creeds. Much of the desperate doctrinal confusion within the church came with the rise of modern religious Liberalism,[113] and even of Humanism which pitted anti-Christian doc-

---

113. It cannot be controverted, of course, that serious doctrinal confusion existed before the rise of Liberalism. The Roman Catholic church had been rocked again and again by doctrinal controversies; there was the Rites controversy on the mission field in post-Reformation days, the suppression of neo-Augustinianism in the form of Port Royal Jansenism by the Jesuits, and the fight of the spiritual Franciscans against the Pope. The Reformers had serious disputes, as over the significance of the Lord's Supper; as late as 1613 a Thuringian minister of state was put to death for crypto-Calvinism in Lutheran territory. Orthodoxy has had sad chapters; German Baptists and other 19th century dissenters in Germany and Scandinavia suffered the bitterest persecution from orthodox, not liberal, preachers, for men like Ernst Troeltsch played fair with the Anabaptists and Baptists in their struggle for soul liberty. But it remains that Liberalism introduced a new type of confusion into the doctrinal scene — it declared that all doctrines are of secondary significance (except this doctrine, that doctrine is not primary) — and the modern world has inherited, as a consequence, the problem of making men see that everything turns on the truth of the Biblical ideology, as well as the reality of the Christian life. The continuing controversies in post-Reformation thought did not endanger the fundamental structure of Christian faith, whereas modern Liberalism constituted an attack upon what had been historically conceived as the essence of the Biblical message. The minor unitarian movement on the Continent in the post-Reformation period, especially in Poland and Hungary, came to major expression. Even the post-apostolic Arianism was far higher in its doctrinal claims

trines against Christian doctrine, in the name of Christian doctrine, while at the same time professing to disparage doctrine. Thus a flexible view of doctrine, on the part of one who is calling the liberalist movement to higher ground, may be strategic in enlisting a hearing, but the danger is that it will crystallize in a flexible view of the Living Word, and in a doctrinal flimsiness which provides no adequate safeguard against subjective Mysticism, however much one may cry out against that alternative.[114] One does not need, in order to stress the need for theological caution on secondary issues, to throw a reserve over the great verities on which the Christian movement came to concurrence long centuries ago—not if one's appeal is to Biblical theology, and he means by that the theology of an unreconstructed Bible.

Again, it is true that theologians have sometimes, in the name of dogmatic theology, imposed upon the data of Biblical theology a rigid yoke, pursuing an extreme systematization around some one principle, too restricted to do full justice to the rich comprehensiveness of Bible content. But, is the cure for such excess a renunciation of the unity of Biblical doctrine, or rather the quest for that organic unity which, without doing violence to some phases of the divine activity and self-disclosure, finds as the all-sufficient key a Living Word with its well-defined implications for the totality of existence?[115] There is a reawaken-

than classic religious Modernism, for the new stress on historical consciousness and on scientific method was pressed with such a naturalistic bias that it inevitably became part-cause of the modern religious confusion.

114. W. A. Visser 't Hooft's *The Kingship of Christ* suggests the formulated confessions "are the signposts which the church puts up to indicate the way along which it is led by its Lord, as it pursues its pilgrimage in the world. Signposts — serious warnings as to what is the true and what is the false road. But *only* signposts — not to be confused with the place to which they point . . . In (a confessionalist church) the formulated confession is considered as an ultimate criterion. One cannot get around it. It stands between the church and its Lord as he speaks in the Scriptures" (pp. 107f. New York: Harper and Bros., 1948). It is clear that here too the revolt against the lordship of doctrine rather than the lordship of Christ follows too much of a doctrine-at-a-distance pattern.

115. The dangers of dogmatic theology are not as present to groups like the Baptists who subscribe to "no creed but the New Testament", and who therefore are preoccupied with systematic rather than dogmatic theology. (And the danger of having "no creed but the New Testament" is seen in the present theological flux of the Northern Baptist Convention, where the New Testament is appealed to in the interest of theological vagueness rather than doctrinal precision.)

ing, in recent literature, to the doctrinal unity of the Bible. But even the rediscovered unity is frequently compromised, because of evolutionary assumptions; one cannot contrast without profit the minimal postulates of *The Christian View of God and the World*,[116] set forward in James Orr's book a half century ago, with the modern reductions, even in the reactions against classic Liberalism. And Orr was, for all that, a theistic evolutionist. The only adequate substitute for a disproportionate systematic theology is one Biblically proportioned, and not one which makes the Living Word, without clearly defined implications, the reservoir for multitudinous ripples of paradox.

2. *Appeal to Spirit Perilous Apart from A Trustworthy Book.*

In proportion as those who seek to test such views by the only available historical records do so, in that proportion they will be driven to the established exegetical results to which the evangelical movement in recent generations, outside the arena of destructive higher criticism, has committed itself. But Brunner cannot accept this test: the Scriptures for him are not identical with the Word of God. The question then arises, whether the Word of God is identical with the word of Brunner. The appeal to the *testimonium spiritus sancti* is here a perilous* one, on the precise word of the Scriptures. For the spirits are themselves to be tried, and if no objective word is given, it is barely possible that one will mistake the spirits of Wellhausen, Harnack and Herrmann, Calvin, and Luther, in a mystical composite, for a revelational event. The time has come for dealing severely with this dialectical speaking in tongues.

D. *Difficulties Inherent in the Mid-Century View of Revelation.*

As one surveys the history of the modern rupture with the belief in the verbal inspiration of the Scriptures, he is impressed

---

116. Recently reprinted by William B. Eerdmans Publishing Company.

* Engelder writes that the Barthians "refuse to believe that God performed the miracle of giving us by inspiration an infallible Bible but are ready to believe that God daily performs the greater miracle of enabling men to find and see in the fallible word of man the infallible Word of God" (*op. cit.*, p. 129).

with the fact that liberal Christology was here determinative for Bibliology.[117]

1. *Higher Criticism Required a Fallible Christ and a Fallible Bible.*

The higher critics had "infallibly" shown that Moses could not have written the Pentateuch nor David the Psalms, for[118] monotheism was assumed a late emergent, a view from whose foundation stones the critics are now beginning to retrace their steps.[119] But Jesus had accepted the "now disproved" authorship, hence in the incarnation He possessed neither historical nor scientific omniscience, inspiration being limited to spiritual and moral precepts. Now, if this was the case with Jesus, it could not have been otherwise with prophets and apostles, in whom the union of the divine and human was not as intimate. Here by a single movement as it were, under the compulsion of presuppositions, and not because of a weight of minor con-

---

117. J. S. Lawton, *Conflict in Christology*, pp. 44ff. New York: Macmillan and Co., 1947. Emil Brunner remarks: "What I said of God incarnate is true of the revelation in the Bible; to be a real revelation it must be veiled. The Word of God in the Scriptures is as little to be identified with the words of the Scriptures as the Christ according to the flesh is to be identified with the Christ according to the spirit. The words of the Scriptures are human; that is, God makes use of human and, therefore, frail and fallible words of men who are liable to err" (*The Theology of Crisis*, p. 19. New York: Charles Scribner's Sons, 1929). Cf. Brunner's *Revelation and Reason*: "The Church must develop its doctrine of the Scriptures on the same lines as the doctrine of the two natures" (p. 276). And Karl Heim has said in the same mood: "The historical form of the Bible is a part of the 'form of a servant' which God took upon Himself in order to help us, thereby deliberately laying Himself open to the criticism of man . . . What we have to bring to the world, is not the wonder of an infallible book. We bring the living personality who stands behind the book . . ." ("The Gospel Which Commands Us", in *The Jerusalem Meeting of the International Missionary Council*, March 24-April 8, 1928, vol. VIII, p. 84. New York: 1928).

118. It may of course be argued that the traditional authorship was rejected on independent grounds, and that this rejection created a mood hospitable to evolutionary interpretation, but such a view overlooks the impetus which evolution gave to the whole enterprise of negative higher criticism. A. E. Burtt sees clearly the extent to which Modernism revised theological ideas in conformity with the evolutionary theory, so that a gradual and progressive understanding of God was substituted for a primitive supernatural disclosure of absolute truth (*Types of Religious Philosophy*, pp 315ff. New York: Harper and Brothers. 1939). Kuenen had put the issue clearly: "So long as we attribute a part of Israel's religious life directly to God and allow supernatural or immediate revelation to intervene even in one instance, just so long does our view of the whole remain inexact, and we see ourselves obliged to do violence here or there to the well-assured content of the historical accounts. It is only the assumption of a natural development that takes account of all the phenomena" (*De profeten en de profetie onder Israel*, Vol. I, p. 5. Quoted by Noordtzy, *op. cit.*, Vol. 98. No. 389. p. 104).

119. The retreat in America has been encouraged by the research of William F. Albright, and in Europe by such studies as Wilhelm Schmidt's *The Origin and Growth of Religion.*

tradictions in the records, Liberalism turned its back upon the ideal of Biblical infallibility; particular "inconsistencies" were introduced to confirm, rather than to establish, the broader assumption of fallibility.[120]

a. *Newer Theology Interested in Content Rather Than Form of Scriptures.*

Under the evolutionary bias, which tended to seek a continuity with non-Christian religions for all Biblical doctrine, the essential differences were obscured, and Liberalism was preoccupied with the supposed *form* of the records, rather than the *content*.[121] Liberalism produced no great Biblical theologies in the past generation (Burrows remarks that one must go back to Oehler and Davidson for competent Old Testament theologies),[122] and it is one of the signs of the sterility or preoccupation of conservative scholarship that its record was little better.[123]

The excesses of liberal criticism have become so apparent in recent years that higher critical circles are just now in rather troubled tension.

120. The experiences of Sir William Ramsay in Asia Minor, resulting in the repeated confirmation of the detailed accuracy of the writings of Luke, is a reminder how much the liberal thesis depended on philosophic premises.

121. The present trend is away from a preoccupation with higher criticism rather than with Bible doctrine. The message of the Scriptures as a whole, writes Norman H. Snaith, cannot be discerned while the Bible is appraised "only with respect to its literary sources" (*The Distinctive Ideas of the Old Testament*, p. 112, footnote. Philadelphia: The Westminster Press, 1946). On this account, Fundamentalists are "sometimes nearer to the truth" than the literary critics, he declares, in view of their primary concern for the *message* of the Bible. While retaining an appreciation for literary criticism, Snaith concedes that criticism often forgot that the Old Testament was purposely "pieced . . . together as we have it now . . . The editors had the final say, and they used all the material from its varied sources in order to teach their particular message" (*loc. cit.*). Literary criticism, he remarks, "tended to forget that there might be method even in the madness which so thoroughly dovetailed" the strata; "perhaps after all that madness was divine" (*ibid.*, p. 14).

122. Raymond A. Bowman remarks that "at the end of the nineteenth century the term 'theology' fell into disuse among students of Old Testament; and, under the influence of the prevailing interest in historical criticism of the Bible, a historical and descriptive, rather than a topical and theological, approach to religion was followed. From the time of Davidson's *Theology of the Old Testament* (1904) to Burney's (*Outlines of Old Testament Theology* (1920) this emphasis prevailed, and the term 'theology' was avoided in describing work devoted to Old Testament religion . . . The definite resurgence of the study of Old Testament theology reflects the conviction that the critical, analytical, historical, and descriptive approach to the Bible is not sufficient in itself and that a further approach must be adopted if the entire truth of the Bible is to be known and the full needs of the inner spiritual life of man are to be met" ("Old Testament Research Between the Wars", in *The Study of the Bible Today and Tomorrow*, pp. 30f. Chicago: Univ. of Chicago Press, 1947).

123. A notable exception, Gerhardus Vos' *Biblical Theology*, edited by his son, J. G. Vos, was published in 1948 by Wm. B. Eerdmans Publishing Co.

(1) *Archaelogy Supports the Scriptures.*

In the Old Testament area, archaeologists[124] like Albright reaffirm a Mosaic monotheism, and German theologians (always putting British and American theologians in debt to them for better or worse) have been insisting for a generation that one does violence to the Biblical record without a realistic view of revelation, of election, and of divine covenant. Biblical archaeology has not only dealt a death blow to radical higher criticism, by overthrowing the notion of a legendary patriarchal age,[125] and establishing the antiquity of Hebrew language and writing, but it has demonstrated the correspondence between patriarchal social life as reflected in the Old Testament and patriarchal times as excavations delineate it, has recovered the ancient Hittite empire and the Horites, and by an appeal to the Ras Shamra tablets has proved that the Aramaisms in the Pentateuch do not require late datings.

When one turns to the New Testament, the central interest is leagued now with the literary study encouraged by *Formgeschichte,* and here it may seem at first glance that the main preoccupation is one of form rather than content. But it is, as we shall see, the form of the *tradition,* the form which the central *message* has taken, that justifies in the last resort such intense study of the manuscripts. Even among New Testament scholars who, under the driving spell of higher criticism, coupled their Biblical studies with a "metaphysical agnosticism" there is an occasional uneasiness today, as the deeper question of the value and truth of the Biblical tradition reasserts itself.

(2) *Confirmation of Early Dating of John's Gospel.*

In the New Testament area, the most serious tensions have accrued from the new discoveries bearing on the Fourth Gospel, which liberal criticism had so confidently banished to the post-

---

124. Bowman notes that the archaeological "confirmation of biblical narrative at most points has led to a new respect for biblical tradition and a more conservative conception of biblical history" (*op. cit.,* p. 30).

125. Cf. R. P. R. De Vaux, "Les Patriarches hebreux et les decouvertes modernes," *Revue Biblique,* 53, n. 3, pp. 321-328.

apostolic period, in view of its high Christology. Nothing gave the liberal theologians quite as much assurance in their distinction between a simple apostolic message and a developed post-apostolic theology as the late datings which placed some of the crucial writings at a safe remove from the primitive church. But now a Johannine authorship of the Fourth Gospel is once again a live possibility, although critics prefer yet to speak of a "late first century authorship", which is simply an attempt to let themselves down easily from a distressing speculative altitude. It ought all along to have served as a constraint on this sort of speculation, that it curiously gave us a later John to whom the church stood even more greatly indebted than to the disciple, and yet we know nothing else about him; rather, only the early John found a place in the history of the church. But liberal criticism was scientific, and it needed the confrontation of hard empirical fact. When archaeology provided this, criticism saw the handwriting on the wall. For the fragmentary leaf published in 1935 by C. H. Roberts was a copy dated in the first half of the second century, and hence required a still earlier date for the original; it opened the door to first-century authorship.[126]

The implications of this are clear: the most advanced Christology of the New Testament was the possession of the apostolic church; eyewitnesses of the ministry of Jesus were contemporary with it. The most favorable circumstances for the theory of a gradual development of a post-apostolic doctrinal system were thus removed.

(3) *Formgeschichte Unable to Obscure Early Supernaturalism.*

But higher criticism was able to move mountains, and some of the ingredients which gave encouragement to *Formgeschichte*

126. As Floyd V. Filson commented, the discovered fragments of the Fourth Gospel force us "to date the composition of the Gospel no later than the very beginning of that (i. e., the second) century, while a date further back, toward the end of the first century, would be decidedly preferable . . . We must date the fourth Gospel still earlier, conceivably at the very opening of the second but far more probably in the latter part of the first century" (*Origins of the Gospels*, pp. 40f. New York: The Abingdon Press, 1939).

are here evident, even though that movement traces its beginnings to the 1919 efforts of Dibelius, Bultmann and Schmidt
to rescue criticism from the confusion over the sayings of Jesus
in which Bernard and Johannes Weiss, Holtzmann, Wrede,
Gunkel and Wendlung, not to say Wellhausen, had left it.
For if the formula "apostolic age to post-apostolic age" provides no justification for a rigid distinction between a primitive non-metaphysical Gospel and a subsequent doctrinal
expansion, the distinction can only be maintained—*if maintained it must be*—by a view which goes *behind* the written
sources in an effort to show that they represent a redaction
of a simpler message which characterized the pre-literary or
oral stage of the Gospels and their sources. When the late
date of the manuscripts is overthrown, a primitive doctrinal
message can be disowned only in this way, which accepts the
early dating, but seeks behind this—apart from any such written
records whatever—for a non-theological Gospel. The period
of literary redaction *par excellence* now becomes the twenty
year after the public ministry of Jesus.

b. *The Theology of the Apostles was the Theology of the
Disciples Before Them.*

The extent to which *Formgeschichte* criticism has been
swayed by subjective judgment rather than by true historical
and literary criticism, and its inability to compress into a single
generation the recasting[127] of the Gospel story for which another theory had required several generations plus the removal
of eyewitnesses, as well as specific literary criticism to which
the theory is exposed[128] are difficulties, which have served to

---

127. The difficulty is two-sided. For one thing, as G. Ernest Wright remarks, the
new conservatism regarding oral tradition in the Old Testament "ought to have a
challenging effect on those whose skepticism has viewed the Christian Gospels as
largely the creation of the early church, especially since the period of oral transmission
in this case was so short" ("The Present State of Biblical Archaeology", in *The
Study of the Bible Today and Tomorrow*, p. 88). On the other hand, the apostles were
ready to die for Him, and the slightest suspicion of mythologizing would have undercut the psychology of this mood.

128. Redlich, *op. cit.*, enumerates many of these. One of the main hurdles of *Formgeschichte* is its effort to provide an authoritative history where historical writings are
absent.

show how desperate and how increasingly futile is the determination to drive a wedge between the doctrinal core which links the disciples with the apostles on the one hand, and with the Old Testament witness on the other. Form criticism appears, in view of such facts, often more arbitrary, in the main, than the literary criticism of a generation ago.

2. *Doctrinal Unity of the Bible Is Being Rediscovered.*

The renewal of interest in Biblical theology, as it gains momentum, will serve to bring out more clearly the doctrinal unity of the testaments, proportionately as it divorces itself from liberal critical excesses. Thus one of the key problems of the mid-century restudy of revelation is, as already suggested, a satisfactory alternative to the view championed by Brunner, of a unity of personal confrontation which stops short of propositional revelation.

a. *Personal Revelation Unintelligible Without Propositions.*

Forgetting for a moment the dialecticism of neo-orthodoxy— which A. C. Knudson denominated an "irrationalism and mystery mongering" which "seem to me to be the chief scandal of present day theology,"[129]—the question remains whether, apart from the disclosure of knowledge in the revelational encounter, the whole concept of special revelation is not artificial.

If revelation is confined to the series of redemptive acts, then what do we have more than a *natural theology,** in which

129. A. C. Knudson, in his review of Brunner's *The Divine-Human Encounter (Crozier Quarterly Review,* Vol. XXII, No. 1, Jan., 1945, pp. 71ff.). In a not unsimilar mood, Daniel Williams remarks that "the conclusion must be stated that the theologian who has spent his life in an effort to free Christian theology from entanglement with mysticism and with philosophy has in his own theology developed a perspective which embodies a philosophical mysticism whose classic exponent is a philosopher who does not depend upon the New Testament" ("Brunner and Barth on Philosophy", in *The Journal of Religion,* Vol. XXVII, No. 4, Oct., 1947, p. 251.

* It is not surprising in view of Brunner's low view of Biblical inspiration (contradictory doctrines, erroneous scientific and historical views, etc.), that Horton should inquire—since sin is held to vitiate general revelation outside the Biblical movement— what "would happen to the testimony of the prophets and apostles if the same . . . tests were so rigidly applied" as outside of Biblical tradition? (*op. cit.,* p. 56). Only an adequate view of inspiration can escape the force of this pointed inquiry. And, since Brunner presumes to secure revelation by a divine act without an infallible and clearly authoritative Scripture, it is also not difficult to understand Horton's further question, why, "if by faith it is possible to apprehend a unified revelation of God in the Bible, in spite of the apparent contradiction and admitted sinfulness of the biblical witnesses," may not faith similarly apprehend another form of revelation in the area of general revelation?

the data of physical nature are exchanged for those of history, and the human mind left to formulate its theology subsequent to personal confrontation? Whatever may be said about a special series of divine acts in the Hebrew-Christian tradition, and the immediate confrontation of man by the divine Spirit, while there is no revealed truth it can only be the series of uninterpreted events which is the real core of revelation.[130]

(1) *Religious Agnosticism Not Effectively Dispelled.*

If the theology is an inference, and divine meaning is not *given,* then a religious epistemological dualism is hardly escaped, and the problem of overcoming agnosticism remains.[131]

What objective assurance is there, except propositional revelation be admitted, that the confrontation is genuine, that it is not, indeed, merely a philosophic dramatization of the "I-Thou" relationship as viewed by existential philosophy, or simply a misreading of the subliminal activities of the mind?

Brunner's grandiose assertion that the Church misunderstood the personal character of revelation, and that therefore "it

---

130. C. H. Dodd, in *The Bible Today,* stresses that the prophets would not have accepted an explanation of Hebrew history on the ground that they "worked out a particular interpretation of the course of history, and induced their people to accept it" (p. 51. New York: The Macmillan Co., 1947). Dodd adds: "They were not philosophers, constructing a speculative theory from their observation of events. What they said was 'Thus saith the Lord.' They firmly believed that God spoke to them (spoke to the inward ear, the spiritual sense). He spoke to them out of the events which they experienced. The interpretation of history which they offered was not invented by process of thought; it was the meaning which they experienced in the events, when their minds were opened to God as well as open to the impact of outward facts. Thus the prophetic interpretation of history, and the impetus and direction which that interpretation gave to subsequent history, were alike the Word of God to men" (*ibid.,* p. 51). Dodd combines the insistence on divine disclosure with a critical view in which an *irruptive* evolution displaces unilinear evolution. But it is quite apparent that revelation, even in these terms, is still considerably at the mercy of the human agents, for the prophets appear as much creative as receptive of its content. Again, once divine disclosure is admitted, can any *a priori* objection be raised to the possibility of an initial revelation, or primal monotheism? The notion of progressive revelation demands irruptive evolution only if one is unwilling to divorce himself from critical conclusions with regard to the Scriptures which were derived within assumptions now professed to be abandoned.

131. D. C. Macintosh classified the dialectical theologians with religious epistemological dualists (*The Problem of Religious Knowledge,* pp. 326ff.). N. B. Stonehouse comments, in a symposium by Westminster Theological Seminary faculty members, that "Appearances to the contrary notwithstanding, Barthianism also is fundamentally agnostic; it maintains that God remains wholly hidden in his revelation" (*The Infallible Word,* p. 100).

did not understand that the transition from the 'Thou-form' to the 'It-form,' from personal address to doctrine, was the transition from one dimension to another, namely, the transition from the 'truth as encounter' to that of the 'truth as idea' "[132] can hardly avoid reducing essential Christianity to formless Mysticism and non-doctrinal vagaries.

(2) *Dialectical Paradoxism a Self-Destructive Concept.*

It seems sufficiently important, even if at the cost of seeming repetition, to reintroduce the subject of neo-orthodox dialecticism.[133] For, whatever doctrinal difficulties one may find in the movement are twice-worsened by the insistence that no final, consistent doctrinal position is possible; we have merely pointers,[134] but not metaphysical dogmas. Here the lengthened shadow of Kant is apparent, overcast by which the Neo-Supernaturalists are as much at war with the Hebrew-Christian tradition as allied to it. Their dialectic restatement of the Biblical idea of revelation, with a consequent avoidance of any *revealed truth* (or propositional revelation), leaves their theology with a stuttering deity, a transcendental self who roams about in a super-rational sphere not fully subject to the categories of thought. And critics want to know why one should *think*

---

132. Brunner, *op. cit.*, p. 149.

133. Barth protests an over-distrust of the intellect of man as a center of possible religious experience of the Word of God (*op. cit.*, p. 231). The intellect is no worse off than man's other self-realizations. Barth, championing the view that "the Word of God is quite literally language, not ultimately but primarily and predominantly so, i. e., a spiritual event" argues from this that "the communication of it to man must at least also involve a claim upon the intellect, and the experience of it must at least also actually involve the co-option of the intellect" (*ibid.*, p. 231). But how, in view of the dialectical superstructure, the *yea* ever escapes the force of the *nay*, is not apparent, though assuredly Barth endeavors, for all his doctrine-at-arms-length mood, to conceive revelation with more than a propositional cast than does Brunner. The Word of God, Barth tells us, "is directed to man's *ratio*, by which, of course, we are not to understand the intellect alone, but the intellect at least also and not last of all" (*ibid.*, p. 234). But we are warned that "one can never look back upon the human, even upon the Christian act of knowledge as such, as upon an already successful work which corresponds with is object" (*ibid.*, p. 279).

134. "The object of faith is something which is absurd to reason, i. e. paradox" wrote Brunner a decade ago; "the hall-mark of logical inconsistency clings to all genuine pronouncements of faith" (*The Philosophy of Religion*, p. 55. New York: Charles Scribner's Sons, 1937). Given *that* proposition (which, if genuine, ought itself to be logically inconsistent, on Brunner's own premises), one ought not to be surprised to hear the Neo-Supernaturalist theologians speak in dialectical tongues.

about such a God,[135] and whether the dialectical approach itself is not at the mercy of a deeper dialectical movement.[136]

Hence one cannot but show a certain sympathy for those who feel that, whatever minimum of doctrinal residue remains in a system like Brunner's—even that the *one* doctrine is Jesus Christ, or that God is both holy and merciful—it cannot be treated too seriously while its champions voice their convictions from a dialectical merry-go-round. The rising contemporary interest in the unique ideology of the Hebrew-Christian tradition is reduced to an idle diversion on this pattern, unless the dialecticians do not mean what they so often appear to say.

b. *Recent Theology Centers in Bible-Unifying Beliefs.*

The renewed pursuit of Biblical theology, except as it proceeds on superseded philosophic biases which have progressively come to frustration, will serve to heighten the doctrinal unity of the testaments. One may disbelieve doctrines which the Biblical writers affirm, but if Biblical theology is set in a new perspective this will cease to become a motivation for denying that prophets and apostles proclaimed them as a *sine qua non,* or a motivation for the denial that there is a doctrinal unity. The newer theological interest in the Bible retains higher

---

135. Van Til stresses the influence of Kantian epistomology on Neo-Supernaturalism (cf. *The New Modernism.* Philadelphia: Presbyterian and Reformed Publishing Co., 1946). In *The Infallible Word,* Van Til adds: "Dialectical theology has, to be sure, made the attempt to combine the main *Critique* of Kant and the *Institutes* of Calvin. But the magnitude of its undertaking is itself the best instance in proof that such a thing cannot logically be done. Barth and Brunner have satisfied the requirements of Kant's criticism, but in so doing they have at the same time denied the God of Calvin. Largely influenced by the Phenomenalism or Existentialism of such men as Kierkegaard and Heidegger, Barth and Brunner have been consistently anti-metaphysical in the Kantian sense of the term. That is to say, they have insisted that God is wholly unknown as a numerical individual and that he is wholly identical with his revelation as a specific unity. In other words, the God of the Confession is for Barth and Brunner nothing but an idol. The God of the Confession claims to have revealed himself directly in nature and in Scripture. And all direct revelation, Barth and Brunner continually reassert, is paganism" (pp. 291ff.). Leonard De Moor traces the Barthian defect back to Kantian dualistic epistomology. He declares that Barthianism "fails to give us a solution to the problem of revelation, because, like its predecessors, it fails to weave into an organic and vital unity the divine content or supernatural reality and the historical or empirical medium. Only when a synthesis of these two is maintained do we have a sound and adequate conception of this crucial theological doctrine" ("The Concept of Revelation in Barthianism", *Religious Digest,* Vol. V. (Oct., 1937), p. 21).

136. Why should the dialectical principle itself be static, and not subject to a profounder dialectic?

criticism as a companion rather than as a competitor, and one cannot but ask whether pre-liberalism once explored this same avenue which post-liberalism now traverses, only to slide down the avalanche of subjectivism.[137] Frederick C. Prussner, although sharing the post-liberal mood, remarks that for the past decade a trend has steadily gained strength, in which the Old Testament scholar adds theological interests to his functions, "seeking to present the religious thought of the Old Testament as a unified system of belief and to demonstrate the vitality of this belief for our own day... All trends seem to indicate that the real emphasis of future research will be here."[138]

(1) *But Settles for a Minimal Unity.*

The road back from liberal subjectivism to Biblical faith is, on the empirical route, long and winding and perilous. For Liberalism discovers by surprise in the modern cultural crisis that there is after all a *uniqueness* in the Hebrew-Christian tradition. It must then learn that this uniqueness is not merely in divine disclosure, but in meaningful revelation; it must then learn that granted such revelation, criticism cannot date the sacred books whithersoever the gusts of Naturalism breathe. Then and then alone can the historic conviction of a progressive revelation with doctrinal implications take a compelling form.[139]

---

137. Bowman remarks: "All tendencies are leading to a more conservative attitude in Old Testament study than prevailed among scholars prior to 1919, but there is no sign of an absolute retreat to the earlier uncritical position" (*op cit.*, p. 31). Perhaps the *uncritical* position was that of the Liberalism now being modified, rather than traditional conservatism.

138. Frederick C. Prussner, "Problems in Old Testament Research," *ibid.*, pp. 184ff.

139. Orr wrote sober words for those who disparage the doctrinal side of Christianity: "If there is a religion in the world which exalts the office of teaching, it is safe to say that it is the religion of Jesus Christ. It has been frequently remarked that in pagan religions the doctrinal element is at a minimum—the chief thing there is the performance of a ritual. But this is precisely where Christianity distinguishes itself from other religions — it does contain doctrine. It comes to men with definite, positive teaching; it claims to be the truth; it bases religion on knowledge, though a knowledge which is only attainable under moral conditions. I do not see how any one can deal fairly with the facts as they lie before us in the Gospels and Epistles, without coming to the conclusion that the New Testament is full of doctrine . . . Christianity, therefore, addresses itself to the intelligence as well as to the heart. It sounds plausible indeed to say, Let us avoid all doctrinal subtleties; let us keep to a few plain, easy, simple propositions, in regard to which there will be general agreement. But, unfortunately, men *will* think on those deep problems which lie at the root of religious belief — on the

The recent literature in this area suggests that significant cross-currents of opinion are already present. Although Millar Burrows' *An Outline of Biblical Theology*[140] discloses in places the same over-generalization as some of the dialectical theologians (as when we are told that the unity of the Bible is Christ (p. 5), and that the Bible does not present a doctrine of God so much as a way of thinking about God (p. 63)) and although there is at the same time a link of spirit to the old liberal camps (as when we are told that Fosdick's work is "by all odds" the best volume on Biblical theology as a whole, or that monotheism "emerges" in Hebrew religion, or that the eighth century prophets are "implicitly" monotheistic, and that monotheism appears as a popular "deduction" from the fulfillment of prophecies of judgment) there is nonetheless an awareness of enough ideological unity in the Scriptures so that it is futile to dismiss it simply as the author's teleological bias. The use of Old Testament ideas is clearly seen as a preparation for the New Testament, and indeed has its precedent in the early Christian community. For all of Burrows' underestimation of prophecy and miracle, he is alert to many ideological roots of Christianity, even if inadequately expanded, as seen especially from the treatment of the chapter on "Christ", which recognizes that apart from the Old Testament much of the meaning goes out of concepts like prophet, lawgiver, priest, suffering servant, king, son of man, and son of God.

H. H. Rowley's *The Rediscovery of the Old Testament*[141] goes even further in stressing the theological indispensability of the Old Testament for understanding the New, and insists that the portrait of the suffering servant cannot be explained

---

140. *Op. cit.*, Philadelphia: The Westminster Press, 1946. Burrows' reluctance to invoke special revelation is seen by his suggestion that the apparent antithesis between revelation and discovery is "practically resolved by the biblical conception of all knowledge as ultimately dependent on revelation. From this point of view, discovery is only the recognition of something that has been revealed" (p. 36).
141. Philadelphia: The Westminster Press, 1946.

---

nature of God, His character, His relation to the world and men, sin, the means of deliverance from it, the end to which things are moving, — and if Christianity does not give them an answer, suited to their deeper and more reflective moods, they will simply put it aside as inadequate for their needs." (*The Christian View of God and the World*, pp. 20ff.)

in terms of the historical suffering of Israel (p. 202), and that the Old Testament itself can be properly understood only in terms of a "fuller meaning" in Christ (p. 21). Rowley is alert to some of the necessary corollaries implied in the Biblical concept of revelation, such as a personal God, monotheism, the divine image in man, and yet God as "other" (pp. 187ff.).

Norman H. Snaith's *The Distinctive Ideas of the Old Testament*[142] fixes on the religious ideas which distinguish the Old Testament view of God from that of other religions, and his discussion of God's holiness, righteousness, salvation, covenant-love, election love and spirit—however incomplete and frequently inadequate—serves to fix upon points of ideological unity common to the Hebrew-Christian movement.

(2) *Reraises the Question of Propositional Significance.*

The rising liberal conviction that a preoccupation with the literary forms rather than with content amounted to a wholesale business in husks from which the kernels were missing, cannot but reinstate for the next decade the whole issue of the doctrinal unity of the Hebrew-Christian movement.[143] The lines are already somewhat clearly drawn. Among those who have rebounded from Liberalism in the higher direction, the dialectical theologians by virtue of the very philosophy which overarches their position, cannot assign to doctrine an enduring value, and other higher liberals are seeking to combine a doctrinal minimum with evolutionary anthropology and criticism, even if modified in an *irruptive* rather than unilinear

---

142. Philadelphia: The Westminster Press, 1946.

143. The similarities of Barth and Brunner in the stream of mid-century religious thought are more impressive than their differences, though their disagreements involve major issues also. The main agreements are (*against classical liberalism*) first, that Christianity is not merely a higher expression of an essence shared in common with other religions but is essentially unique in view of a once-for-all historical revelation; second, that Christian experience is not intelligible in terms of categories derived from the psychology of experience outside the Hebrew-Christian tradition, in view of a supernatural work of regeneration by the Holy Spirit; third, Christianity involves a theology of special revelation (the Word) and at the center of this divine self-utterance is Jesus Christ; (*against orthodoxy*) first, divine revelation is not inscripturated in the sense of an infallible, trustworthy Bible in view of higher criticism; second, divine revelation is not conveyed in propositional doctrinal statements, but rather in terms of an "I-Thou" faith dialectic in which thesis and antithesis do not merge in a rational synthesis.

direction; on the other hand, the evangelical movement insists that in neither of these upward thrusts is there a sufficiently objective authority to safeguard against a declension in terms of subjectivistic predilections.

3. *The Study of Special Revelation and Inspiration Inseparable.*

It is at this point that the second tensional factor, once special propositional revelation is affirmed—and one which engages the attention of those whose convictions have attained to evangelical altitudes—presses into view. That is the question of an adequate statement of Biblical inspiration, or of the precise significance of the words of Scripture.[144] That the plenary view, with an insistence that the very words are free from error,[145] is both the view of the traditional church and of the writings themselves, has been abundantly demonstrated in Warfield's monumental work, *Revelation and Inspiration.* The appeal to human fallibility, to sustain the case for Biblical fallibility, cannot safeguard itself against the consequences of this same assault on the inerrancy of Christ. In both cases—and it is remarkable how Christology has been reflected in Bibliology—the insistence on "infallibility in spiritual and moral con-

---

144. Prussner emphasizes that a distinctive part of the post-liberal enterprise will be "the formulation of a doctrine of Sacred Scripture," but he also makes clear that, so far as post-liberalism is concerned, this view must be an alternative to the traditional view of Biblical authority. The obligation to formulate a new position, he affirms, exists "because most of contemporary Protestantism urgently requires something that will take the place of the Reformation teachings concerning the place and meaning of the Bible — teachings which, to a large extent, were robbed of their strength by the work of the biblical critics. Having torn down, we also have the responsibility of building up again" (*op. cit.,* p. 189). In the same volume, Baab remarks that the modern educated churchman "finds it impossible to follow the ultra-conservatives, to whom the unquestioned Bible is the very word of life. However wistfully he regards the simple biblical faith of his conservative contemporary, he is unable to enter into that faith" (*op. cit.,* p. 403). The use of the term "ultra-conservative" may be a device for anticipating an identification of post-liberalism with a conservative position, but whatever charm new labels may have, they cannot conceal the fact that the Reformation position is continuous with that of the apostolic church and the Scriptures' self-view of revelation and inspiration.

145. Orr, while preferring to speak of plenary rather than of verbal inspiration, conceded that a "true and important" significance of the latter was its opposition to "the theory that revelation and inspiration have regard only to thoughts and ideas, while the language in which these ideas are clothed is left to the unaided faculty of the sacred penman . . . Thought of necessity takes shape and is expressed in words. If there is inspiration at all, it must penetrate words as well as thought, must mould the expression, and make the language employed the living medium of the idea to be conveyed" (*Revelation and Inspiration,* p. 209).

cerns" proved an ineffective stop-gap which finally displaced Biblical theology with profoundly non-Biblical philosophy.

Can it ever be forgotten that the Hebrew-Christian movement issued in the conviction that there exists a *literature*, a corpus of *writings*, a record in words, set apart from all the literatures of world history because in them God speaks the *message*, the *good tidings?* The concept of *divine oracles* is not foreign to the Hebrew-Christian tradition.

THE MID-TWENTIETH CENTURY
VIEW OF SIN

III

The Mid-Twentieth Century View of Sin

IT was Hegelian philosophy which, a century ago, suggested that the event known traditionally as the "fall of man" should be an occasion for singing the Doxology, rather than for the provision of atonement.

A. Idealistic Philosophy Stressed Man's Moral Continuity with the Divine.

For in the logical evolution of the universe as the self-manifestation of the Absolute, as Hegel pictured it, the birth of a sense of guilt was a memorable happening indeed. Prior to that event, the Absolute was externalized only in a non-moral and a-moral way, but the sense of guilt marks the appearance of a moral being. Hence the moral struggle and failure of the first man is not regarded, in idealistic Liberalism, as a frustration of the divine plan for man. Instead it marks the normal process by which the moral develops logically from the a-moral, and is the sign of a forward movement in the externalization of the Absolute.

1. *Evil Only a Finite Abstraction Overcome in the Absolute.*

Actually, in such a view, it was the *sense of guilt,* rather than *guilt* itself, to which significance attached. For, in the Hegelian philosophy of optimism, all reality—including man and his struggles—were parts of the Absolute; evil and error were only finite abstractions, for in the Absolute they disappeared in an all-embracing harmony. Therefore, there was no need to defeat or conquer sin; rather, it was transformed in the experience of the Absolute. All sins are, basically, good; understood from the viewpoint of the Absolute, they are necessary parts of an ultimate whole. Evil loses its specific nature as evil in the being of the Absolute.

2. *Hence No Sense of Divine Condemnation.*

The implications of pantheistic Idealism, in terms of the problem of sin, are immediately apparent. There is here no sense of God's moral "otherness" except in terms of completion or fulness, i.e., of more of the same experience. In fact, if all reality is an externalizing of the Absolute, and if the Absolute comes to self-consciousness in the nature of man, it is impossible to think of man as depraved or sinful at the core of his personality, for it is the Absolute who is at the core. God can be view only as man's moral ally, not as man's moral condemner. For man is the highest immanent expression of the Absolute; God is morally continuous with man's highest efforts and fulfills them. The only meaning that sin can have is the denial by the empirical or individual self of the essential self, self in its wholeness, i.e., of that infinite morality in which all finite moralities are included. God is not man's judge, but a friendly cosmic creative spirit; man is not a sinner in need of a Saviour, but is morally continuous with the Absolute. Between man's highest achievement and the divine righteousness there is continuity; there is here no genuine discontinuity, for the disparity is but one of degree, of all-inclusiveness, of fulfillment. The terminology of sin is here retained only by way of accommodation, for the notion of moral revolt is afforded no place.

This post-Hegelian mood, not without vigorous champions in Germany, England and the United States at the beginning of the century, had antecedent relations also to the ancient Greek thought of Plato and Aristotle, and also to that of Hegel's modern predecessor, Kant. For in classic Greek idealism it was assumed that man is morally continuous with God; here there was room only for the concept of maladjustment, but never for the notion of sin. And while Kant paid his respects to the notion of radical evil, in deference to the Lutheran theology of his homeland, he did not treat the concept with adequate philosophic seriousness;[1] rather, the moral nature of man is assumed to be so continuous with the divine nature that Kant's chief argument for God is from the moral law within to the Lawgiver which it demands as a necessary postulate.

B. *Liberalism Modified Biblical Anthropology with Both Idealistic and Naturalistic Emphases.*

But when one thinks of the religious Modernism of a generation ago—that temper which, where it survives today, is often denominated unreconstructed or unrepentant Liberalism—one finds an optimistic anthropology related to the idealistic mood, yet somewhat compromised. For, whereas idealistic Liberalism was fashioned under the impulse of Hegelian logical evolutionism—with its view of all reality as the progressive unfolding of spirit—religious Modernism stood in closer interaction with the Hebrew-Christian tradition, though compromising its essence in deference to the presuppositions of evolutionary Naturalism. Here the supposed origin of man from a brute ancestry served to color the resultant anthropology as much as Hegelian Idealism.

1. *Sin a Positive Evil, but Traced to Brute Impulses.*

Classic Liberalism, championed still by contemporary unreconstructed Liberalism, viewed sin not merely as something transformed and automatically overcome in the Absolute, i.e., as incipient or latent good, but rather as a positive evil. Liberalism believed in a militant warfare against sin and vice; it

---

1. Kant's theory of *radical evil* is the erratic block in his thought, but he does not take it seriously enough, from the Christian standpoint. His insistence on the autonomy of reason — on reason which gives itself the moral law — makes all heteronomously imposed (divine) law impossible. Moreover, while Kant held that radical evil is a disorder of the instincts, a wrongness and perversion of the human heart, he finally resolved man's ethical contradiction into an opposition between the intelligible and the empirical ego: one cannot truthfully speak of guilt because the intelligible ego is guiltless since it is virtue, while the empirical is without guilt because it is in essence mechanistic.

decried anything that encouraged a "moral holiday." Here
sin was not merely the difference between a finite and an
infinite interpretation of the same set of facts, but rather could
be explained only in terms of man's sensuousness, i.e., the
remnants of the brute instincts which survive in him as a
consequence of his animal ancestry.

2. *Sin to be Overcome by the Upward Movement of History.*

And yet for all of this, classic Liberalism championed an
optimistic view of sin, in contrast with the Hebrew-Christian
tradition with which it had largely broken. For, even if sin
was delineated as something positive, rather than as a negation or lack of absoluteness, this Liberalism as much as post-
Hegelian Idealism assumed that evil is being overcome by an
automatic movement of history.[2] In the case of classic Liberalism, this tendency to minimize the significance of sin arose from
an inter-action with the Spencerian notion of historical progress, and from the assumption of the essential goodness of
man which furnished an ideological link to Darwin as well as
to Kant and Hegel. For if the sweep of history is inevitably
upward, and if the production of man from the animals is
indicative of the ethical tendency of nature, sin would be
overcome by an automatic movement or reality which man
himself could hardly resist. The key to moral advance was
not the crucifixion of natural tendencies, but the proper har-

---

2. It is true that a more moderate view was sometimes championed, even among
"social Gospel" formulators like Walter Rauschenbusch, who stressed the perniciousness
of evil, and the relentless fight it requires on both the personal and the social plane.
But many of Rauschenbusch's disciples lost the depth dimension of sin which he constantly emphasized, and already the attempt to resolve social problems without a primary reference to individual regeneration by a supernatural rebirth involved a new
optimism about human nature. Among evangelicals, the moderate view reflected itself
in post-millennialism, although the necessity of supernatural regeneration was insisted
on. James Orr concluded his famous 1890-91 Kerr Lectures on *The Christian View
of God and the World* with a supplement on "The Idea of the Kingdom of God", in
which he declared to his British audience: "It is difficult to avoid the belief that the
singular development of conditions in this century, its unexampled progress in discovery and in the practical mastery of nature, the marvelous opening up of the world
which has been the result, and the extraordinary multiplication of the means and agen-
cies of rapid communication, together portend some striking development of the kingdom
of God which shall cast all others into the shade, — a crisis, perhaps, which shall have
the most profound effect upon the future of humanity" (pp. 360f.). He adds a footnote
associating "the feeling of an impending crisis" with "apocalyptic reveries" and, in
view of Orr's post-millennialism, he can only have in view the bringing in of the divine
kingdom.

The Story in Readers Pr...

The instance of Lenny H...

II Peter 1:3 — 19

THE PROTESTANT DILEMMA

An Analysis of the Current Impasse in Theology

by CARL F. H. HENRY, TH.D.

Modern man is suddenly aware that the great Hebrew-Christian convictions which have shaped the culture of his western world are altogether incompatible to the naturalistic pathway he is following. He stands bewildered under the impact of two world wars. His leaders anxiously, frantically scan their limited horizons to find a new way. Some, already, suggest the nihilistic alternative as inevitable. How dire the impasse!

"Ours is a frightened age," says the author as in this volume he brings into clear focus the swiftly changing thought of our modern day. Then, skilfully delineating the kaleidoscopic world of current theology, he believingly, convincingly marks the path of Biblical truth with wisdom and sobriety.

"Dr. Henry gives a clear picture of the changing estimates of man, of sin, of the Bible, and of Jesus Christ," says Dr. Wm. Childs Robinson in his Foreword to this penetrating study. "These studies reveal the author's familiarity with current theological thought and provide a sound basis for evaluating this thought, namely the Biblical faith. *I know of no other such comprehensive presentation of the current theological situation.* Among the treasures that linger in the memory are the New Testament study on the Word of God and the insight that the Christian pathway of faith has always pursued a Christological course.

"Here is indeed a vital, up-to-date work in which the thoughtful reader will find rich food for his meditation. for his classroom discussion, and for his pulpit ministrations."

The Author...

Dr. Carl F. H. Henry is Professor of Philosophy of Religion at Fuller Theological Seminary, Pasadena, California, and has served the Northern Baptist Theological Seminary, Chicago, in a similar capacity. He has also served as visiting professor at Gordon College Divinity School, Boston, and Wheaton College, Wheaton, Illinois.

A native of New York City, Dr. Henry received the A. B. and M. A. degrees from Wheaton College, the Th. M. and Th. D. degrees from Northern Baptist Theological Seminary, and has done post-graduate work at Loyola University, University of Indiana, and Boston University. He is a member of the American Philosophical Society, the American Theological Society, The Victoria Institute, London, and is also a member of Pi Gamma Mu and Alpha Delta which are national honor societies in the social sciences and journalism.

Two earlier volumes by Dr. Henry on current philosophical-religious thought have received wide recognition for their clear analysis and discernment of contemporary thought. These are *Remaking the Modern Mind* (Eerdmans, Rev. Ed., 1948, $3.00), which analyzes the basic assumptions of modern philosophy and shows the vital relevance of the Christian view of God and the world; and *The Uneasy Conscience of Modern Fundamentalism* (Eerdmans, 1947, $1.00) which calls for an evangelical ecumenicalism and the application of evangelical Christian fundamentals of faith to the solution of world problems.

monization of them with the moral movement of reality. The philosophy of progress thus overarched the modern hamartiology. Whereas in idealistic Liberalism, the Absolute automatically commuted sin into good, for classic Liberalism history itself was an evil-eliminating mechanism.

a. *Continuity With the Divine the Main Mood.*

Thus classic Liberalism after all, whatever it made of sin as a positive evil, deep down assumed man's essential moral continuity with God. For the assumption of non-miraculous theistic evolution, that man appeared by a process of emergence through the brutes, in the plan of God, meant also that the survival of brute impulses in man must be treated as a normal moral condition for him at this stage of advancement. The discard of the Biblical view of an originally perfect man, divinely created, who later disturbed his proper relationship to God by virtue of a moral revolt, was discarded in deference to the evolutionary insistence that no primally perfect man ever existed, and that evolutionary anthropology knew only of the arrival of man by the slow birth of a moral consciousness which succeeded gradually in bringing the naturalistic or brute impulses under the domination of a higher ideal or spiritual impulses; i.e., the suppression of egoistic motivations for altruistic motivations. Thus the present condition of man, with his moral and spiritual tensions, was regarded, from a sufficiently broad view, as normal, in contrast with the traditional Biblical anthropology, which insisted that historic man since the Fall has been in an abnormal state of spiritual revolt.

b. *Sin Not Lodged in Man's Will.*

This is clear from another consideration. For as classic Liberalism framed its anthropology, the principle of sin was not lodged in the human will, contrary to the Hebrew-Christian tradition. The concept of sin had dimensions very much reduced from the Biblical outlines. For sin now was viewed in terms of an inertia of nature, which explained man's indisposition to his potential role as an immanent channel of divine love. It was the drag of brute instincts on the higher spiritual ideals which pulled men down. Sin was centered in man's "animal" or bodily—rather than his spiritual—activity. But the essential man, once again, as in the Hegelian tradition, was identified with the higher or ideal self; at the core of personality, man was essentially good and perfectible, whatever moral torpor or spiritual sluggishness may accrue to him as a consequence of his brute ancestry. If, after all, this was the means by which God had chosen to bring man into existence, it could not be put to man's account that the inertia of his nature should slack the subservience of the natural sensuous impulses to the higher altruistic ends. Sin was indeed a betrayal of our best selves, it was a lack of love for humanity, it was an enthronement of egoism at the expense of utilitarianism, it was (in a word) *selfishness;* more than this, it was ingratitude in the light of Christ's selfgiving on Calvary,[3] and hence a failure to respond to God's love—but for all that, it was the struggle proper to humanity at this stage of its advance.

But as this view of sin as a drag of animal inheritance interacted with the convictions of progress and essential goodness, sin came also to be viewed as a culture lag, or the failure to transcend the limitations of one's particular environment or his immediate behavior patterns. Thus education was looked upon as the solution to the sin-problem; in the final analysis, sin was evaluated in terms of ignorance. Hence classic Liberalism fluctuated, in its final moods, between a view of sin as sensuousness and as ignorance, and found the key to both notions in the conviction of an animal ancestry in the course of evolutionary advance. But ignorance too, like the survival of animal drives, was not an abnormal predicament for one implicated in evolutionary process; here also the moral predicament of man was consistent with an easy conscience and an undisturbed finiteness. For perfection was appropriate only to the end of the evolutionary process; *in medias res,* it was but an impractical ideal.

------

3. The significance of Christ, on this view, was that of example. He best shows how integration of character is achieved by supreme devotion to the highest spiritual ends.

(1) *Moral Law Treated Impersonally.*

From another vantage point, this complacent view of sin can be studied in relation to classic Liberalism's tendency to view God impersonally—a not wholly unintelligible phenomenon wherever the moral nature of man is regarded as continuous with that of God, and not without anticipations in Plato, Kant and Hegel. Man's disparity was determined in view of the highest social ideals,[4] or the moral law with a certain impersonal cast—so that while God was viewed as the creator and sustainer of the moral law, in an evolutionary context the moral law came to be viewed in detachment from Him so far as involving direct divine confrontation of man. (Man loitered behind the loftiest ideals, but he was hardly in revolt against God.) Precisely this element of confrontation was lacking. For God was viewed as man's moral equal, endowed only with larger perfections. In the realm of morals, the voice of God was equated with the voice of conscience.[5] Deity never demanded more than the higher self, except in terms of other higher human selves. God's thoughts and ways are our highest thoughts and ways, except on a grander scale. Thus theological students were told that "God is at least as good as the Red Cross, or as the Y. W. C. A." and not infrequently the deity concept was impersonally merged with "the sum total of the forces at work for righteousness in our environment." The moral "otherness" or holiness of God was obscured.

(2) *Ability the Measure of Responsibility.*

This assumption of moral continuity between God and man worked itself out, in classic Liberalism, in a doctrine of sin somewhat different from Kant's formulation. The philosopher

4. Niebuhr came to see that Liberalism had more affinity with modern Naturalism than with classic Christianity, with its affirmation that "man remains a sinner in spite of all moral achievements" *Reflections on the End of an Era,* p. 204. New York: Charles Scribner's Sons, 1934).

5. The presupposition was, of course, that any special revelation by a personal God would add nothing to the moral law within. Niebuhr later saw how the liberals identified with "the absolute and transcendent ethic of Jesus" such momentary utilitarian goals as "democracy, mutual cooperation, the League of Nations, international trade reciprocity, and other similar ideals", whereas they were but "the relative moral standards of a commercial age" obscuring the "transcendent ideals of Christian morality" (*An Interpretation of Christian Ethics,* pp. 9ff. New York: Harper and Bros. 1935.)

of ethical Idealism, it will be recalled, developed the sense of *ought*, which is not merely hypothetical nor indicative but a "categorical imperative", in a direction quite different from the Biblical tradition. For Protestant orthodoxy, dealing in stark realism with the Biblical doctrine of the fall of man, affirmed the inability of man to fufill the moral *ought*, as a consequence of his implication in original sin; the *ought* indicated that man *could have;* it declared both his responsibility and his inability. But Kant reasoned from the moral *ought* not to the inability but to the ability of man; *I ought,* he affirmed, *therefore I can.* Whereas Biblical thought declared that the *ought* is fulfilled by the life and death of Jesus Christ for all believers, and could never be fulfilled by sinful man, Kant's ethical Idealism interpreted the *ought* in an optimistic direction, so that oughtness implied moral ability.

Now classic religious Modernism, it has been suggested, gave Kant's formulation a somewhat different turn, in which F. R. Tennant was the wayshower.[6] Tennant, like Kant, was in revolt against the doctrine of human depravity. If every human being *"always* turns to evil"*, he protested, then both ethics and Christian theology are destroyed.[7] Thereupon Tennant appropriated the Kantian formula in an even more optimistic way: whereas Kant had said that "I ought, therefore I can," Tennant insisted that "if I cannot, I ought not"; that is, for Tennant, ability is the measure of moral obligation. This was substantially the view of sin held by leading liberal thinkers at the beginning of the generation now closing, among them W. A. Brown, E. W. Lyman, D. C. Macintosh, John C. Bennett, Walter M. Horton, and Reinhold Niebuhr. On this pattern, man was not a sinner at the core of his personality; sin was computed no longer by reference to an ideal standard of perfection, but in terms of the present possibility of the moral agent. It was impossible to denominate an act sinful, insisted the liberal hamartiology, unless freedom of performance was demonstrably

---

6. See Tennant's works in this area: *The Sources of the Doctrine of the Fall and Original Sin, The Origin and Propagation of Sin, The Concept of Sin.*

7. *The Concept of Sin,* p. 265.

present. Wherever inability prevailed, the ought was presumed to be nonexistent.

It is apparent that the modernist view—that God does not require perfection of man, yet does call man to follow the example of Jesus Christ in whom the ideal is fully enthroned over other impulses — is directly connected with the evolutionary view of man's origin. For if in the course of the divine plan man came into being through an animal ancestry, the survival of wicked impulses is to be viewed as normal, rather than as penal. The whole notion of an original righteousness subsequently undercut by a fall is discarded. To take evolution seriously meant to reject any literal history of perfection before the Fall, that is, it involved the necessity for interpreting the Bible mythically and rejecting it literally in its testimony to primal man. Genesis three was to be treated with neither historical nor symbolical seriousness. For it was not to a "fallen Adam" so much as to the "Second Adam", Jesus Christ, that religious Modernism related the modern man; they were separated, indeed, but only by degree. In deference to evolutionary anthropology, the notion of a fall from primitive righteousness was abandoned; instead, a trial-and-error moral being, produced in the course of theistic evolution, was substituted. This being was not, in virtue of a fall, essentially a sinner; rather, the core of his personality enjoyed divine approval, and contemplated the prospect of ultimate control, by natural striving, over the surviving brute instincts. But in principle, the battle was already won. Man was not any longer the perpetual sinner without hope apart from a divinely provided redemption; in fact, he had a bias to good rather than a bias to evil—in the liberal view—for sin was not put to his account except where he was responsible and, where the brute impulses prevailed, man was but struggling against a normal aspect of his nature. This gave rise to the modernist use of psychology and psychiatry; personality sickness was differentiated from sin—for it had its roots in an evolutionary heritage, rather than in a moral revolt against God. Within such predilections, sin was foredoomed to consignment with morbid and antiquated concepts.

The classic modernist view of sin, therefore, while it protested in word against the optimistic Idealism which said that sin was automatically commuted into good in the Absolute, nonetheless shared a highly optimistic view of man—when contrasted with the Hebrew-Christian tradition—and in its identification of sin in terms of culture lag or brute drag hardly regarded sin an ultimate seriousness, for God stood behind the evolutionary process.

3. *Optimistic Anthropology Discredited by Contemporary History.*

What shook this optimistic philosophy was not so much a resurgence of Biblical faith as the empirical happenings of two world wars, horrible in their toll of both life and security. The rise of a "reconstructed Liberalism" came from a consideration of the implications of war-torn western culture, which had served, in the case of the evangelical movement, merely to comfirm, rather than to establish, the need for a non-optimistic anthropology.[8]

C. *Neo-Supernaturalism's Assertion of Man's Essential Sinfulness.*

The influential figures in the rise of a more realistic anthropology were Soren Kierkegaard in Denmark, Karl Barth and Emil Brunner in Germany and, in America, Reinhold Niebuhr. Barth saw the emptiness of liberal optimism already during World War I, when Germany was drenched in blood. Wearing Kierkegaard's mantle, he fired the theological guns against

---

8. One of the finest treatments of the reversal of Liberalism in its view of sin, as a result of the war years, is found in Mary F. Thelen's *Man as Sinner* (New York: King's Crown Press, 1946), to which the author acknowledges his debt. There the shift to a less optimistic anthropology is traced rightly to (1) the course of world events resulting from the social behavior of the past generation; (2) the fact that leaders who absolutized their finite programs as "the will of God", and who thought that only those in opposition to such programs were infected by sin, were themselves seen to be guilty; (3) the lessons learned from Freudian "depth" psychology; (4) the revival of continental anthropological thought in a context of supernatural Absolutism.

Modernism, and charged that liberal theologians were especially perverse, proudly maintaining an optimistic anthropology even when the empirical facts to which they presumably appealed were lacking. But England and America were the victor nations, and the implications of the first World War in terms of anthropology were not so readily apparent. Here clear signs of an almost inevitable drift to a second and vastly more devasting war were necessary before the liberal view of man was questioned. True, throughout the whole generation of liberal optimism, evangelicals vigorously assailed and challenged the modernist view, but they were given no hearing; the fundamentalist anthropology seemed too much like an echo of "original sin mythology" which Liberalism had discarded in deference to an evolutionary view of origins.

1. *Niebuhr on the Discontinuity of the Human and the Divine.*

The most important American work in the field of theological and philosophical anthropology for a generation is Reinhold Niebuhr's *The Nature and Destiny of Man,* the two-volume statement of his 1939 Gifford Lectures, which has become the rallying point of a restatement of the doctrine of original sin. The implications of this position are being worked out, by various American theologians and philosophers of religion, in the areas of metaphysics and epistemology, Christology and sociology. If one takes the 1914-46 generation of two world wars as a unit, the rise of the so-called reconstructed Liberalism may be placed just about at the mid-generation point. For from 1932 the revolt against the older liberal optimism about man has included such prominent modernist figures, formerly identified with the classic liberal viewpoint, as the two Niebuhrs, Bennett, Calhoun and Walter M. Horton.

Niebuhr saw, as against the liberal idealists, that particular sin could not be transmuted merely by its inclusion in an absolute or all-inclusive will. His *Moral Man and Immoral Society* underscored the thesis that the collective will is more immoral than the individual will, as seen in the fact that state absolutisms involved the most perverse type of idolatry. The political absolutisms of Europe, in the dictator countries, dealt harshly with the optimism that the collective will transformed evil into good.

Now if the liberal romanticizing of human nature had as its setting a reduction of sin from voluntary revolt to involuntary inertia, which the progress of history would inevitably overcome; if it assumed man's moral continuity with God, even if this meant the discard of the doctrine of original sin, the denial that man is a sinner at the core of his personality, and the depersonalization of the God-idea; if it reduced the *ought* to the limits of present ability, and refused to trace personality sickness to sin—then it is precisely at these points that reconstructed Liberalism manifests its revolt. For the recent anthropology, motivated by the events of the generation of world warring, renounced the modernist sentimentality about man and declared, in bold type, *man is a sinner!*

a. *Man's Will in Revolt Against God.*

Reconstructed Liberalism lodged the principle of sin squarely within the human *will;* extra-volitional aspects — as sensuous impulses—are merely the occasions of moral revolt against God.

The implications of this view are immediately apparent:

The sin struggle is viewed as an encounter between man and God. In fact, as Brunner has put it, it is only when man sees himself in such revolt, sees himself a condemned sinner before a holy God, that the sense of human personality and of the personality of God stands forth in clearest outline. Philosophically, this marks the rise of a new Personalism in which man comes to a personal God not by an argument from ethical values in the course of moral human-divine continuity (as in personalistic Idealism) but by way of moral discontinuity.[9] It is not the implacability of an impersonal moral law, but the implacability of God Himself, which confronts man. Nor can man's predicament be resolved on the naturalistic premises that men are essentially animals, are basically egoistic; rather, Neo-Supernaturalism proclaims, "Men are egoists in contradistinction to their essential nature." Man's moral relationship to God, rather than his physical relationship to the brutes, is definitive in principle for human nature.

b. *God as Man's Judge.*

To say this means also that God not only is man's source and goal, but also man's enemy and judge. Man's ethical default has supracosmic repercussions. God takes sin seriously; no longer is man His moral equal. Rather, it is *immoral* man, every man a sinner and under condemnation of God, not moral man able to divest himself of responsibility in *immoral society*, as Niebuhr once thought. God's reaction to sin is active, not passive; He *causes* men and nations persisting in sin to perish. Human achievement in history—as apparent from the successive ruin of cultures—is discontinuous with deity; divine judgment rests on all behavior patterns, including the highest human achievements. Precisely those achievements which were identified with the divine, those temporary idealistic expedients which were confused with the will of God, are twice condemned, for the judgment of God strikes with dual force against self-righteousness and spiritual pride, especially such righteousness and pride which repudiates the sinfulness of man and his moral discontinuity with God.

---

9. A truly evangelical statement of man's present moral predicament denies man's total discontinuity as well as man's total continuity with God. A total discontinuity would make it impossible for man to distinguish even formally between right and wrong. But the discontinuity is sufficiently serious so that man cannot reconstruct the Good without special divine initiative; it is not a universal possession of human reason, or an *a priori* idea. Man is a sinner, and hence is locked up to divine disclosure for a true knowledge of the Good. But he is a *sinner*—that is, he is still morally responsible; hence the discontinuity is not entire. The divine image is distorted, but not destroyed. Despite his inherent sinfulness and waywardness, man retains the capacity to respond to God. Even in this fallen nature, man is within God's grasp, either for grace or for judgment.

c. *Significance of Subconscious Impulses.*

The dismissal of sin as a pathological condition, as a sense of guilt which conforms to no real guilt, is indeed one of the worst manifestations of sin. The sinner who accepts this alternative not only complicates his mental illness, but multiplies his guilt. For personality sickness, and many types of mental disease, have a religious reference. Thus Neo-Supernaturalism tends to view the sense of guilt as irreducible, however one may suppress it in deference to pathological interpretations; subconscious guilt finds no adequate relief by repression, for apart from forgiveness it but multiplies itself, and involves complex personality disorders. More human behavior is traceable to unconscious compulsions than classic Liberalism admitted under the demand that man can be charged with sin only where immediate conscious responsibility is evident. Even in many acts devoid of freedom and immediate responsibility, the sense of religious guilt is appropriately present.[10]

d. *Reaffirmation of Original Sin and Responsible Inability.*

Man is "inevitably and always a sinner" Hence, for Neo-Supernaturalism, the doctrine of original sin comes into clearer focus. The doctrine of the fall of man is to be treated with symbolical seriousness, versus optimistic Liberalism.

(1) *The Fall as Trans-Historical.*

The fall is not, indeed, historically true—for Neo-Supernaturalism retains an evolutionary anthropology. The case against an evolutionary origin is lost, shouts Brunner. But Genesis three is not thereby invalidated; rather, it is symbolically true.[11] It is a temporal picture of a timeless truth.

For man, despite the animal drag due to a brute ancestry, has the symptoms of a *fallen* rather than an ascending creature. His predicament is not merely *I ought if I can*—that is ethical double-talk—but rather, it is *I ought and I cannot;*

---

10. Niebuhr, *An Interpretation of Christian Ethics,* pp. 77f.

11. Niebuhr's stress that the early Genesis story must be taken "seriously but not historically" is found in *The Nature and Destiny of Man,* I, pp. 50, 289f.

both Kant and Tennant are wrong, are, in fact, most sinful where they deny sin, in assuming man's moral competence.

Since the revival by Neo-Supernaturalism of the terminology of original sin is a serious bone of theological contention, inviting attack from unreconstructed Liberalism with its less positive view of sin, and also from traditional Evangelicalism which claims that neo-orthodoxy falsifies the Biblical view of sin, it is important to examine this aspect of the system in detail.

Reconstructed Liberalism discards, as has been said, the Biblical idea of a historic primal perfection of the first man, which was lost in a historic fall, so that all humanity by virtue of implication in Adam is devoid of original righteousness but shares in original sin. Evolutionary anthropology, it is held, demands the surrender of the historicity of this narrative. Instead, the narrative is held to be symbolically or mythically true. It depicts, not the loss of original righteousness by a primal Adam, but rather the story of all humanity: all men possess original righteousness, and all men possess original sin. The story of Adam is simply the story of the human race. In *Beyond Tragedy* the sin-salvation drama is localized in each human act, rather than in the full sweep of history, a theme reechoed in Niebuhr's *The Nature and Destiny of Man;* perfection before the fall is a mythological symbol for "perfection before the act."[12] The fall is not a historical event, but rather the "presupposition" of action and belongs to the "transhistorical" realm of human freedom. Original sin is not an inherited corruption, Niebuhr tells us also elsewhere, but is "an inevitable fact of human existence, the inevitability of which is given by the nature of man's spirituality. It is true in every moment of existence, but it has no history."[13]

---

12. *Beyond Tragedy*, pp. 11ff.

13. *An Interpretation of Christian Ethics*, p. 90. The use of the traditional phrase "original sin" gains a certain propriety because of the failure of the neo-orthodox thinkers to distinguish, as the older theologians did, between *peccatum originans*, that is, Adam's fall, and *peccatum originatum seu originals*, that is, inherited sin due to Adam's original sin, and *peccatum actuale*, that is, our individual sin.

(a) *Original Sin is the Failure to Translate Ideals into Actuality.*

Original sin is simply the failure of man to translate his ideals into actuality. Between our ideals and original righteousness there is continuity, but between our acts and original righteousness there is discontinuity. Man's best acts are still the performances of a sinner, not of an unfallen agent. This fact—that man constantly translates his ideals into activity by a process of reduction—is his predicament; man shows himself to be "always and inevitably" a sinner. Thus man remains a sinner despite all moral achievement.

(b) *Original Righteousness is Man's Ideal Continuity with God.*

Our ideals are continuous with the divine goodness, even if our achievements in history are discontinuous with the will of God. For God's ways are other than ours; between the highest human goodness and the divine goodness there is disjunction. But our ideals are continuous with God.

The reason for the failure to realize ideals without perverting them is not some external drag on the human will, but is due to a defect in the will itself. The "Fall myth" suggests that sin does not follow inevitably from temporal existence, from an inertia of nature, from sheer finiteness, but rather that man is responsible for sin, for temptation is there represented as coming to man from outside, and as involving him in decision.

(2) *The Inevitability of Man's Fall.*

Now, it is clear that this anthropology poses an immediate problem. For if each man possesses original righteousness (continuity of ideals with the divine goodness), how does it come that each man in turn falls into original sin (discontinuity of human achievement with the divine will) —that man is inevitably and always a sinner? If man's sinfulness is not contingently necessitated by virtue of his link to fallen Adam as the Hebrew-Christian tradition contended, is it actually necessitated by the original constitution of man's nature, or is the "inevitable" fall nonetheless free?

The discussion of this problem requires some detail in the statement of Niebuhr's view. For everything turns upon the definition of the nature of man.

(a) *The Pretensions of Finite Spirits.*

In the pre-Gifford Lecture mood,[14] Niebuhr traced sin to the weakness of man's reason as against his egoistic impulse. Though reason affirms life in its most inclusive terms, voicing man's altruistic impulses and reflecting his self-transcendence, yet the principle of rational universality is frustrated by an incurable egoistic impulse, by an evil will which undercuts pure altruism in deference to egoism.

Beginning with his Gifford Lectures, Niebuhr traces sin to spiritual more than to rational failure; sin arises from the pretensions of spirit, for man tends to mix the eternal with the finite, tends to absolutize his finite claims, tends to make himself God.

Let us look then to Niebuhr's statement of the essence of the Biblical view of man:

Man is neither essentially a part of nature nor essentially rational, but rather belongs to both realms—stands, in fact, at the juncture of the realms of nature and spirit. His creatureliness is not sinful, for finite man was declared good at his "creation" and his creatureliness is never to be revoked. At this juncture of the natural and spiritual worlds, man apparently possesses unlimited possibility in the choice of ends. He has the capacity for infinite self-transcendence, or perfect altruism.

But this capacity, Niebuhr hastens to add, is not the same as "reason" or the capacity to deal with universals. For, following Soren Kierkegaard and Max Scheler, he distinguishes between rationality and spirit. Man is a creature of nature, of rationality, and of super-rationality (i.e., a freedom of spirit to trans-

---

14. The progression in Niebuhr's thought is carefully analyzed by Thelen.

cend rationality by reaching upward for a principle which com-
pletes human nature—for the God "beyond reason" disclosed
in the Hebrew-Christian revelation). Thus it is seen that man's
spiritual nature, for Niebuhr, outreaches the categories of
thought and hence spills over the law of rational non-contra-
diction; theology is at home in paradox and irrationalism, and
limiting concepts.

(b) *Anxiety as the Psychological Condition Preceding
Sin.*

Sin occurs when man's reason universalizes a particular, and
when the spirit infinitizes a finite. But what is the occasion
for such? It is man's insecurity. For evil arises in the human
will because of the anxiety of man in view of his ambiguous
situation at the conjunction of nature and spirit. Man's ignorance, at this juncture, of the final meaning of life, begets an
anxiety which constitutes the state of temptation out of which
either faith or sin may arise. Man's love is universally cor-
rupted by self-seeking. The moment man *acts,* he corrupts the
divine ideal; a defect of will corrupts all human behavior.

Anxiety is "the inevitable spiritual state of man standing in
the paradoxical situation of freedom and finiteness."[15] Anxiety itself is not the cause of sin but only—as Kierkegaard held—
the psychological condition which precedes sin. It does not
make sin necessary, for the ideal possibility exists that its tension might be surmounted by faith in God—thus fulfilling the
"original righteousness" by love of men as God's creatures.
There is the "ideal possibility" that man might accept insecurity and anxiety as inescapable implications of human existence, and find in God both moral security and the meaning
of existence, rather than to seek security in society. But while
anxiety is a neutral state of temptation and is inevitable and
necessary, the sin which follows it is unnecessitated, yet "inevitable though not necessary." Thus anxiety leads to sin, while
not necessarily begetting it. In Niebuhr's words, sin ensues

---

15. *The Nature and Destiny of Man,* I, p. 182.

from man's "inevitable though not necessary unwillingness to acknowledge his dependence, to accept his finiteness and to admit his insecurity, an unwillingness which involves him in the vicious circle of accentuating the insecurity from which he seeks to escape."[16] That the fall occurs in every act is not fortuitous but inevitable, yet the inevitability arises in a context of freedom and hence is not determined. Hence man, instead of acting altruistically, of his own free will—not necessitated by his nature—falls into *sin in every act,* seeking security by a course other than the acceptance of his weakness and ignorance and trusting God for security. History proves inescapably evil, disclosing man in the service of false gods. Original sin thus is a bias of will before action, inferred to be present from the universality of sin. It is not an act, but the presupposition of every act. The fact that in the "Fall myth" temptation is depicted as coming to man from outside, in a distortion of God's command, suggests to Niebuhr that man always deceives himself into projecting the proposed evil as a good before he acts. Man seeks to save his life *by saving it,* by spiritual pretension: rather than admitting his creatureliness and enthroning the will of God, he seeks to infinitize his finiteness. His virtues become a cloak for his will-to-power, his generosities a screen for his injustices.

(c) *Original Righteousness and Conscience.*

Now, if man's behavior is consistently sinful, and if by original sin is intended not the fall of a primal man in which all humanity was so implicated as to render human nature guilty and corrupt, but rather that each man creatively corrupts the divine ideal, the question arises, what is the neo-supernaturalist view of original righteousness? Again here, original righteousness is viewed not as an exclusive possession of a primal man, but as a possession of every man. For while man is held to be discontinuous with God in behavior and act, he is held to be continuous in his ideals. On the level

---

16. *The Nature and Destiny of Man,* I, p. 150.

of moral idealism—before human behavior endeavors to trans-
mute altruism into reality only to find that the mood of
anxiety encourages an infection of altruism with egoism, "before the Fall"—God's love and man's are not different, but
rather God's thoughts are our thoughts, even if His ways are
not our ways, because of the inevitability of sin. The goodness
of God is continuous with man's "original righteousness" but
not with man's behavior. Man's conscience is continuous with
divine goodness;[17] conscience as pure contemplation prior to
action is the "memory of original perfection" for it represents
a rising above anxiety and the projection of a right general
intuition. Man still possesses the sense of obligation toward
his essential nature; the law is still written on his heart.

The phrase "after the fall" denotes for Neo-Supernaturalism,
therefore, not a once-for-all fallen condition which looks back
to primal human innocence, but rather the contrast between
ideal human nature and empirical sinfulness. The "fall myth",
we are told, "does justice to the actual facts which a rational
conception of human imperfection fails to reveal", i.e., that
"the egoism of natural impulse is actually transmuted into a
willful conflict of life with life."[18] But orthodoxy has "mis-
interpreted" the significance of the fall in terms of primal
anthropology.

2. *Difficulties in Niebuhr's Anthropology.*

After this survey, we are ready for a recapitulation of the
neo-supernaturalist view of sin, and also an evaluation of it.

The view itself is, as we have seen, higher than that of
unreconstructed Liberalism. Sin is a personal revolt not against
an impersonal moral law but against a personal God; man's
acts, even at his best, are morally discontinuous with God;
man's guilt has its subconscious as well as its conscious roots;
man is inevitably and inescapably a sinner, though not necessarily so; man's inability to achieve perfection of activity does

---

17. *The Nature and Destiny of Man*, I, p. 272.
18. *Reflections on the End of an Era*, p. 291.

not exempt him from responsibility; man is a "fallen" creature, even if the notion of primal perfection must be surrendered to evolution, for he always translates his altruistic ideals into a behavior tempered with egoism.

But is the view able to sustain itself at so high a level? Does it possess an inner coherence which makes possible so much of an advance from the liberal to the Biblical definition, and how far short of that Biblical view of sin does it halt? These are questions which remain for our appraisal. Important questions indeed they are, for if the neo-supernaturalist mood succeeds in its effort to win the committment of a significant majority, it can render effective service only if its evaluation of sin is sufficiently realistic and ultimately adequate.

a. *The Connection Between Freedom and Anxiety as Primitive.*

The first difficulty in the Niebuhr formulation is its suggestion of a necessary connection between freedom and anxiety —a notion carried over from Kierkegaard, and to be found also in Freud, Adler, and other psychologists who made an intensive study of modern man and assumed that he was in all respects representative. Anxiety is viewed as a concomitant of creatureliness, arising out of the possession of finiteness and freedom.

Now, while anxiety appears characteristic of modern man, the question arises whether such anxiety is normal, is indeed an attribute of creatureliness? May it not be that the key to sin is found, not in anxiety as a normal accompaniment of creatureliness, but in the explanation of anxiety as an abnormal state? Is anxiety a prerequisite of creatureliness? Or is it the sign of an uneasy creature, the sign of a moral and spiritual creature in abnormal relationship to God?

For it is precisely as an abnormal experience that anxiety is presented in the Scriptures themselves; here we are told to "be anxious for nothing" and that "perfect love casteth out fear". Rather than the Niebuhr pattern—that "anxiety is a concomitant of finite and insecure existence"—we find the suggestion that anxiety is characteristic of insecure, but not a necessity of finite existence; that indeed it is man as fallen, man in a state of suspended or interrupted security, who is so delineated. The Biblical man lacks "peace with God" because he is in moral revolt, not because he is a man. On the Biblical pattern, Niebuhr's "ideal possibility"—a finite being who finds his security in God—is indeed a "primal actuality", the first Adam created in the divine likeness, and reposing his trust in his Maker. Anxiety comes into this story not as a normal element in it, but rather in terms of a rupture of an original and normative relationship; anxiety itself is as abnormal as sin, and indeed is not without its direct relations to sin. The loss of an anxiety-less state is itself the result of sin; the presence of anxiety is not the prelude to, but the accompaniment or aftermath of sin.

Thus, from a Biblical viewpoint, Niebuhr's distinction between a sinless state of creaturely anxiety, and a subsequent state in which anxiety leads inevitably to sin, is without justification.[19] The Scriptures teach nothing of mankind becoming sinful, each man in his turn, by the conversion of a normal state of creaturely anxiety, into an inevitable state of anxious sin. Anxiety was not a characteristic of the original nature or destiny of man.

In fact, it is precisely the Biblical view which gains support from Neo-Freudian psychology. That anxiety results from a previous rupture in inter-personal relations is a common-

---

19. The insistence on anxiety as a concomitant of finiteness stems out of the existentialist revolt of Soren Kierkegaard against Hegelian philosophy, which looked upon every aspect of man's experience as an expression of a universal logical necessity. The Kierkegaardian movement, developed by Martin Heidegger and Karl Jaspers in Germany and Gabriel Marcel in France, minimized reason and idealized man's existence in its irrationality. For man in the existentialist predicament anxiety and suffering is a continual state which becomes almost the essential proof of man's very existence. For an acute criticism of existentialist philosophy on this approach see Guido de Ruggiero's *Existentialism: Disintegration of Man's Soul* (New York: Social Science Publishers Inc., 1948).

place insistence of this school.[20] Now, while the Neo-Freudian psychology has no use for a non-evolutionary view of origins, its interpretation of anxiety is congruous with the Genesis account, in which the anxiety of the first man is depicted first in connection with a moral revolt which reverses his previous state of acceptability with God, and not as characteristic of his original nature and destiny. On this pattern, one finds in the abnormal relationship between man and God the sufficient reason why finiteness is not now emancipated from anxiety. It is not in a genuinely Biblical context that one finds creatureliness aflux with anxiety as the normal and primal human mood. For here *Urangst,* or cosmic helplessness, is not without its relations to a sense of divine wrath.

b. *The Inevitability of Sin Traced to Anxiety.*

But apart from Niebuhr's confused treatment of "primitive anxiety," his derivation of sin from anxiety by a process which renders sin inevitable yet unnecessary has a curiosity all its own. The difficulties are best brought to light if one considers first the Niebuhr recast of "original righteousness" and then his statement of "original sin."

(1) *Conscience Not Man's Original Righteousness.*

With reference to "original righteousness", or the continuity of our highest altruistic ideals with the divine, Niebuhr takes ground which falls short of the seriousness of the Biblical view of sin.[21] For the notion that each man possesses "original righteousness (continuity with divine ideals) falsifies the Biblical insistence that men are *by nature* (and not only by deed)

---

20. Cf. Gregory Vlastos, in *Christian Century,* "Sin and Anxiety in Niebuhr's Religion," Oct. 1, 1941. Thelen comments that "Vlastos is probably right that Niebuhr's anxiety is already sin, but is anxiety really avoidable in our attitude toward the Creator of the universe?" (*op. cit.,* p. 182, footnote). The key question, however, is whether our attitude is normative. For the Hebrew-Christian tradition, metaphysical and psychological anxiety are not unrelated.

21. Alan Richardson writes, in this mood, that human reason and conscience are the disfigured remnants of God's image in man—are "his 'original righteousness,' which should be mentioned also every time we speak of his 'original sin.' . . . The high achievements of many forms of non-Christian humanism and of non-Christian ethical and religious systems demonstrate the reality of man's original righteousness and the fact that it has not been altogether lost . . ." (*Christian Apologetics,* p. 132).

children of wrath. While it is an insistence true to Biblical theology that the divine image in man is not destroyed—so that man retains the conviction of the good, and the conscience is prebent so that it formally points in the general direction of the good—nonetheless it is also a Biblical insistence that man's thoughts as well as his ways are not God's, and that his knowledge of the good is falsified and vitiated because of sin. In other words, the notion of a moral mind and a sinful will is hardly Biblically adequate; it reflects, in fact, an over-optimistic view of man.

(a) *Niebuhr's Awareness of This Problem.*

There are aspects of Niebuhr's thought which indicate Niebuhr's awareness of this problem, and which indeed indicate a serious effort to come to terms with it. For Niebuhr stresses also the supra-morality of God, in his stress upon the divine "otherness." Thus we are told that there is a higher goodness of God which "negates" even man's original righteousness.[22] Even the divine goodness known through special revelation, Niebuhr affirms, transcends our corrupt human goodness.

(b) *Suggestions of an Irrationalistic Solution.*

But this emphasis on the supra-morality of God comes, in Niebuhr's thought, not in the spirit of the Hebrew-Christian tradition, with its antithesis between the divine goodness (which man may possess only by imputation and the energizing of the Holy Spirit) and the fallen nature of man (constituting his need for supernatural regeneration); rather it comes in the course of his epistemological dialecticism, under which— leaning on Kant—the nature of God defies the categories of human thought. As was noted in the discussion of Niebuhr's definition of the essential nature of man, the spiritual is placed

---

22. *An Interpretation of Christian Ethics,* pp. 230ff: "A too strongly humanistic theism cannot possibly comprehend the whole world into its universe of meaning, because there are processes in nature which are in obvious conflict with the highest human purposes. Such a theism, therefore, tends to perpetual dissolution into a humanistic dualism in which man is persuaded to rebel against the world as nothing more than 'the trampling march of unconscious power.' A genuine prophetic faith reaches a transcendence in which the conflict between man and nature is overcome, even when the conflict defies every effort of rational comprehension."

above the rational as though it escapes the limits of conception. As Thelen acutely notes: "Niebuhr's insistence upon infinite self-transcendence is nothing less than an insistence upon the super-rational and is consequently fundamental to his epistemology, his doctrine of God, and his ethics. It is tantamount to saying that reason is not the essence of either divinity or humanity, nor the medium of communication between God and man, nor the principle of worth."[23] On such a view, obviously, any notion of propositional revelation must be discarded, and hence Niebuhr stands firmly with the Barth-Brunner neo-supernaturalist movement in the insistence that whereas there are revelational events, there is no such thing as revealed truth.[24] Thus, under the influence of Kant, the neo-supernaturalistic temper goes beyond the historic insistence of the Christian movement that whereas the Christian-self-as-transscendent has spiritual implications beyond reasoning, beyond philosophic contemplation, it does not have implications beyond rationality.

It is from this vantage point that one must understand the accusations leveled by critics of the Barth-Brunner movement, such as Van Til,[25] who contend that their dialecticism does not, except in a verbal way, get beyond the tendency of classic Modernism to settle for an impersonal god. The thrust of Kant's system was that, since the limits of human knowledge preclude a theoretical knowledge of deity, it is only by way of regulative judgment, or as a limiting concept, that one can speak of a personal God. It is difficult to see how, in view

---

23. Thelen, *op. cit.*, p. 89.

24. Thus the other Niebuhr, H. Richard, holds that God transcends all our ideas including doctrines like that of atonement, derived from special revelation. The actual content of revelation, we are told, is not intellectual truth, but rather forces the continual revision of ideas derived from other sources—merely affording us tools with which to accomplish self-made corrections. In revelation we encounter the Self behind all truth; ideas belong not to revelation, but are part of the apparatus of human reason. Revelation conveys an awareness of our sinfulness, not propositional truth concerning the divine will; revelation results in doctrinal thought, but is not identical with it. One does not need to look far into this mood to discern the lengthened shadow of Barth and Brunner, and behind that, Kierkegaard and Bergson, and behind that, Kant.

25. Cornelius Van Til, *The New Modernism*. Philadelphia: Christian and Reformed Publishing Co., 1946.

of the neo-supernaturalistic reduction of the significance of rationality, this criticism can be successfully combatted. In the final analysis, the two moods expressed by Niebuhr with reference to man's "original righteousness", its continuity and its discontinuity with the divine, must be regarded as simply two movements of the neo-orthodox dialecticism, which dance onward in paradox, with no ultimate resolution. Indeed, if spirituality spills over the bounds of rationality, it is futile to seek a synthesis; such irrationalism is the playground of paradox and mysticism, but not of clear concepts.[26]

(2) *Inevitability a Postulate from Empirical Probability.*

But now, assuming Niebuhr's formulation of original righteousness as the acceptability of man's ideals before he acts, and of original sin as the unnecessitated inevitability of translating altruistic ideals into an egoistic-tainted reduction, what problems crucial for the doctrine of sin remain? It is precisely the notion of a normal "unnecessitated inevitability" which is the vulnerable point.

It is clear, of course, that "inevitability" is on Niebuhr's profession an empirically-based concept; it is derived not from an authoritative *a priori* revelation, but rather is taken as implied in the downward drift of all human cultures, without exception. When this is kept in mind, it is clear that all Niebuhr can philosophically champion is a "tentative inevitability," and doubly so on an evolutionary scheme, if the possibility of significant advance is still open. But the seriousness of sin, on the neo-supernaturalist formula, is main-

---

26. Arthur E. Murphy expresses this complaint well, although from a vantage point of unrepentant Liberalism. Writing of Niebuhr's treatment of Bible doctrines as symbolically but not literally true, he remarks: "What this seems to mean . . . is that these doctrines have some important element of truth in them but are not true in the form in which they were traditionally accepted, while any attempt to say what *is* true in them ends in logical incoherence. It ought to follow from this that Dr. Niebuhr cannot conceive them in any way that does not violate the principles of logic, and hence, on these crucial matters, literally does not know what it is that he believes, except that it is something strongly suggested to his mind as true by these traditional doctrines, but something which turns out, in every attempt to think it through, to be either false or logically inconceivable" (*Religious Liberals Reply*, p. 19). In the same volume, Henry Nelson Wieman declares that neo-orthodoxy "tries to live under the guidance of an incoherent mixture" of myth and intellectual understanding (p. 13).

tained by elevating the "inevitability probability" into an "inevitability actuality"—"I ought, and I cannot."

c. *Inevitability as Destructive of Responsibility.*

More pointedly, it may be questioned whether the insistence on the inevitability of sin, as a normal experience of human nature, does not in itself destroy the very notion of sin,[27] If the classic religious Modernism against which Neo-Supernaturalism is in revolt tended to regard sin as both inevitable and necessary in view of its normal existence as an animal drag on man's nature, the question arises whether Neo-Supernaturalism succeeds in maintaining an essentially higher view of sin, despite its insistence that sin must be localized in man's personal will, and that while inevitable it is yet not necessitated.

(1) *Undercuts Free Moral Revolt.*

For on both views, sin is taken to be a normal experience for the nature of man as constituted. And, from the standpoint of the Hebrew-Christian tradition, this concession to evolutionary philosophy precludes an adequate definition of the nature of sin. Sin, in the Biblical estimate, is not ultimately reducible to a normal experience—one which is inevitable in view of man's consistent reduction of altruism in egoistic terms—but is, in its roots, the turning aside by primal man of his own free will and *without an inevitability of nature* from a proper and normative relationship to God. It is precisely this fact, that man primally stood in free moral revolt against his Lord, that defines sin in its dread proportions for the Hebrew-Christian tradition. The attempt to take sin seriously while regarding it as normal, as inevitable, cannot sustain itself, for it works itself around to the denial of the seriousness of sin. Here the evolutionary hypothesis succeeds finally in rising above the optimistic view of unreconstructed Liberalism

---

27. It is not intended here, of course, that the neo-orthodox thinkers intend to deny the seriousness of sin, but rather that, despite their intention to take it with an extreme seriousness, they are foredoomed to failure because of the concessions already made in the context of their argument.

only by a dialectic of words which the moral experience of man cannot countenance.

(2) *Implications for Christology.*

It has been pointed out elsewhere—as by Thelen[28]—that the reconciliation of Niebuhr's hamartiology and Christology is still awaited. Niebuhr insists that the divine perfection enters into human history in Jesus Christ. But now, either perfection has entered in our nature, or it has not; the question then is, is sin *inevitable,* granted human nature, or is it *contingent?* In *Beyond Tragedy,* Niebuhr comments that the sinlessness of Christ proves that sin is not an inherent defect, but is a contingency in each soul.[29] The extended emphasis on the sins of the righteous, especially of the wise and pious, and their especial susceptibility to spiritual pride, comes here to crucial focus: "The greater the avoidance of conscious wrong-doing and the self-discipline for the sake of a cause believed to be the will of God, the greater the danger of sin; for the more difficult it becomes to see that the cause is only a part of the will of God (because of our finiteness) and is only partly the will of God (because of our sin)."[30] If, then, the sinlessness of Christ is explained without a reference to a divine incarnation (Niebuhr rejects the two-nature Christology as "logical nonsense") , the whole notion of the inevitability of sin, and the heightened susceptibility to it of the righteous, is left in a perilous mid-air. "It is doubtful," writes Thelen, "whether Niebuhr has reconciled the sinlessness of Jesus with the universality of sin in every act. Perhaps the renunciation of all struggle for the survival of the self could be construed as wholly passive and the sinlessness of such a passive act might not contradict original sin."[31] Is it then that the most promising means by which Niebuhr can retain Christ's sinlessness is to deny His essential deity—for the divine-human ego of the

---

28. *Op. cit.,* p. 84, footnote.
29. *Niebuhr, op. cit.,* p. 95.
30. Cf. Thelen, *op. cit.,* p. 187.
31. *Ibid.,* p. 105.

Biblical incarnation never struggled for survival on the strictly so-called human plane of anxiety,[32] but rather was the entrance of the pre-existent Christ into history for purposes of atonement? Here the dialectical seems to require the denial of Christ's deity to preserve His sinlessness, a strange Biblical theology indeed. But there is no true incarnation-consciousness in the Niebuhr formulation. As Thelen comments, "The reconciliation between original sin and the Incarnation is similarly left at loose ends; Niebuhr does not believe that a theory of the Incarnation 'in metaphysical terms' is possible and confines himself to presenting Jesus as a revelation rather than as an incarnation of deity."[33]

But we are not yet through with the difficulties of the Niebuhr sin-formula, in terms of interaction with the Biblical view.

d. *Requires a Non-Biblical View of Redemption.*

For, on neo-supernaturalist assumptions, the whole notion of redemption is emptied of meaning. It is true, of course, that the stress on the mercy and holiness of God vibrates through literature from the Barth-Brunner-Niebuhr fold; that God is both judge and redeemer is an emphasis which contrasts with the smug last-generation Liberalism. God redeems; the solution to man's moral predicament is found alone in the Hebrew-Christian movement. Only from outside man, by the energy of a transcendent holy and merciful God, comes deliverance from the corruption with which sin infects human activity. The one redemptive word which God speaks in His self-revelation is "Jesus Christ." One does not long read the literature of neo-orthodoxy without living and moving in such phraseology. How then can it be said that redemption is here emptied of its content?

---

32. Niebuhr says: "His life culminates in an act of self-abnegation in which the individual will ceases to be a protagonist of the individual life; and the life ends upon the Cross" (*The Nature and Destiny of Man,* II, p. 74). But the will of Jesus Christ, if He is the incarnation of a pre-existent being seeking man's redemption, was at no time during the incarnation "a protagonist of the individual life."

33. Thelen, *op. cit.,* p. 105.

(1) *No Adequate Doctrine of Sanctification.*

It is not merely that Niebuhr has no adequate doctrine of sanctification, although there is indeed a serious lack in his development of Christian ethics. In the thought of H. Richard Niebuhr even more than of Reinhold, worldliness and corruption are viewed as so deep rooted even in the church that the righteousness of redeemed and unredeemed is despaired of alike. The church is pictured in the sinner's role, and redemption bears no peculiar ethical fruit, though it affords a heritage and tie for the Christian community, Salvation is not treated in a sanctification mood; if redemption is not glorification neither indeed is it sanctification. In Reinhold Niebuhr's treatment, there is more room for moral transformation; contrition is the forerunner of a curtailment of egoism and pride. But, in contrast to the "Jesus ethics" of past-generation Liberalism, Niebuhr swings to an opposite pole, affirming the irrelevance of "Jesus ethics" to the church, and dismisses it as an impractical ideal. What is needed, we are told, is an "interim ethics."[34] Ideal perfection is unattainable in history, in view of the universality and ineradicability of original sin, hence it is an illegitimate contemporary objective.[35]

---

34. In *Religious Liberals Reply*, Arthur E. Murphy notes that Niebuhr hardly does justice to the Biblical tradition by his "attempt to combine a rejection of the perfectionist teachings of that tradition as actual guides for conduct with a reaffirmation of their ultimate validity as norms of righteous action, and to find in the resulting impossibility of action rightly conforming to its own 'highest' goal a proof both of the inherent sinfulness of man and of the incomprehensible transcendence of the standpoint from which ultimately he is judged" (p. 31). He adds that the good news of the Gospel was "more straightforward news than this declaration that something is profoundly true," in a fashion which negates its literal assertions and precepts, and which is in any case beyond our capacity to understand, and that we must accept its apparent incoherence with humility as the basis for a moral judgment . . ." (p. 32).

35. Thelen acutely criticizes a notion which "identifies the will of God with perfection to the exclusion of any direct concern on his part with the immediate possibilities which make up the substance of life within history" (*op. cit.*, p. 200). The evangelical formulation of the doctrines of justification and sanctification, as will be seen, affirms such concern. Only one who comes out of overoptimistic Liberalism, rather than Biblical theology, could be disappointed that there is no *glorification* in contemporary human history; Evangelicalism reserved such optimism for the future divine kingdom. But Thelen's complaint grows rather out of a desire to retain more of the liberal optimism about history; she finds a little of the Unmoved Mover, in Niebuhr's conception of God as the perfection beyond history, since for Perfection to enter into history only long enough to die on a cross is too thin a doctrine of the Incarnation" (p. 207).

Now it is true, against the perfectionist traditions, that sin is so deep rooted, even in the redeemed life, that a state of sinless perfection is never attained; there is a disjunction between sanctification and glorification. Sin continues to corrupt practise; grace does not make sinlessness possible. But, in Niebuhr, one senses the lack of any sufficient distinction between justification and sanctification; it is as if the believer's acts are wholly discontinuous with the divine.

True, Niebuhr tells us that grace provides resources for constantly higher moral achievement, for a state far surpassing that of one who is a stranger both to despair and to divine mercy, for "infinite development" toward a more perfect brotherhood in history (p. 85).* For sin is broken in principle and the self becomes righteous in intention. In prayer, the self may rise above egoistic concern to a volitional identification with impartial divine love.

But for all this, there is in Niebuhr no adequate doctrine of sanctification, no alertness to the transforming power of the Holy Spirit over the behaviour of the redeemed. The Christian anticipates not perfection but sin. For sin is not broken at all in fact, but merely in principle (p. 114); the regenerated self is a self of intention rather than an actual achievement; its continuity with God in "beyond history" extends to intention, but not to action. In fact, sin intrudes already into the formulation of a course of action, in which self-concern is merged with the service of God. For Niebuhr, it might be said in a preliminary way, the new self has an existence only in justification, not in sanctification: "It is the self only by grace, in the sense that the divine mercy 'imputes' the perfection of Christ and accepts the self's intentions for achievements" (p. 114). Niebuhr thinks the Pauline epistles bequeath us an uncertainty whether the regenerate self is "by faith" in the sense (1) of an imputation of Christ's righteousness, or (2) of a new power to become Christlike (pp. 107ff); yet he feels Paul regards grace as a power to make us sinless, without recon-

---

*References are to Niebuhr, *op. cit.*

ciling this with the Christian's sinning. One senses here no victorious life emphasis with which the Pauline as well as Johannine letters throb on occasion; it is Romans six and seven, but not Romans eight, which paces the Christian experience for Niebuhr.[36] There is in the New Testament the believer's *possession* of the more abundant life, as John puts it; or his partaking of the divine life, as Peter phrases it; or the indwelling Christ, of the Pauline mysticism. It is not sinless perfection, but for all that it is victory, it is sin broken in fact as well as principle, for sin no longer lords it over the believer.[37] The moral dynamic of the Holy Spirit finds no adequate place in Niebuhr's theology. The tension in his ethical system grows out of a sub-Christian view of regeneration, resulting in turn from a distorted soteriology.[38]

(2) *No Satisfactory Doctrine of Justification.*

But if we have found fault with Niebuhr's treatment of sanctification, it remains to be said that the neo-supernaturalist failure to provide a Biblical doctrine of redemption grows even more out of its distorted view of justification. The notion of atonement is here appropriated in a wholly non-Biblical way. For *redemption* means, in the plan of salvation outlined in the Scriptures, a restoration to the privileges of a previous state; the whole notion of Biblical redemption turns on the idea, not of a lifting of man to a level of possibility above an

---

36. Augustine's contrast between the final perfection of man, and the present life of righteousness in Christ, is sketched in *On the Spirit and the Letter* (especially chapters 65 and 66) and makes for interesting contrast with the notion of a life in which sin is still lord in fact.

37. R. Newton Flew points out that while the epistle to the Romans, with its "most explicit statements of the freedom from sin possible for the believer" need not be equated with the impossibility of sin in the life of the believer, yet Paul demonstrates "how incompatible the evangelical experience is with continuance in sin" (*The Idea of Perfection in Christian Theology,* p. 57. London: Oxford University Press, 1934).

38. The same failure to make sufficient room for the dynamic of the Holy Spirit in the regenerate believer's life also characterizes Bennett, who not only finds sin present "on every level of moral and spiritual growth," but stresses the need for "continuous *repentance*" whereas the evangelical tradition would speak of continuous *surrender* (cf. Bennett, *Liberal Theology—An Appraisal,* pp. 199ff). Assuredly the Scriptures exhort believers to "crucify the flesh" (Gal. 2:20) and suggest that the regenerate man, daily involved in some sin, should resurrender himself to God's will, but there is more of a mood of triumph than among recent writers. Calhoun and Horton, on the other hand, retain the liberal optimism about the degree of moral change possible—despite the impossibility of sinlessness—though there is no adequate sensitivity to sanctification in the evangelical sense.

inevitability which accompanies a normative anxiety, but rather of overcoming a defection from a prior acceptability in spiritual privilege, a deliverance from an abnormal predicament. The Bible has to do not with *demption* merely, but with *re*demption; not with conciliation, but with *re*conciliation. Christ is not merely *deemer,* but *Re*deemer.[39] Hence a sound Biblical theology is driven to a higher notion of atonement than one which sees in Calvary—true as such an insight may be—the contrast of the altruistic self-giving of Jesus Christ with the self-withholding with which the rest of mankind vitiates even the most utilitarian behavior. For there is here no notion of ransom, of rescue; the deliverance is a one-sided affair, having to do with a lifting to higher potentialities, but the notion of lostness, of unacceptability with God, of condemnation, is minimized. God is judge—but we are not enemies; that is why Neo-Supernaturalism deals lightly with expiation and propitiation,[40]

---

39. On the modern view, redemption is never an act objective to us, but a subjective experience; it becomes futile to speak of Christ acomplishing by one act our eternal redemption, for this scheme of Biblical redemption rests likewise on the Biblical doctrine of original sin. Christ's atonement regains, recovers, restores something which man once possessed in Adam, but ever since has been without; we are *re*deemed from the curse of the law, are bought back.

40. The Swedish reinterpretation of Luther's theology of the atonement, in the interest of the "classic" view (cf. G. Aulen's *Christus Victor* (London: S. P. C. K., 1931) is a deliberate attempt to minimize the "satisfaction" aspect of Luther's theory in deference to the emphasis on the divine conflict with and victory over evil powers. The Swedish theologians in the Aulen tradition (e.g., Ragnar Bring, Arvid Runestam, Gustaf Ljunggren) object to the "static" orthodox doctrine of substitutionary atonement, on the ground that it involves a bifurcation of the divine nature in which God's love and justice are at odds; the true theory, they stress, represents the atonement as the provision of divine love which is at the same time righteous. American orthodoxy is familiar with the criticisms which A. H. Strong, Charles Hodge, and William G. T. Shedd leveled at Anselm's view, while preserving the emphasis on satisfaction and at the same time viewing the atonement not as a "third-party" transaction (so that the Son demonstrates the divine love as against the Father in the role of divine justice) but rather as a "first-party" provision, in which God Himself suffers in the provision of atonement. The Swedish theologians in Aulen's tradition make it appear that the holy love of God cannot be adequately represented without submerging the satisfaction elements in Luther's view, and their attitude here proves only their hostility to the Pauline emphasis on satisfaction. For an understanding of recent trends in Swedish theology at this point, Edgar M. Carlson's *The Reinterpretation of Luther* (Philadelphia: The Westminster Press, 1948) is indispensable. Carlson is clearly sympathetic to the so-called "classic" view, but he concedes that an investigation remaining to be made is "a study of Luther's atonement theory from the point of view of the idea of satisfaction, attempting to interpret the motif of conflict in the context of the satisfaction theory" (*ibid.,* p. 184). The Norwegian theologian, O. Hallesby, has levelled forceful criticisms against contentions of the "classic" school, especially charging that the objective character of the atonement is surrendered by them. The prominence of satisfaction in Luther's view of atonement is emphasized by Swedish theologians like Arvid Sjostrand.

and tends to dismiss as parable the insistence on substitutionary atonement. The oversimplification of divine love and wrath, since they are regarded as phases of a single movement which does away with the need for expiation, here becomes part of a familiar liberal pattern, in which justice and love become interchangeable descriptions of a single divine activity with which substitution is incompatible. What need of expiation, if man's bondage is not an unnatural state to which penalty accrues; if, rather, he is "on the way up", in a spiritual evolutionary movement in which Christ is but the wayshower in the conquest of egoism. But it is not such a view which can deal realistically with the Biblical stress on justification, as the imputation to us of Christ's righteousness in view of His vicarious death; and on sanctification,[41] as the inner working of the Holy Spirit in a progressive, even if incomplete, realization of the divine ideal.

It is in this evolutionary mood also that one needs to understand the modern attempts to explain the predicament of man in terms of an ultimate metaphysical flaw, rather than a primal moral revolt. The "creature feeling" which begets anxiety, and which in turn issues inevitably in sin: what is this, stated in these terms, but a turn in man's constitution which makes sin quite intelligible; which, indeed, refers moral revolt to a metaphysical predicament? In the long run, however great the contrast, one cannot obscure the similarity between a view which evaluates sin in terms of a drag outside the will of man, and a

---

41. The newer, dynamic theories of justification all tend to merge justification with sanctification, and thus to move in a Roman Catholic direction; justification does not involve the imputation of Christ's righteousness to the believer, but rather is the outworking in the believer's life of the triumph which Christ won on the Cross over evil powers. As in the incarnation Christ assumed human nature and conquered the tyranny of evil, so in us he overcomes evil. The believer's relationship to God is also overshadowed by this dynamic view. The regenerate individual is not permanently a "new creature", but is engaged in constant warfare; as egocentric, he stands under divine judgment. Here the emphasis on a state of justification vanishes, and justification and sanctification are merged in the progressive control which Christ gains in the believer's life. It is clear how, on this view, while the atonement may be regarded as a divine provision (as against the subjectivistic view it is simply a human achievement) yet it denies that there are hindrances on God's side to divine fellowship with man which require propitiation. The dynamic views gain their sympathy, as against evangelical views, by the fallacious charge that the orthodox view of justification is disinterested in personal holiness.

view which places it inside the will of man by an inevitability of his nature as normally constituted. Both views explain the origin and persistence of sin in some other way than the Biblical account, in which the moral revolt of man is not depicted as inevitable in view of the constitution of human nature.

There is in neo-supernaturalist theology, it is plain, an impressive inheritance of liberal teaching.[42] The formulation of the doctrine of sin in this tradition is involved in philosophic tensions which preclude its satisfactoriness, for the merger of elements from Biblical theology and from non-Biblical sources fails to satisfy either the theologian alert to the Hebrew-Christian tradition, or the philosopher alert to the history of philosophy.

D. New Relevance of Biblical Anthropology.

But the heightened view of sin in the neo-supernaturalist movement brings into new relevance the Biblical emphasis apart from which an adequate anthropology is impossible. A treatment of this emphasis merely in a symbolic mood can hardly satisfy the claim of a sound Biblical theology. One cannot stop where the Niebuhr dialectic stops and hope to sustain permanently the case for the sinfulness of sin and the desperate predicament of man *qua* man.

Hence it is that the Biblical view of man, without its modern incrustations even of the neo-supernaturalist variety, regains a new significance. For here we are introduced frankly to the fact that man is not a sinner in virtue of his humanity, as though sin were a normal inevitability, but rather we are instructed that all men are implicated in a primal moral revolt against

---

42. Neo-supernaturalistic thought on the atonement is a difficult study, mainly because no work dedicated specifically to the atonement has yet appeared by Barth or Brunner. One often finds in Brunner two moods which seem to cancel each other out (as in so much of the dialectical presentation); thus he writes in *The Mediator* of the parabolic statements of the atonement in the New Testament in terms of ransom and substitution, which the orthodox views take too literally, whereas in *Revelation and Reason* he writes that "The Lord's Cross reveals both the sternness of the divine righteousness, in its penal aspect, and in the demand for expiation, and the unfathomable, generous love of God, and thus the union of the holiness and the mercy of God" (p. 106). But Brunner adds, almost at once, that Christ's vicarious penal suffering does not involve "the non-Biblical objective doctrine of satisfaction . . . according to which God Himself had to be reconciled" (p. 107).

the Creator. The consequences of this revolt are of such dimensions that man's ideals as well as his acts are discontinuous with God, though contact with general revelation is not destroyed. Though no original righteousness remains, the divine image is not obliterated, however distorted. But man is at enmity with God—in a state of enmity which he ratifies by the successive choices of His will. History, apart from the regenerating grace of God, is the story of man's moral revolt, the story of the pursuit of secondary ends rather than the End, the story of having other gods before Jehovah. If therefore God is a holy God, and sin is an abomination to Him, there is no antecedent outside ground on which forgiveness may be "expected" from Him; if there is divine grace, it comes not by necessity but as a gift. And if there is forgiveness, it comes on God's terms alone. That God is merciful as well as holy is one of the focii of the Biblical ellipse; that in Jesus Christ He provides the sufficient atonement for the sins of men, is the other. An adequate view of sin has implications also for the whole of Christian theology; man is a sinner indeed—so much modern thought has learned; man is the heir of the grace of God—this it needs to learn, yet cannot until first it unlearns the non-Biblical understanding of his sinfulness.

THE MID-TWENTIETH CENTURY
VIEW OF CHRIST

IV

The Mid-Twentieth Century View of Christ

THE differentiating datum of Christianity is Jesus Christ. Since His crucifixion on that middle Golgotha cross, He has been the center of reference for the Christian movement, as its Founder and as its indispensable core.[1] From John the Baptist to John the Beloved, from the first gospel to the apocalypse, from Paul to Athanasius to Calvin, the Christian pathway of faith has been a "Christological course." The striking claim made by Christianity was that "God is come in Christ."

Christianity did not mean by this what other religions, outside the Biblical tradition, meant, when they said God was manifested somewhere. For, wherever one begins by saying that nature, as in the Oriental Pantheisms, or the reason of man, as in the Greek Idealisms, is a part of God, there one already obscures the immense gulf spanned by the event of incarnation. The Christian faith begins by declaring that God is creator. He is other than nature and man; they are not parts of God. Christianity reaches its high point in the declaration that God was *in Christ,* that in the historic Jesus, the fulness of the Godhead dwells in a body. The Christian faith stands or falls with the truth of that affirmation.

---

1. Oswald Spengler remarks that the "incomparable thing which lifted the infant Christianity above all religions (of the first century) is the figure of Jesus. Tame and empty all the holy legends . . . must have seemed to any man reading or listening to the still recent story of Jesus' sufferings—the last journey to Jerusalem, the last anxious supper, the hours of despair in Gethsemane, and the death on the cross. . . . Christianity is the one religion in the history of the world in which the fate of a man of the immediate present has become the emblem and the central point of the whole creation" (*The Decline of the West,* vol. ii, p. 212. New York: Alfred A. Knopf, 1945).

A. The Mid-Century Christology Is a Reaction From Critical Confusion.

By a strange concourse of events, the contemporary religious mind has been beset by a Christiological agnosticism. It is almost as if the coming of Jesus into the world, and the New Testament writings, constitute a burden, divinely imposed upon mankind.[2] There is, in representative modern faith, little spontaneous, unhesitating "Thou are the Christ, the Son of the Living God" (Mt. 16:16), nor a whole-hearted "Not in the words which man's wisdom teacheth, but which the Holy Ghost teacheth (I Cor. 2:13).

1. *Skepticism About New Testament Led to Christological Agnosticism.*

Rather, we read in our generation of "the search for the real Jesus."[3] We have the witness of the evangelists and the significant apostolic writings, yet the mid-twentieth century appears at times to confess—for all this—less certainty as to the defining outlines of the Redeemer than some of the Old Testament prophets.

a. It Led to Competing Views of Jesus.

Arthur C. McGiffert Jr. affirms that "within the Christian movement, the name of Jesus has been used with reference to at least seven different figures"[4] and he cites "the literary Jesus of the Gospels, the dogmatic Jesus of the Gospels, the ecclesiastical Jesus of the Gospels, the invisible but living comrade, the communal Jesus, the symbolic Jesus and the historic Jesus."

---

2. True, scholars like John Knox reject the Skepticism which holds that we have no trustworthy indications of the character, teaching and career of Jesus, and insist that we can trust the "impression of the person which the Gospels convey to us," yet they concede, as does Knox in his latest book, "that there are not many points where we can feel absolute assurance" and that "we have reason to doubt the accuracy of many of the reports" of Jesus' words and acts (*On the Meaning of Christ*, pp. 62f. New York: Charles Scribner's Sons, 1947). R. H. Lightfoot comments in *History and Interpretation in the Gospels* (Bampton Lectures) that "It seems to me, then, that the form of the earthly no less than of the heavenly Christ is for the most part hidden from us. For all the inestimable value of the gospels, they yield us little more than a whisper of his voice; we trace in them but the outskirts of his ways" (p. 255).

3. As Chester C. McCown titled his book (New York: Charles Scribner's Sons, 1940).

4. Quoted by Thomas S. Kepler, *Contemporary Thinking About Jesus*, p. 341 (New York: Abingdon-Cokesbury Press, 1938).

G. K. Chesterton recalled how, in his own studies, he was confronted by the contradictory christs which the critical experts solemnly pronounced as the latest assured result of scholarship:

> "The first rational explanation of his life was that he never lived. And this in turn gave opportunity for three or four different explanations; as that he was a sun-myth or a corn-myth, or any other kind of myth that is also a monomania. Then the idea that he was a divine being who did not exist gave place to the idea that he was a human being who did exist. In my youth it was the fashion to say that he was merely an ethical teacher... Then somebody said he was a madman with a Messianic delusion. Then others said he was indeed an original teacher because he cared about nothing but Socialism; or (as others said) about nothing but Pacifism. Then a more grimly scientific character appeared who said that Jesus would never have been heard of at all except for his prophecies of the end of the world... Among other variants on the same theme was the theory that he was a spiritual healer and nothing else..."[5]

There was hardly a world vocation in which Jesus was not cast. The eighteenth century hailed Him as a noble ethicist, and the nineteenth as an enlightened liberal democrat; everywhere He was projected in the image of the prevailing temper, so that one may speak of the revolutionary Jesus of the Communist Barbusse; the bourgeois Jesus of Bruce Barton; the pacifist Jesus of Tolstoy; the militarist Jesus of the late Kaiser Wilhelm; the Aryan Jesus of Hitler's Alfred Rosenberg; the liberal Unitarian Jew of Joseph Klausner—everywhere the moderns sought to trace in Him the lineaments of their particular ideals. Then, in 1934 came D. Rudolf Bultmann's Jesus—born of form criticism—of whose life almost nothing could be known except that His early ministry was linked with John the

---

5. Quoted from *The Everlasting Man*, in Ralph L. Woods' *Behold The Man*, p. 138 (New York: The Macmillan Company, 1944). Used by permission of Dodd, Mead and Co., Inc.

Baptist's Messianic movement, and that He was crucified as an insurrectionist.[6]

b. *It Resulted in Disinterest in Christology.*

Despite the extensive modern literature—the cumulative library index indicated annually that authors produced more writings relating to Jesus Christ than to any other topic—the modern mood imposed a moratorium on Christology. A serious and detailed interest in the unique person and work of Christ was hardly to be expected among those who were so eager to identify Jesus with their own ideals. The picture was somewhat better in Great Britain than in America; there, in 1909, came P. T. Forsyth's *The Person and Place of Jesus Christ;* in 1912, H. R. Mackintosh's *The Doctrine of the Person of Christ;* in 1916, T. R. Glover's *The Jesus of History;* in 1922, Charles Gore's *Belief in Christ;* in 1924, Arthur W. Robinson's *The Christ of the Gospels;* and in 1933, L. W. Grensted's *The Person of Christ.* And out of Germany, in 1927, came Emil Brunner's *Der Mittler.* But American thought was clasped by the extended grasp of Ritschlianism, which plunged liberal Protestantism into a subjectivistic and antimetaphysical mood.[7] Presupposing that Jesus was a man only, it was preoccupied only

---

6. Bultmann knows much more, however: Jesus "did not believe himself to be the Messiah" (*Jesus and the Word,* p. 9. New York: Charles Scribner's Sons, 1934). Bultmann refuses to deal with the subject of Christ's Messiahship, because he feels nothing certain or conclusive can be found pertaining to it. The subject is "of secondary importance," he remarks (p. 9). It would be interesting to know how he found out.

7. John Baillie's *The Place of Jesus Christ in Modern Christianity* (New York: Charles Scribner's Sons, 1929) was one of the few serious American efforts in Christology, and this came during the Canadian service of the former Edinburgh professor, who returned to the Scotch university later as professor of divinity. And Baillie's Christology was hardly lofty: "However sorely puzzled our day and generation may find itself over the Catholic Christology taken as a whole, yet I believe that it is making such a rediscovery of *the spirit of the man Jesus* as has hardly been made in all Christian ages" (*ibid.,* p. 19). Modern Christianity was to give Jesus a very much reduced place indeed: ". . . We must radically revise our old conception of deity in the light of the new predicate of Christlikeness" (p. 147). ". . . The New Testament claim that 'neither is there salvation in any other' is not in its essence an *a priori* theological dogma, such as it too readily became in later centuries, but rather a declaration of personal experience. . . . The New Testament writers were not academic philosophers but hard-working missionaries. . . . And their common declaration is that, whatever philosophic minds may say about degrees of truth and the like, yet in *their* experience not one of the many religious alternatives that were at that time before the Mediterranean world could in practice be relied upon (if we may allow ourselves this phrase) for 'doing the trick,' save only the faith of Jesus Christ" (*ibid.,* pp. 204f.).

with whatever peculiar endowments could be conceded to Him within that premise.

2. *Yet Christ Was Assigned a High Place Among Mankind.*

This does not mean that men pronounced no judgments, and even singularly high estimates, on the person and work of Christ. Except among the left-wing humanists and naturalists and a few pessimists, the loftiest words of praise were reserved for the man of Galilee.

a. *Moods Which Depreciated Him Were Unpopular.*

Although the modern temper was prevailingly naturalistic, thinkers who rejected Jesus as the highest moral and social ideal did not[8] carry the multitudes with them.

There is indeed Harry Elmer Barnes' *The Twilight of Christianity,* which discards not only the divine sonship of Christ, but tells us that Jesus knew very little about God, that Jesus' teachings are archaic and destructive of any advance in civilization, and that Jesus knew less than Plato about human personality.[9] Bertrand Russell felt that Jesus could profit from Buddha and Socrates; Middleton Murry thought Him deceived in trusting God as His Father; and outside the humanistic sphere came the attacks of Jewish scholars—Claude Montefiore in England, Joseph Klausner in the States—on His sinlessness and perfection. The readiness of the religious humanists to discard any absoluteness for Jesus has been pointedly expressed by Edwin A. Burtt: "He does not embody all the values that are religiously significant today, and the attempt to find them in him is historically unwarranted."[10] The humanists complain, as Burtt puts it, that:

"Jesus had no appreciation for the value of intelligence
as the most dependable human faculty for analyzing the

---

8. Nietzsche saw much more clearly than inarticulate, sophomoric Liberalism that one who discards Christian metaphysics ought to disown Biblical values also. Jesus, he said, is the bait which makes people nibble at the wrong values.

9. Harry Elmer Barnes, *The Twilight of Christianity,* pp. 405ff. New York: R. R. Smith, 1929.

10. Edwin A. Burtt, *Types of Religious Philosophy,* p. 359. New York: Harper and Brothers, 1939.

perplexities into which men fall and for providing wise guidance in dealing with them. Simple and childlike trust in the Heavenly Father and humble obedience to His will was the sum and substance of life's wisdom to him. His theory of the world, which to his mind justified this confident faith, is squarely opposed to the scientific naturalism that a frank assessment of experience increasingly compels modern men to accept. Far from thinking of nature as an objective, law-abiding order, to which man must patiently learn how to adjust himself while assuming responsibility intelligently to transform those parts of it that are amenable to human control, he believed it to be directly subject in all its details to the purposive care of a personal being ... As for economic relations Jesus took entirely for granted and without criticism the economic structure prevalent in his day ... In fact, God's relations with men are often compared with those of a haughty and capricious employer with his workmen ... He is subject to no standard of right beyond his own arbitrary will ... Add to these considerations the surge of self-exaltation that occasionally found expression through Jesus' lips—the claim to a unique familiarity with God, control of the powers of nature, and ultimate authority over mankind ... does not the deepest ethical insight of modern times feel it to be inconsistent with the modesty of true friendliness, the humility appropriate to consciousness of one's many limitations, and the genial readiness, demanded of moral leadership in a democratic age, to learn from the deeper experiences of others while teaching them the significance of one's own?"[11]

b. *Religious Modernism Both Depreciated and Exalted Him.*

Religious Modernism, while resisting such depreciation of Jesus, reconstructed the gospel figure in the reflection of modern presuppositions, but soon found that it had only complicated the Christological dilemma. It was unhappy over a supernatural

11. *Op. cit.*, pp. 359 ff.

Jesus, but also over a Jesus who could not somehow be detached from his own age; the tension pushed either toward humanist depreciation or toward evangelical exaltation.[12] But the failure of the humanist's attempt to discredit the person of Jesus is conceded, even if inadvertently, in their own writings. It forms the background for Barnes' declaration that the central figure still, in the conflict of science and social change today, is Jesus; therefore He continues to plead for an abandonment of the "Jesus stereotype."[13]

The dilemma of higher Liberalism was its espousal of the scientific method, at the core of which is *tentativity, uniformity,* and the notion of *repeatableness,* and the contradictory affirmation that Jesus is the *final,* the *unique,* the *unrepeatable* religious personality. As Liberalism wedded itself wholly to scientific method, it narrowed the distance between Jesus and other men and regarded Him as matchless only in a context of caution and hesitancy. Here men, as P. T. Forsythe put it, could show sympathy only for a Christ they did not worship, and bestow praise upon a Christ to whom they did not pray.

(1. *Representative American Tributes to Uniqueness.*

On both sides of the Atlantic, theologians, Biblical critics, and philosophers penned their glowing tributes to Christ in a frame of thought considerably different from that to be found in the only written sources reaching back to the early church.

We read that Christ Jesus "is highest and completest person" and that in Him "we see what God is like" and "know at last what it means to be a completely normal human person" (Rufus

---

12. C. E. M. Joad, critical of the wrath, sensitivity, failure to practise his doctrine of love, and anti-intellectual bias which he attributes to Jesus, confesses "a certain disquietude at the high-handedness of those critics who, whenever Christ says anything which seems to be more than usually at variance with modern modes of thought, dismiss it on the ground either that He didn't say it, or that it means something quite different from what it seems to mean" (*God and Evil,* p. 309. New York: Harper and Brothers, 1943).

13. *Op. cit.,* pp. 367ff. Some naturalists refused to be caught up in this depreciatory impulse. Henry Nelson Wieman, though of course not absolutizing Jesus, declares that the "living Christ" is not merely an influence, nor ideal inherited from Him, but "a reality which works in the world today," a historical, psychological condition for a higher way of living, a magnified power of the creativity of God in history, community, and personality" (*Encyclopedia of Religion,* "The living Christ," p. 159. New York: The Philosophical Library, 1945).

Jones, [14] *The Trail of Life in the Middle Years,* p. 234) "a very good man, perhaps the best man who ever lived" (C. E. M. Joad, *God and Evil,* p. 329); is the "leading exponent of prophetic religion" ... is the one in Whom "the Eternal has spoken" ... is the one in Whom "God has revealed his purpose and his life for men" (Harris Franklin Rall, *Christianity,* pp. 146, 162;) is the one in Whom God so indwelt that he is rightly regarded as *the* divine man, as *the* historic revelation of God in man (Douglas Clyde Macintosh, *The Reasonableness of Christianity,* p. 154); is the "supreme religious genius," who exhibited "unequalled purity of life, singleness of purpose, and devotion to God's will unto the last supreme sacrifice" (Chester C. McCown, *The Search for the Real Jesus,* p. 302); is the one in Whom God made himself known as a God of love, willing to endure suffering if need be, if only He could thereby lay hold on the heart of man (Robert H. Beaven, *In Him Is Life,* p. 167); is the bearer of that personal life which Christians recognize as the supreme revelation of God, and as the final test by which all mankind is judged (Frederick E. Grant, *Encyclopedia of Religion*: "Jesus Christ", p. 394)

(2. *Involved Contradictory Views of the 'Historical Jesus.'*

In more recent days numerous writers, once identified with religious Liberalism of last generation's attempt to discover the so-called "historical Jesus", have severely castigated this naturalistic portrait.[15] The stirrings of Barth and Brunner rumbled

---

14. In *A Preface to Christian Faith in a New Age,* Rufus Jones remarks that "the most sensitive interpreters . . . feel satisfied that in this Person of Galilee and Judea we see what the Heart of God is like" (p. 127, New York: The Macmillan Company, 1932).

15. G. K. Chesterton emphasized the obvious fact that "a man reading the New Testament frankly and freshly would *not* get the impression of what is now often meant by a human Christ. The merely human Christ is a made-up figure, a piece of artificial selection . . ." (*op. cit.,* p. 238). Liberalism was preoccupied with a Christ that was quite unlike the central Figure in the Gospels, yet decried the "mythologizing" mood of orthodoxy. Emil Brunner, himself given to a rather radical critical view, declared that even extreme criticism left the Biblical picture of Jesus essentially unaltered from that of pre-critical days. C. J. Cadoux expressed the same mood: "The very attempt to get behind the gospel records to a real 'historic Jesus' distinguishable from the Christ of faith is itself an illegitimate attempt, because it means transporting the records to an alien atmosphere, and ignoring the only interpretation of them in which their authors and first readers were interested" (*The Historic Mission of Jesus,* p. 335. New York: Harper and Brothers, n.d.).

across the Atlantic to American shores. [16] Men like Walter Marshall Horton called for an end of the Christological moratorium which expressed the protracted dilemma of a hesitant Modernism. Even the most extreme higher criticism found itself unable to sustain the so-called "liberal Jesus."[17] Horton declares bluntly that the modern portrait now has been "irretrievably condemned by New Testament criticism, as a spurious modernization which falsifies the Great Master it purports to represent."[18]

Actually, as already suggested, liberal scholarship had issued not in any *one* "historical Jesus", but in *many*—often mutually contradictory, and having in common no one element so much as their mutual difference from the Jesus of the New Testament manuscripts. The "historical Jesus" was always some vague figure brought to terms with the prejudices of the American naturalistic-empirical school of thought. Although Christological investigation was ostensibly conducted in the name of "presuppositionless inquiry", there remained the same fundamental

16. Reinhold Seeberg, too, indicted the liberal assumption of a merely human consciousness as a disregard for the historically given starting point for Christology: "Investigators, in my opinion, are as a rule led into error by this—that they make the 'Historical Jesus' their starting-point by simple assumption, and treat all expressions which go beyond this as attributes added to him in gradual precipitation on the ground of faith in his resurrection. The historical starting-point is, however, in reality contained in three facts: (1) That Jesus in his earthy life manifested a superhuman self-consciousness; (2) that his disciples were convinced by him, *after* his resurrection, not precisely *by* it, that they had directly experienced and received the proof of his divine nature; and (3) that they accordingly honored and proclaimed him as the heavenly Spirit-Lord. These facts are, in my opinion, indisputable, and from these facts as a starting-point—they are simply 'given' and not deducible—the entire thought development can be fully explained. . . . Christ is ever both: Spirit, Lord and God, and He has become a real man" (*Lehrbuch der Dogmengeschichte*, I, p. 134. Quoted from Robinson's *Our Lord: An Affirmation of the Deity of Christ*, pp. 24ff.).

17. Robinson had stated neatly the liberal embarrassment in terms of paucity of supporting documents: "Every early document that we possess witnesses to a Divine Christ. Therefore, those who profess that the merely human figure is the historic Jesus have not a single first century document on which to rest their claim. Now the primary dictum of all historical methodology is, 'No documents, no history.' Applying this universally accredited canon, may we not properly say to the naturalistic critic: Sir, show us your documents, before you ask us to accept your history?" (*op. cit.*, p. 42).

18. *Our Eternal Contemporary*, p. xv (New York: Harper and Brothers, 1943). In his earlier *Realistic Theology* (New York: Harper and Brothers, 1943) Horton reported that the newly emerging portrait of Jesus was "of One who felt the heaped-up tragedy of our human predicament as no one else had ever felt it; who believed in the near coming of the End of the Age because he saw the Providence of God lowering like a storm-cloud over his time; who yearned over the fate of foolish and perverse mankind, wandering toward their doom like sheep without a shepherd, and interceded for them with strong crying and tears, until there came to him from God, as he believed, a message of forgiveness and deliverance for all who would receive it" (pp. 196 ff.). But it was not, he warned, the portrait of "an Omniscient Deity masquerading as a man."

difficulty of the rationalistic research of a century ago, and that difficulty, as McCown states "is philosophical."[19]

(3. *Reduced the Supernaturalistic Claim of the New Testament.*

The rise of a new Christological literature is being witnessed on the American scene. In this, a more conscious effort is being made to articulate a suprahistorical as well as a historical significance for Jesus Christ.[20] To a great extent this interest in Christology is an overflow of the Neo-Supernaturalist movement in Germany, where Barth and Brunner vanguard the attack on immanentistic Liberalism. The prevailing German humanitarian Christology—divided mainly over whether the human Jesus is a special organ of God, or a God-seeking man only—was here pushed to higher ground; belief in Jesus' Messiahship confirmed by his death and resurrection, is viewed as the prerequisite for understanding the New Testament. But to identify the newer Christology wholly with any one movement would be uncritical; it represents departures from, as well as agreements with, the continental mood,[21] and even more so because American think-

---

19. *The Search for the Real Jesus,* pp. 388ff. McCown's own view is that "empirical religious realism is the path to the truth" in the search for the "real Jesus." It will "not serve the world to claim for Christianity exemption from the laws of nature, the processes of a reasonable reason, or the methods of historical research." McCown seems never to question the possible fallibility of his own philosophic bias—an anti-Supernaturalism which rejects the Fourth Gospel as critically demonstrated to have been written to supplant the Synoptics (p. 160)—a rather bold claim indeed. The naturalistic bias leads McCown to reject Synoptic passages pointing to a suprahuman Jesus (p. 291).

20. It is recognized by conservative, mediating and liberal scholars alike, as Robinson has pointed out (*op. cit.,* p. 73), that every book of the New Testament is written from the standpoint of faith in Jesus Christ. He reiterates that "modern scholars representing diverse points of view either hold that the Lord Jesus Christ is the Lord of the Old Testament, or that this is the doctrine of the New Testament writers. In the former group B. B. Warfield, T. C. Johnson and Professor Louis Berkhof sufficiently represent the Reformed Faith; Francis J. Hall, the Anglo-Catholic; Milton Valentine, the Lutheran; Professor Karl Adam, the Roman Catholic; and Reinhold Seeberg and C. A. Briggs what may roughly be described as mediating groups. A. C. McGiffert, a leading American 'liberal,' acknowledged that this was Paul's doctrine" (*ibid.,* p. 147).

21. Horton claims that Karl Barth's view of Christ is inadequate (*op. cit.,* p. 23). The attempt by some contemporary theologians—he names Barth especially—"to combine utter reverence for the unique divine revelation in personality" is, in Horton's view, an impossible one; God's supreme revelation cannot have been made through a commonplace man. He shares John C. Bennett's view (*Christian Realism,* pp. 121 f.) that Barth so disparages Jesus in the following sentence that he undermines faith in Christ as the unique Mediator between God and man: "Jesus Christ in fact is also the Rabbi of Nazareth, historically so difficult to get information about, and when it is got, one whose activity is so easily a little commonplace alongside more than one founder of a religion and even alongside many representatives of his own religion" (*The Doctrine of the Word of God,* p. 188).

ers, even in their latest turn, represent many shades of thought, agreed mainly in the conviction that Jesus must be granted a singular suprahistorical as well as historical role.[22]

The American view of Jesus in the mid-twentieth century in its main outlines is, if anything, in many ways more supernaturally appreciative. But even in the mood of a generation ago, the loftiest adjectives in the human vocabulary were reserved for Jesus; He was singled out as the most towering religious and moral genius in the centuries of human history. But, in recent years, there is a movement to lessen the obscurity about his relationship to eternity as well as to time.

Let us look more carefully for a moment at the tribute proferred Christ, first in appreciative unreconstructed Liberalism and then in the recent higher mood, and ask whether the mid-twentieth century Christ, in both expressions, is not usually a variant of one and the same figure—and that figure is *not* the Christ of the New Testament. The striking fact about contemporary Christologians is that, with remarkably few exceptions, their statements of the person and work of Christ are so many ways of saying that Christ is unique without affirming a genuine uniqueness. In countless patterns, declaring that Christ is "the *son* of God," they declare actually that Christ is *not "the* Son of God." They afford Jesus a triumphal entry into their discussions, but if one lingers long enough, he can hear them testify to the Sanhedrin that "he spoke blasphemy" or mutter at the tomb that "the disciples must have stolen the body". They marshall a glittering vocabulary of spangled adjectives, but if one looks through the heavenly words and beyond the starry clusters, he

---

22. A curious contrast with Bultmann's indifference to the Messianic significance of Jesus was Arthur C. Headlam's affirmation: ". . . Let us be quite clear about this: you cannot understand the narrative unless you recognize that He thought himself to be the Messiah, and that from the beginning He had thought thus of His ministry. . . . The total impression which is left upon us by the actions and words of Jesus, by His teaching and His claims, is of someone who transcends the conditions of human life. We may be able to get rid of this conception by eliminating much of the narrative, but let us be quite clear that we eliminate it, not on critical grounds, but because we do not like the conclusion to which we are forced" (*Jesus Christ in History and Faith* (Noble Lectures, 1924), pp. 120, 125. Cambridge: Harvard Univ. Press, 1925).

will find concealed in the inter-stellar spaces an obscure caveat, a submerged denial, a series of quotation marks which retracts what apparently has been affirmed.

When, for example, Rufus Jones affirms the singularity of Jesus, there is really none of the Biblical *otherness* about Him at all. Jesus is not, to Jones, one who has invaded the stream of humanity from without, as the pre-existent Logos who assumes the form of a servant; rather, we are told, "here in Christ the universe has produced a Person who made the supremacy of love vivid and vocal and victorious, a Person whom multitudes of men and women have felt to be good enough and noble enough to express the highest human ideal of God's nature."[23] It is not Christ as different in kind, but only as different in degree, that we find, for the incarnation is not to Rufus Jones an irrepeatable, once-for-all fact: "It may well be that God is all along endeavoring to break through, and reveal His presence and character, the only difficulty being that He finds such poor, self-filled instruments for any true revelation to break through."[24]

When Joad pays tribute to Jesus, he makes it clear that it is unreasonable, in his view, "to hold that Christ is a divine person in a sense in which no other man is divine";[25] and therefore unreasonable to hold that he is God's son.

When Grant eulogizes Jesus, he does so with insistence that the idea of a divine incarnation "does not depend upon history or historical records for its support" and that He "did not proclaim himself as Messiah."[26] The context lifts Him above other prophets and men only relatively.

----

23. Rufus Jones, *A Preface to Christian Faith in a New Age,* p. 127.

24. *Op. cit.,* p. 128.

25. "He was a man—and not more than a man—in precisely the same sense in which Confucius, Lao Tsi, Buddha, Socrates and Saint Francis were men—and not more than men" (*op. cit.,* p. 329).

26. *Op. cit.,* pp. 392ff. Grant remarks: "Undoubtedly Jesus was conscious of a divine call, at least as strong and clear as that of any of the O. T. prophets" (p. 393). He adds that Jesus "taught that God is the father of all men and that they are brothers in the one great human family."

This attitude of affirming some absoluteness for Jesus in the very process of rejecting His absoluteness in the Biblical sense is a characteristic of almost[27] all published theological effort which attempted to be creative during the past generation. The citations here given are not conspicuous exceptions from the predominant mood of religious leaders who had gained recognition from the leading publishing houses, but are random selections from the prevalent attitude, dominated as it was by post-Hegelian Immanentism, post-Darwinian Evolutionism, and post-Comtean Naturalism. The formula is everywhere the same; if one turns to Kirsopp Lake, he reads that "the experimentalist will certainly rank Jesus among the great prophets of all history"[28] and also that "no one way is *the* way any more than one kind of test tube is *the* test tube[29] or, if as in the case of J. E. Turner the compromised absoluteness is not so overt, it is still true that his chapter on "The Supreme Revelation of Deity[30] might more appropriately have been captioned *a* supreme revelation of deity, for Jesus appears only as the best among many, and not as the one among all.

When Douglas Clyde Macintosh lauds Jesus, he cautions that he is merely affirming a "special" immanence of the divine in Him; hence this uniqueness reduces for Macintosh to a "higher degree."[31] Macintosh specifically affirms that "it is increasingly possible for the Christian to be united to God the Holy Spirit

---

27. Only among the old line evangelicals did there appear an unflinching insistence on His essential deity. Cf. Geerhardus Vos, *The Self-Disclosure of Jesus* (New York: George H. Doran Co., 1926); B. B. Warfield, *The Lord of Glory* (New York, American Tract Society, n.d.), and *Christology and Criticism* (New York: Oxford Univ. Press, 1929); W. H. Griffith Thomas, *Christianity Is Christ* (Grand Rapids: Zondervan Pub. House); Wm. Childs Robinson, *Our Lord: An Affirmation of the Deity of Christ* (Grand Rapids: Wm. B. Eerdmans Pub. Co., 1937); Wilbur M. Smith, *The Supernaturalness of Christ* (Boston: W. A. Wilde Co., 1940); Louis Berkhof, *Reformed Dogmatics* (Grand Rapids: Wm. B. Eerdmans Pub. Co., 1937) and *Systematic Theology* (1941); Loraine Boettner, *The Person of Christ* (Grand Rapids: Wm. B. Eerdmans Pub. Co., 1943).

28. Kirsopp Lake, *The Religion of Yesterday and Tomorrow*, p. 154 (Boston: Houghton Mifflin Co., 1926).

29. *Ibid.*, p. 66.

30. J. E. Turner, *The Revelation of Deity* (New York: The Macmillan Co., 1930).

31. *Op. cit.*, p. 153.

in essentially the same way in which the human nature of Jesus was united with his divine nature."[32]

When McCown exalts Jesus, it is a person who is a "product of his times"[33] and whose ultimacy is accepted until a higher than Jesus appears.[34]

When Beaven exalts Jesus, it is not on the New Testament pattern of the incarnate Logos; rather, Jesus is affirmed to be divine because God "raised" Him to a new level of life.[35] The essential deity of Christ is expressly denied; it is "in experience" alone that Jesus is divine. Christ is not truly unique, for we are invited to reproduce His life level in every sense.[36]

3. *Christological Descent Encouraged by Higher Criticism.*

The process of this declension in Christology, in which a divine Christ who assumed human nature was replaced by a religious genius whose ego was human rather than essentially divine, is told competently in John Stewart Lawton's *Conflict in Christology,* which surveys English theology from the publication in 1889 of *Lux Mundi* to the appearance in 1912 of *Foundations,* in which the former "uneasiness" had settled into "unbroken gloom." The pattern of descent from higher to

---

32. D. C. Macintosh, *Personal Religion,* p. 115 (New York: Charles Scribner's Sons, 1942). Macintosh adds that "the secret of his saviorhood is to be found in the natural but God-initiated and God-directed effect of the right religious adjustment (spiritual aspiration, faith in God and surrender to His will), made thorough going and maintained (with the assisting grace of God) by the human Jesus throughout his life on earth, so far as that is known to us" *ibid.,* p. 119). So little sense of mediation is found in Macintosh's view that in *The Problem of Religious Knowledge* he declares that there would be no embarrassment if criticism should eliminate the figure of Jesus entirely (p. 341).

33. *Op. cit.,* p. 115.

34. *Ibid.,* pp. 300ff.

35. *Op. cit.,* p. 126. The title of Beaven's volume *In Him Is Life* is taken from the Fourth Gospel, but there it pictures the relationship of the pre-incarnate Logos to the created universe, whereas in Beaven only the earthly Jesus is in view. A rather devastating review of Beaven's treatment of the doctrine of the Trinity appears in *Crozer Quarterly,* Vol. XXIII, No. 3, July, 1946. There Rowland Gray-Smith, a liberal, describes as "absurd" the attempt to derive a doctrine of the Trinity (Beaven does not intend an ontological Trinity, of course) out of an analysis of human love.

36. Georgia Harkness writes: "If one believes . . . he will affirm belief in Christ as the Son of God. This does not mean that Jesus *was* God. It means that his life was so filled with the character and power of God that when men have seen him, they have seen the Father" (*Understanding the Christian Faith,* p. 74. New York: Abingdon-Cokesbury Press, 1947). Miss Harkness tells us that the death of Christ discloses what God is *always* doing for us. On such an approach, the cross loses its essential uniqueness for another uniqueness which is not truly unique. The doctrine of the Trinity is reduced to God expressing Himself "in three ways" (p. 73).

lower Christology views has its traces on both side of the Atlantic, and in Germany no less than in England.

The Chalcedonian orthodoxy, championed by Reformation Protestantism, by Roman Catholicism, and by Greek Catholicism, had insisted on the basis of Biblical theology that Christ Jesus is a divine person, His ego being resident in His deity, who later "inpersonalized" human nature by the divine ego. On this view, in the incarnation He retains divine no less than human attributes, though the incarnation has a bearing on their use.

But higher criticism[37] insisted that Jesus had wrongly championed Mosaic and Davidic authorships, that He had assumed the existence of patriarchal cities and persons now thought to be legendary. Hence, it was said, his knowledge was limited in the area of historical and scientific truth, and his authority could be invoked only in spiritual and moral matters. Evangelical theologians who accepted the new criticism took two alternatives, neither of them a logical halting-place. Some contended that Jesus merely "accommodated" His teaching to the scientific and historical limits of the times, but the specific use to which he put many of the passages made this untenable, as also did the fact that elsewhere He refused to condone misbeliefs. Others championed a *kenosis* Christology, insisting also upon a divine Christ, but declaring that in the incarnation He set aside not merely the exercise of certain attributes, but some of the attributes themselves, so that the God-man is limited, is a reduced deity.[38] For those who embraced higher

---

37. *Conflict in Christology.* Among that majority of thinkers who resisted the German leftist philosophies, by which Biblical supernaturalism was waved aside under the one grand assumption of Enlightenment philosophy, the Christological descent began with problems of the nature here suggested.

38. H. R. Mackintosh, with English thinkers like D. W. Forrest, W. L. Walker, and P. T. Forsyth, leaned to the *kenosis* view espoused by German theologians. Forsyth held that, to do justice to the historical Jesus, some form of self-divesting Godhead must be affirmed, but rather than to accept the older *kenosis* view that he *set aside* certain attributes (the absolute attributes, e.g., omniscience, or omnipotence), Forsyth suggests that we should view the attributes as taking on *a new mode of being,* a human rather than divine mode of existence, in which the attributes are reduced to potentiality, are self-retracted, rather than renounced (*The Person and Place of Jesus Christ,* pp. 305ff. Boston: Pilgrim Press, 1909). We are told that "If the infinite God was so constituted that He could not live also as a finite man, then He was not infinite"

criticism, this was a favorite option, for it enabled its proponents to insist on an ego resident on the divine rather than
human side, and yet to accept views of the earthly ministry
of Jesus which made somewhat intelligible his supposed limitations of knowledge in the realms of historical and scientific
truth.

But such sub-Chalcedonian formulations proved ineffective
stop-gaps, since English liberals, however reluctant to accept
the destructive views of radical German critics, cast their lots
with two determinative presuppositions: 1) the study of Jesus
Christ must be carried forward by the application of the historical method, with its implication that He is examinable as a
psychological unity, as with all other men; and 2) that He
must have possessed indubitably a human nature not vitiated
by the intrusion of alien attributes. In Lawton's words, the
twin liberal postulates were that "Christ must be truly one,
and truly human."[39] This was, of course, a Chalcedonian insistence also, but for Liberalism it meant that the categories of
modern psychology could be applied to Him without reserve,
and that whatever else might be said of his divinity, the initial
insistence must be upon a human ego. Coupled with this, was
the impetus from Kant which discouraged metaphysical speculation, and which encouraged definition of the divine in ethical
terms.

In point of fact, the *kenosis* Christology had already assumed
what was latent in the liberal movement, in the assumption
that Christ's knowing, thinking and willing must be *one*—that

---

39. *Op. cit.*, p. 24. Lawton comments that "the conjunction of the two axioms, unity
and humanity, tended to heighten the tension between the divinity and the humanity in
Christ a thousandfold . . . The natures, or two sides of his being, possessed no separate
significance for liberal theology — just as the modern biologist or psychiatrist can
conceive no effective distinction between body and 'soul'. This view had a profound
effect upon the idea of the mode and content of revelation" (*ibid.*, p. 43).

(p. 315). But to this self-reduction, on the side of deity, Forsyth would add a self-
fulfillment on the side of Christ's humanity; thus we have in Christ a divine *kenosis*
and a human *plerosis*—"within one single increate person the mutual involution of two
personal acts or movements supreme in spiritual being" (p. 344). Mackintosh, who contributed the foreword to the English translation of Brunner's *Der Mittler*, likewise
thought the humiliation of Christ to consist not in the surrender of some attributes, but
rather in the modification of all—possessed "in the form of concentrated potency rather
than of full actuality" (*op. cit.*, p. 447).

the unity of His being could not be of such complexity as to allow the operation of two wills, contrary to the orthodox formulation.[40] Thus the conservatives who sought to reconcile Christology with a higher critical view of Bibliology already had accepted the structure of the new psychology which made inevitable a break with the orthodox patristic formulation. Yet Kenoticism took its stand firmly against the notion of a human ego only; it was, in fact, a compromise movement within orthodoxy.[41]

American Christology was more prone to make the descent from orthodoxy directly to the more humanistic constructions of Jesus, partly under the influence of scholars who received instruction under more radical Ritschlians in Germany. They were fully aware, therefore, of the difficulties of a *kenosis* Christology which also troubled some of the higher liberals in Great Britain. For while *kenosis* flourished in Germany not much less than a century ago, and carried along with it Godet of France and Martensen of Denmark, it was already well on the decline on the continent when on British soil it was championed by Charles Gore,[42] A. B. Bruce, A. M. Fairbairn,[43] and

40. Lawton acutely notes the significance of this: "It was accepted, virtually as an axiom, that two natures so united as in the Person of Christ must integrate themselves into one single conscious unit if they are to form one person and not some divided self. What in fact it amounts to, expressed in yet another form, is that we have an admission that the old term 'Nature' has for all practical purposes vanished — it has coalesced with the term 'Person'. Owing to the change in the definition of the term person, the older term, nature, human nature, contained elements which could not be present without the possession of individual personality. This fact explains, among other things, the failure to comprehend the conciliar doctrines of the impersonal manhood, and the Two Wills in Christ. A being who possessed two sets of psychological functions, two wills, for example, would to these thinkers have been not simply one person, but two. Person was no longer a principle of individualization, an ego, but a set of psychological functions, in particular the self-consciousness, which was commonly believed to be that element which furnished continuity of personal existence and hence moral responsibility. One person cannot possess two sets of memories, two personal continuities, two separate self-realizations, but one: nothing but a monophysitism in modern dress was intelligible; for the two natures even if separated in but the slightest degree as regards psychical operation would have dissipated the unity of Christ's person" (*ibid.*, pp. 116f.)

41. A. B. Bruce's *The Humiliation of Christ*, (1881) is, of course, a classic treatment of types of kenotic theory, providing an excellent summary of continental European Christology of two generations and more ago.

42. Charles Gore, *Dissertations on Subjects Connected with the Incarnation*. New York: Charles Scribner's Sons, 1895.

43. A. M. Fairbairn, *The Place of Christ in Modern Theology*. New York: Charles Scribner's Sons, 1894.

a half generation later by P. T. Forsyth,[44] and then shortly before World War I by H. R. Mackintosh. There were, of course, repercussions on American soil, with William Newton Clarke[45]furnishing a representative point of contact. But the American scene had no state church whose orthodox creeds acted as a check on Protestant Christological descent, and with the domination of large universities by naturalistic presuppositions imported from Germany, by the first World War many of the old-line divinity schools stood solidly with the concept of a humanitarian, rather than of a *kenosis,* Christ. For, beginning with the assumption that a genuine humanity of Jesus required an essentially human consciousness, and alert to the fact that kenosis Christology had already pared down the consciousness of Jesus so that despite the ascription of deity, it was no longer a fully divine consciousness, this movement insisted that the divinity of Jesus was not to be found in an eternal divine ego, but rather in the communication to Him, in a supreme degree, of a divine quality accessible also to other men. Here an ethical sonship was substituted for a metaphysical sonship, and the human Christ replaced the essentially divine Christ—a view espoused, under many variations, by representative American Liberalism of the generation past. It was the view no less of Edwin Lewis, in his earlier writing,[46] than of Harry Emerson Fosdick,[47] or Shirley Jackson

----

44. P. T. Forsyth, *The Person and Place of Jesus Christ.*

45. Clarke writes: "Consciousness that he was divine is to be carefully distinguished, however, from the eternal consciousness of God not incarnate. The two are not one, and the eternal consciousness of God, he did not possess. Divine consciousness in Jesus was necessarily the consciousness of divinity within human limits: it could be nothing more. It was such divine consciousness as is possible within humanity" (*An Outline of Christian Theology,* p. 298. New York: Charles Scribner's Sons, 1911).

46. Edwin Lewis, *A Manual of Christian Belief,* p. 97: "He (Christ) was like us because he came into existence and remained in existence according to the same laws which make any human life possible." "He was unlike us as every man is unlike every other, except that in his case this unlikeness was such as to fit him to do something which none other was ever fitted to do." "God was in Christ.'" "He is in every man in some sense, and according to that divine indwelling the man is able to do this or that work. God was in Plato — to make him a philosopher; in Shakespeare — to make him a poet; in Bach — to make him a musician; in Jesus Christ — to make him the supreme exponent of the religious life, the Author and Finisher of Faith, the world's all-sufficient Saviour and Lord." (New York: Charles Scribner's Sons, 1927).

47. Harry Emerson Fosdick, *A Guide to Understanding the Bible,* where there is a representative liberal treatment of the "deification" of Jesus: "In this process by which Jesus was progressively reinterpreted in new patterns of thought, it is customary to see the gradual elevation of a man to the divine realm" (p. 46).

Case.[48] Here the most distinctive adjectives in human speech were still reserved for Jesus but, as has been noted, always in a context of denial with regard to his essential deity, and intending only his superlative humanity.[49]

4. The Question of a Divine or Human Ego The Turning-Point.

It is really this issue—whether the personal center of Christ's consciousness is on the side of His deity or humanity—which is the turning point of all Christological controversies.[50] Those Christologies inspired by Schleiermacher and Ritschl interpreted Christ's "divinity" in terms of a degree of excellence which separates him from us as highest among many—in terms, that is, of a denial that His personality exists on the side of

---

48. Shirley Jackson Case, *Jesus—A New Biography*, written "with a single purpose . . . to depict Jesus as he actually appeared" (p. v), in which Case declares that "In the period following the crucifixion the disciples were, both historically and psychologically, far more abundantly supplied with christological stimuli than ever Jesus had been. . . . It remained for Christianity to invest the figure of a new transcendental Messiah with real popularity in the person of the risen and glorified Jesus" (pp. 376f. Chicago: University of Chicago Press, 1927).

49. The same formula is found in Gordon Pratt Baker's *The Witness of the Prophets*, in which Jesus is heralded as "the prince of the prophets," but the Chalcedonian view is equated with Docetism, or the equivalent of a denial of a genuine humanity. But the development of Baker's view hardly conceals the clear rupture with New Testament thought: "This is not to deny the divinity of Jesus. It is to assert the divinity of men. . . . It is to disclose that he is the God-man who preferred to remain divine while we are the God-men who have preferred to become human" (p. 192. New York: Abingdon-Cokesbury Press, 1948).

50. Edwin Lewis came to see how clearly the repudiation of evangelical doctrines was involved in the exchange of a divine for a humanitarian Christ. "There is a way of regarding Jesus Christ which most indubitably *is* essential to Christianity; and the evidence is overwhelming that when men begin to surrender belief in the Virgin Birth and the Resurrection, they are also getting ready to surrender that belief regarding Christ himself which is the vital center of the whole body of faith . . . If a person wants a purely humanitarian Christology, well and good; but let him face honestly all that that implies. Let him admit that it changes radically the whole Christian belief as to God. Let him admit that it calls for the surrender of the Incarnation, and of the Atonement, and of Christ as living reality accessible and available here and now. Indeed, it may well be that the fundamental difficulty is not with the Virgin Birth and the Resurrection at all, but with the historical doctrine of the Person of Christ, and that these two are being let go because they are seen to be serious obstacles to the abandonment of the other . . . Deny that the subject of it was such a One as is presented in the New Testament and as was proclaimed in the earliest preaching of which we have any record, and the credibility of the Resurrection evaporates just as inevitably as does the credibility of the Virgin Birth. Affirm that he was such a One, and what has been called above 'The Supreme Acquiesence' — which is the yielding by our stubborn human minds to the miracle of his Birth and the miracle of his Return from Death — becomes a possibility completely sincere" (*A Philosophy of the Christian Revelation*, pp. 186ff). Lewis put the issue bluntly, as against the liberal Christological redactions of the essential divinity concept: "When the *idea* itself is objectionable, of what use is it to seek to evade the force of the objection by some ambiguous linguistic 're-statement'?" (*ibid.*, p. 201).

an essentially divine nature. Thus it was modern philosophy which prevailed over Biblical Theology. The mediating Christologies, which sought to appease both Biblical Theology and modern philosophy, projected two views. One was the Kenotist theory, the various forms of which included champions like Fairbairn, Forrest, Forsyth, Gore, H. R. Mackintosh, Moberly and Weston. Here they turned to a Christology, rejected in its Apollinarian form as early as 381 A. D., under the influence of German Lutheran theologians of a century ago.* It is the divine *within* the human, rather than united with it, that is stressed, yet the *ego* of His self-consciousness is placed as in traditional Christology, in the divine. But, the incarnation appears on this view to involve *"a new personal center of God's consciousness, Divine-human as distinct from purely Divine,"* as has been pointed out by J. Vernon Bartlet,[51] and hence DuBose declared for a "double personality" Christology, which the early Christian consciousness had rejected by condemning Nestorianism. The second mediating view was that of progressive incarnation, championed by August Dorner, and caught up in Germany by Loofs, and given some philosophic lodging in England by the theory of emergent evolution, which is compatible with the notion of reciprocal interaction of higher and lower natures leading to the emergence of a higher.[52] The view of a progressive coalescence of the divine and human in Christ is the last word of the "fresh approach to the incarnation" projected under the title of *The Lord of Life* (New York: the Macmillan Company, 1929), and appearing under the auspices of the Student Christian Movement in the British Isles. In this, D. Miall Edwards, contributing the essay on "A Christology in Modern Terms," upholds the view of Christ's divinity as "a spiritual achievement." The burdens with which such a theory is freighted, if taken literally—the addition of a person to the Godhead, the possibility of additional "pro-

---

*Thomasius of Erlangen, father of the kenotic theory, conceded the lack of patristic support for the view, which is distinctively modern; the nearest approach was Apollinarianism (cf. J. M. Creed, *The Divinity of Jesus Christ*, p. 77).

51. *The Lord of Life*, p. 175.
52. Scott Lidgett, *God, Christ, and the Church*, chapter 9.

gressive incarnations", etc.—were pointed out long ago by James Orr,[53] and it is scarcely a wonder that in America, at least, those who assigned to Jesus an ego grounded initially in His humanity only, were hesitant to speak of divinity in anything other than a metaphorical or ethical sense. Hence it is hardly surprising that Edwards distinguishes his position from the metaphysical implications which the "progressive incarnation" view bore in Dorner's formulation: "Christ's divinity, then, means," we are told, "that the values incarnated in His character and the quality of His will are Divine, and reveal to us the nature of Ultimate Reality in so far as it can be revealed to man" (*op. cit.,* p. 218) . . . (but) "to call this unity 'merely ethical,' as if that were something short of metaphysical unity, is to fail to appreciate the centrality and ultimacy of ethical values in a Christian philosophy of the universe" (p. 217). Clearly the divinity which is here affirmed of Jesus sets Him off from mankind only in degree, however high.[54]

Thus the traditional Christology found its support mainly in Catholic and in Protestant evangelical circles. Many Anglo-Catholics in England upheld the two-nature doctrine while yet conceding limitations of knowledge "proper to the human form of consciousness"—so that the God-man somehow was without full knowledge of science, history, yet properly divine, including His inability to sin.[55] The so-called Evangelical Kenotists (e. g., H. R. Macintosh and Forsyth) felt their view but a step removed from this—for Kenotism placed the seat of Christ's personality in His divinity. But champions of the orthodox

---

53. Orr, *Christian View of God and the World,* 239ff.

54. E. L. Allen acknowledges that if the three considerations which to many scholars have seemed to point beyond a humanitarian Christology — virgin birth, resurrection and sinlessness — are supplemented by pre-existence, the case for a truly divine Christ is quite inescapable. But he thinks Paul assumed pre-existence and hence invoked kenosis as a theory (*Hibbert Journal:* "Suggestions for a Revised Christology", Vol. XL, No. 1, Oct. 1941, p. 70). Of his proposed view, Allen remarks that "The word 'Incarnation' is scarcely applicable to such a conception, and in any case there is much to be said for abandoning it as misleading. It is not that the Logos takes to Himself a body, but that God chooses a man and equips him for service; others are His servants, but this one stands so near to Him that we cannot speak of him except as His Son" (*ibid.,* p. 72).

55. J. K. Mozley, *Journal of Theological Studies,* No. 12, p. 300. In his *Essays Catholic and Critical,* Mozley expressed doubt as to the philosophic satisfactoriness of the Chalcedonian view of personality.

theology continued to point out how such a view, with its insistence on reduction of the divine nature in view of the incarnation, seemed to require a second divine-human ego, which theological conservatives could not square with the Biblical narratives. J. S. Lawton's *Conflict in Christology* makes abundantly clear the latent disturbances which involved the kenosis formula in an inability to avoid a descent to lower views. It may have appeared momentarily attractive to conservative theologians, who accepted the restrictions within which contemporary thought sought to establish the psychological unity of Jesus by eliminating any tension between an omniscient Deity and a finite manhood. The case against Chalcedonian Christology was pursued presumably in the interest of historical and scriptural induction as against *a priori* dogmas but, as Lawton questions, "what could be more speculative or more metaphysical than the kenotic theory? Conjectures regarding the possibility of the dividing up of God's attributes, or the supposition that divine attributes can be controlled, dispensed with, and regained, by the divine volition: such things can scarcely be termed inductions from the testimony of Scripture."[56] Garvie noted that the idea of a depotentiating Logos with a view to Incarnation was "not only a speculative curiosity, but has even a mythological aspect."[57] And if orthodox theologians were quick to see that the theory jeopardized the essential deity of Christ, the liberal thinkers hardly felt that on this pattern a satisfactory statement of the genuine humanity of Christ could be found, any more than the Chalcedonian view seemed to them to afford it. The door was now opened to the humanitarian views of Christ, and with it, to the discard of His authority and infallibility. The *kenosis* thinkers had granted fallibility in historical and scientific matters, but sought to champion a spiritual and ethical absoluteness—but a humanity such as ours, if such He had, required more restriction than this. A relative absoluteness, that was conceivable—and liberal state-

56. *Op. cit.,* p. 162.
57. A. E. Garvie, *Studies in the Inner Life of Jesus,* p. 517.

ments of Christology expostulated on this kind of absoluteness, all the while unaware that the words were insufficient to overcome the hearer's discerning impression of relativeness.

The mid-twentieth century Christ is a reaction from critical confusion and, while enmeshed still in presuppositions involving concession, is given a heightened supernatural reference.

B. Mid-Century Christology Takes Higher Supernatural Ground.

If then those who resisted the humanistic depreciation of Jesus depreciated Him nonetheless, despite gracious and complimentary ascriptions, has it been better with the newer Christology, which has revolted against the naturalistic "historical Jesus" and claims to become more explicit about his suprahistorical uniqueness? Is the newer Jesus really set off from humanity in a truly unique manner?

1. Yet Often Stops Short of New Testament Uniqueness.

It may be well to begin with Walter Marshall Horton, who has pleaded so eloquently for an end to the Christological moratorium. In his *Realistic Theology* (1934) occurred passages which made inadequate room for a suprahistorical Christ:

> "Step by step, not knowing whither he went nor what the outcome would be, he followed the guidance of the Spirit in the pursuit of his mission of deliverance, until it led him to a death whose meaning and necessity he did not himself fully understand, save that it was the cup which his Father had given him to drink. The remark has sometimes been made that the world has yet to see what God can do with a man wholly surrendered to his will. The world *has* seen; Jesus was that man."[58]

_____

58. *Realistic Theology*, p. 133. In this volume Horton declares that "long before Jesus became conscious of his mission, long before he was born, God had purposed to reveal Himself as Love to close the gap of alienation between Himself and man, to "get inside" humanity as Life of its life. Yes, and must we not add that, long before the soul of Jesus began to reach up to God in eager devotion, God had begun to fashion for Himself the soul of Jesus, and set the stage for his coming? Through Moses, Amos, and the Prophet of the Exile, God was preparing the way for the incarnation; for such a personality as that of Jesus is not made in a day" (pp. 140ff.)

In *Our Eternal Contemporary* one senses the higher note.
Here we are told not only that Jesus is "the supreme Prophet
of all mankind, the One who definitely revealed the will of
God in word and deed, the effective Founder on earth of
God's eternal Kingdom,"[59] but we are instructed that "it was
a truly Christian religious consciousness that actually prevailed
at Nicaea and Chalcedon" and that "the main line of fruitful
development in Christian theology passes straight through
Nicaea and Chalcedon."[60]

But if one stays with Horton to the end, he discovers the
same repudiation of a New Testament once-for-allness; however higher may be the new uniqueness, it is not a uniqueness
which is affirmed of Jesus after all. In an epilogue for non-
Christians, Horton insists that "nothing herein is meant to
disparage the faith of Jews in their Torah, the faith of Bud-
dhists in the Dharma, or any other honest faith which is
truly good and holy. That same wisdom and power of God
which Christians themselves believe that the divine Word
pervades all places and is accessible to all peoples" (p. 153).
"Orthodoxy and Reform, Catholicism and Protestantism, continuity and change, are... both included in the divine strategy"
(p. 99). Horton defines the true nature of the Christian life
as *ethical mysticism*, i.e., a life of deep mystical faith-union
with God in Christ, a mystical and metaphysical union with
God as the *root* of a transformed life. This conception of the
Christian life, to Horton, reflects the Chalcedonian formula
of the "two natures" in Jesus (pp. 173f). Then he adds that
"though I still prefer the language of Scripture to that of
Nicaea and Chalcedon, I now believe that these and other

---

59. *Our Eternal Contemporary*, p. 15. In the same volume Horton declares that Jesus
is "our Eternal Contemporary, God's incarnate wisdom and power not only to his own
age but to our age as well" (p. 24), and that "Jesus is the wisdom and power of God,
the redemptive mercy of God, coming forth 'in the form of a servant' for the salvation of mankind. The possibility of such a coming forth, such a coming down of God
to the level of His creatures, to do them good, is essential to the Hebrew and Christian idea of God; there is from all eternity a manward motion in the depths of God's
being, a motion which apart from the Incarnation would remain abortive and defeated"
(pp. 127f.) . . . "Jesus is the One through whom the redemptive power of God found
entrance into the rebellious City of Man, and began to renew and reorder the whole
human race" (p. 134).
60. *Ibid.*, p. 171.

creeds of the Church Universal clarify the meaning of Scripture in valuable and important ways" (p. 175). Jesus is thus reduced after all, with whatever supra-historical meaning, to simply the best—if that permanently—among many.[61]

When one turns to John Knox, he finds a higher view of Christ, in which a once-for-allness is professed, and a metaphysical reference is fixed for the life of Jesus. Knox thinks he finds adoption tendencies in apostolic preaching and Mark's gospel, and that Paul held to a *kenosis* theory that the pre-existent Christ renounced Godhood and assumed the nature of a common man.[62] The discontinuity, says Knox, stopped "only just short of a complete break."[63] But the Synoptic Gospels, we are told, disclose by the pre-resurrection miracles a tendency to deny the normality of Jesus' manhood. Knox declares:

> "Really great ideas can never be tolerated very long, and the conception of a God who became veritable man was too great to be long borne... And since a

---

61. See Appendix, Note E, for further comment on Horton's Christology. It is not strange that his plea for a renewed Christological interest met with curious reaction even in his own circles. Remarked Wilhelm Pauck, in an incisive review of *Our Eternal Contemporary*: "It is my impression that the import of his answers is homiletical rather than theological . . . Horton's theology can hardly be called consistent . . ." Pauck asked whether Horton was not using the traditional formulas "as a means of inducing certain emotional attitudes toward Christ", since along with the plea for Nicean and Chalcedonian reinterest, Horton was also "able to make Christological assertions in line with the tradition of Schleiermacher, Ritschl and Hermann" (*Journal of Religion*, Vol. XXIII, No. 2, April, 1943, pp. 138f.).

62. Knox declares Paul would have distrusted the doctrine of the "two natures" as involving too important a qualification of Jesus' humanity. Paul knew the earthly Jesus not as God, not even as a God-man; he was in every sense a man" (*The Man Christ Jesus*, p. 84). Knox grants, in *Christ the Lord*, that "in the years 40-60 A. D. the idea of the preexistence of Christ was accepted not only by Paul himself, but also by the churches generally" (p. 95. New York: Willett, Clark and Co., 1945). Knox ascribes to Paul a *kenosis* view that the Son of God "surrendered his deity and entered upon an altogether different mode of existence" (*The Man Christ Jesus*, p. 86). And yet, we are told, Paul would not have pressed the interpretation that "a divine person has ceased being a divine person and has become a human person" to its logical extreme. "He took for granted some kind of continuity between the heavenly and earthly phases . . . The same person, in some deep naked essential of personality, who emptied himself of his deity also humbled himself to the death of the cross. This essential identity, without qualifying the genuineness of Jesus' humanity, explains the fact that he was a unique man, able to conquer sin and to redeem other men from its power. Nevertheless, the discontinuity between the two phases of this person's experience is so great as to stop only just short of a complete break between the two" (pp. 88f.).

63. Knox thinks Paul teaches that Christ's final exaltation was "not the resumption of a temporarily surrendered Godhood — his renunciation had been complete and irrevocable; it was the apotheosis of a manhood which had become inalienably his own" (*ibid.*, p. 89.)

denial of the divinity of Christ was out of the question, the trend was toward a qualification of his
humanity. This trend achieves its fullest expression,
in the Fourth Gospel, where a divine being is represented as becoming human, but without in any sense
ceasing to be divine, and is carried to its extreme
limits in the heretical teachings of the Docetists, who
denied the reality of Jesus' humanity altogether. But
Paul either antedated or repudiated this trend."[64]

The new significance of Christ for faith has come about, in
a more recent mood, by a renewed awareness that the Christian
church has its historical roots in a "revelational event" which includes, as John Knox has put it, "the personality, life and teaching of Jesus, the response of loyalty he awakened, his death, his
resurrection, the coming of the Spirit, the faith with which the
Spirit was received, the creation of the community" as its irreducible unity. [65] Thus, in view of the critical weakening of the
trustworthiness of the Scriptures, the tendency increases to emphasize our continuity with the primitive church (as does Knox)
or to find a heightened significance for the testimony of the
Spirit (as do the neo-supernaturalists).

The God of the Christian church "first made Himself known
in Christ" (p. 6). Christ is the center of "a new kind of human
community", of "a distinctive kind of human fellowship" (p. 8);
in Him, "God revealed Himself in a supremely authentic way"
(p. 13); He is "the innermost central event" of the divine revelational event (p. 33),[66] in which His death "has a place of special
significance" (p. 38). The early church was convinced of His
resurrection not because of visual experiences, "but because the
Spirit had come upon them" (p. 39), and because of this abiding
presence we too believe He died and lived again. This faith in

---

64. *Ibid.*, pp. 89ff.

65. Knox, *On the Meaning of Christ*, p. 34.

66. Knox remarks that God's disclosure in Christ "does not shut out the possibility
of other revelations, although it is hard to see how the particular reality, the God and
Father of our Lord Jesus Christ, could be known elsewhere or otherwise than in and
through Christ" (p. 17). Is the sentence remarkable for circumlocution? Knox concedes Montefiore's contention that Jesus was unforgiving toward His enemies until
the last tragic moment on the Cross, whereas Horton will not go that far.

His resurrection is not merely subjective, but has an objective occasion (p. 41), for "the resurrection was a genuine occurrence" (p. 68). Its intrinsic nature cannot be defined, but the fact of the resurrection is indisputable (p. 69). "The *risen* Christ, Christ the Spirit, is as truly a reality as Jesus of Nazareth" (p. 70). But the resurrection miracle is not to be confused with other miracles of the Gospel narratives, for it belongs to a different category; those other miracles, speaking broadly, did not happen (though Jesus cured by non-miraculous means) —so that the historicity of miracles in the accepted sense is ruled out (p. 76). The resurrection is a part of the whole revelational event —the miracle—the divine saving act, with its irreducible unity— but it is not a miracle in the sense in which the miraculous has been historically formulated.[67]

What are the implications of all this for Christology, which Knox concedes to be "the most important area of Christian theology and, in virtue of that very fact, the most dangerous" (p. 2)? To begin with, Knox disclaims any purpose of developing a logically consistent Christology (p. 36). But, while the revelational event has an essential minimum, some factors which the New Testament and the creeds have affirmed, e.g., the pre-existence of Christ and the ascension, do not belong to the revelational event. They are part of the Gospel story, but not part of the Gospel history (p. 86). The birth stories are legendary (pp. 81ff). Paul's picture in Philippians 2:6-11 is story, not history (p. 87). The pre-existence, the decision to come into this world as a man, the struggle with and triumph over demonic powers, the ascension: these are true, but in a different way from the events of His earthly life and resurrection (p. 89). "The story is not an account of the event, but a representation of the *meaning* of the event" (p. 89), and to forget that it is a story betrays us "not only into a sterile and irrelevant literalism, but

---

67. Knox says the miraculous element in the Gospels is a transfiguration of the early ministry of Jesus under the aspect of His resurrection; it represents "falsification at one level for the sake of truth at another" (p. 80). The Fourth Gospel reports not what the author remembers of the historic ministry of Jesus Christ, but what He has heard the risen Christ say in Ephesus or Alexandria—and these truths he recasts in dramatic form (p. 71).

also into an unnecessarily rigid and divisive dogmatism" (p. 90) ; the story attempts to express a meaning which was too great for merely historical terms (p. 93). Thus the story provides, along with the historical and ontological elements, the mythological formulation expressing the transcendent and redemptive meaning of the event (pp. 94f).

It becomes clear that, for Knox, the heightened significance given Jesus is one which is hesitantly negative about His pre-existence, and that the doctrine of resurrection* which is affirmed is that not of a bodily, but of a spiritual resurrection, and even this conviction is severed from objective manifestations of the type portrayed in the Gospels. The refusal to accept an actual pre-existence obviously has implications for one's view of the person and nature of Christ. Knox contends that the divisiveness of the Christological issue has resulted from the church's effort "to define abstractly in terms of the metaphysical essence of a person's nature what was at first received concretely as the divine meaning of an historical event", to interpret the revelation in Christ as a static thing residing in a person when it was really a dynamic thing taking place in an event" (p. 44). The all-absorbing thing in the Old and New Testaments, suggests Knox, is the work, rather than the person, of the Messiah. The initial Christological question was "What is God doing through Christ?" (p. 49). Once the revealing and saving character of the event was seen, however, it involved an affirmation of the divine role, if not the divine nature, of Christ (p. 50). The identification of Jesus with the Logos of Hellenistic Jewish teachers takes place in the New Testament period (p. 55), and the question about the eschatological and soteriological significance of an event becomes a question about the metaphysical nature of a person (p. 56). The Chalcedonian formulation, while it satisfied the great majority of Christians, has always been "either unintelligible or incredible" for a significant minority in the church (p. 56). That Knox

_____

*How, with his critical view of the Scriptures, Knox can safeguard the resurrection event from being merely a resurrection faith, as Harnack held, is not apparent.

repudiates the metaphysical deity of Christ is clear from his declaration:

> "If Christians are ever to be united credally, it will be upon the basis of these ancient creeds. But that can happen only if these creeds are recognized to be the symbols of God's revealing and saving *action,* not metaphysically accurate descriptions of the nature of His agent. Christ *is* 'of one substance with the Father'; but the utmost, and inmost, it is given us to know of God's 'substance' is that He is love—as such He is revealed in Christ—and love is not a metaphysical essence but personal moral will and action."[68]

2. Discontent with Chalcedonian Christology.

So that, after all, the pattern remains the same—a new appreciation of the historic creeds[69] (as against the former uncompromising attitude of the older Liberalism), but an insistence also upon their non-literal meaning—and upon mythological or symbolic or parabolic elements in Christianity.

It is the emphasis on a "hidden divinity"[70] which furnishes

---

68. *Ibid.,* p. 57.

69. Arthur C. Headlam closed his Noble Lectures (1924) with a nod in the direction of the traditional creeds. After expressing disbelief that Christ's earthly manifestation of knowledge need have been more than "that of a man inspired by the Spirit of God," Headlam added his disbelief that the true interpretation of His life and teaching "may be best studied and summed up in the words of the Christian creed" (*Jesus Christ in History and Faith,* p. 227. Cambridge: Harvard University Press, 1925). Yet he conceded that his lectures did not include the aim of carefully delineating the Divine and human elements in Christ's life (*loc. cit.*).

70. The recent volume on *The Kingship of Christ* (Stone Lectures) by W. A. Visser 't Hooft (New York: Harper and Bros., 1948) indicates how complex is the task of Christological reconstruction. Dr. Visser 't Hooft, in a volume significant in its implications for Christian social action, criticizes the liberalist preoccupation with the prophetic ministry of Christ, and declares that in the tensions and shambles of World War II the Protestants of Europe began to discern anew the *present kingship* of Christ. There is an excellent emphasis on the reality of a *present* kingship, and a yet *future* kingship when the victory of Christ shall be fully manifest. But the priestly aspect of Christ's ministry is hardly treated with a Reformation or Biblical alertness to the need for substitutionary atonement. The whole statement of the lordship of Christ is argued on the basis of Biblical theology, but the latent metaphysical problems—the essential deity of Christ, His pre-existence, the doctrine of the Trinity—are scrupulously out of sight. Yet the cosmic kingship of Christ is affirmed in no uncertain terms. The Lordship of Christ is declared to be both the simplest and the commonest New Testament affirmation, and it was "a strange error to suppose that the title '*Kurios*' was introduced into the Church under Hellenistic auspices . . . In that case the Lordship of Christ means no more than yet another apotheosis of a prophet or teacher. It is, however, very clear that nothing was farther from the thought of the New Testament authors. . . . The Lordship of Jesus Christ is then meant as an absolutely unique Lordship" (pp. 67ff.).

the point of transition to the neo-supernaturalist thinkers, who insist, however, on a metaphysical ground, or genuine pre-existence, of Christ. Yet the "Chalcedonian settlement,"[71] for 15 centuries the standard statement of the doctrine of the person of Jesus Christ, is regarded likewise by many of the neo-supernaturalists, as a contemporary source of theological un-settlement.[72] Wilhelm Pauck pithily expresses the prevailing mood: "Today, the church is in need of a new Christology".[73]

---

71. The Chalcedonian council affirmed in 451: ". . . Our Lord Jesus Christ, the same perfect in Godhead and also perfect in manhood; truly God and truly man, of a reasonable (rational) soul and body; consubstantial (coessential) with the Father according to the Godhead, and consubstantial with us according to the Manhood; in all things like unto us, without sin . . . one and the same Christ, Son, Lord, Only-begotten, to be acknowledged in two natures, inconfusedly, unchangeably, indivisibly, insepar-ably; the distinction of natures being by no means taken away by the union, but rather the property of each nature being preserved, and concurring in one Person and one Subsistence, not parted or divided into two persons, but one and the same Son, and only begotten, God the Word, the Lord Jesus Christ . . ." (Philip Schaff, *The Creeds of Christendom,* II p. 62. New York: Harper and Bros., 1889).

72. H. R. Mackintosh remarked that "For modern thought, the chief defect in strictly traditional Christology has been its insistence, not accidentally but on principle, upon what for brevity is called the doctrine of the two natures," a view which he felt hovered between the Scylla of a duplex personality and the Charybdis of a denial of Christ's real manhood *(The Doctrine of the Person of Christ,* pp. 292ff. New York: Charles Scribner's Sons, 1942).

Almost everywhere among theologians today the Chalcedonian statement is in the winds. There have been, in almost every period of church history, some dissatisfied voices, the most significant comprising the Socinian movement, then Enlightenment Naturalism, later modern religious Liberalism, and now the crisis theologians. Just before World-War I, Professor Friedrich Loofs, the right-wing Ritschlian of the University of Halle, acknowledged that he did not know a single German professor of evangelical theology not seeking "a new path in Christology" on the ground that the traditional theory provided an inadequate view of Jesus' human nature. Philippi (1882) is the German named as the last respected theologian who taught the "two natures" in a coherent manner.

Among almost all the most vocal theologians today, the Chalcedonian theory is spoken of appreciatively only if it can be taken to mean something other than was intended. Writes D. C. Macintosh: "The famous statement . . . would be satisfactory from the point of modern Evangelicalism if the second adverb, 'unchangeable,' could be under-stood as meaning only that the human Jesus remained unchangeably *human* and that the Holy Spirit (or Logos) in him remained unchangeably *God.* . . . As one normal person . . . Jesus must have had one well integrated nature" *(Personal Religion,* pp. 118f.). Or its main value is not found in the doctrine of the "two natures" so much as in the ruling out of certain alternate views, as Ebionitism, Docetism, Eutychianism, Arianism, Nestorianism, Apollinarianism (cf. H. Wheeler Robinson, *Redemption and Revelation,* pp. 29f.: "Whatever the Christian theologian of today may think of the Chalcedonian definition and of its positive contribution to a Christology, it is clear that the clash with views there rejected did define the issue and so far advance the truth. Even a theologian of such broad sympathies as Schleiermacher, recognizes the great value of negative definition in the pursuit of truth").

73. Wilhelm Pauck, article on "Christology," *Encyclopedia of Religion,* p. 167. (New York: The Philosophical Library, 1945.)

Nowhere in our day do we find in reconstructed Liberalism so high an emphasis on the person of Christ, as in the movement associated with the names of Karl Barth and Emil Brunner. It will be interesting, therefore, to observe the dissatisfaction which this movement expresses over the Chalcedonian definition, and to inquire into the adequacy of the proposed alternative.

a. *Niebuhr's Christology Negative.*

It is customary, in America, to link Reinhold Niebuhr with this movement because of the emphasis on the sinfulness of man in his theology of recent years. But there are factors in Niebuhr's thinking which separate him from, as much as link him to, the neo-supernaturalist school, and among these none is so conspicuous as his Christology, however higher this may be than that of left-wing liberal humanism. Niebuhr tells us that "Christ, as the norm of human nature, defines the final perfection of man in history" and that this perfection is "sacrificial love".[74] And yet, we are informed, if Jesus is a God-man, He has no message for us; if He transcends finiteness, we who are finite are prone to be complacent rather than contrite in His presence. "For we must live our life under the conditions of finiteness; and may, therefore, dismiss any ideal or norm as irrevelant which does not meet our conditions."[75] Thereupon the orthodox Christ is repudiated; "all definitions of Christ which affirm both His divinity and humanity in the sense that they ascribe both infinite and historically conditioned and eternal and unconditioned qualities to His nature must verge," we are told, on "logical nonsense."[76] What we have in Niebuhr, clearly, is the doctrine of "one nature", and that nature unqualifiedly human, even if the norm for all human-

---

74. Niebuhr, *The Nature and Destiny of Man,* vol. II, p. 74. New York: Charles Scribner's Sons, 1943.

75. *Op. cit.,* vol. II, p. 68.

76. *Op. cit.,* vol. II, p. 61. Niebuhr's footnote to the Chalcedonian creed is simply: "It is not possible for any person to be historical and unconditioned at the same time."

ity.[77] Moreover, Niebuhr has yet to clear up the implications
for Christology of his insistence that human nature is inevitably and inescapably involved in sinful acts.

b. *Barth and Brunner Insist on a Divine Christ.*

Nothing characterizes the Christology of Barth and Brunner
better, however, than the spirited refusal to reduce the consciousness of Jesus to human limits. Writers like W. Douglas
Mackenzie had struggled heroically but futilely to maintain on
the one hand "a divine consciousness in human experience"
as distinctive of Jesus Christ, while insisting on the other hand
on the full use of "the fundamental ideas of the modern
philosophy of science, and especially of the philosophy under-
lying biology and psychology for the modern restatement of
Christology."[78] But the neo-orthodox mood, with a judgment
thunder, has contested the right of modern science, fashioned
within the limits of the study of specifically human nature,
to give a definitive and final pronouncement with regard to
the constitution of the God-man. Few notes are struck with
more vigor in Brunner's *The Mediator* than the indictment
of the "scientific 'research into the life and the self-consciousness of Jesus,' " which, by its broad humanistic assumption that

---

77. Niebuhr's flirtation with myth at the expense of history leads to astonishing
tensions. Apparently history yields for him only a liberal Jesus, yet one must turn to
the "non-historical" Christ of western faith for "truth" not derivable from the historical Jesus. "The message of the Son of God who dies upon the cross, of a God who
transcends history and is yet in history, who condemns and judges sin and yet suffers
with and for the sinner, this message is the truth about life. It cannot be stated
without deceptions; but the truths which seek to avoid the deceptions are immeasurably
less profound. Compared to this Christ who died for men's sins upon the cross, Jesus,
the good man who tells all men to be good, is more solidly historical. But He is the
bearer of no more than a pale truism" (*Beyond Tragedy*, pp. 20f.).

78. W. Douglas Mackenzie endorses L. S. Thornton's *The Incarnate Lord* (New
York: Longmans Green, 1928) for its awareness that the two-nature doctrine must be
reoriented in such terms (*The Christ of the Christian Faith*, p. 293. New York: The
Macmillan Co., 1933). Mackenzie emphasizes that to understand the Incarnation we
must approach it conditioned not only by the ancient creeds "but with minds which
are aware of the light which the modern sciences of biology and psychology, and a true
philosophy of evolution, may throw upon that supreme act of God in human history"
(*ibid.*, p. 296). Thornton employs the framework of emergent evolution and suggests
that as man represents a new level beyond the animal, "so in Christ the human organism is taken up on to the 'level' of deity" (*op. cit.*, p. 225). Whereupon D. M.
Baillie appropriately inquires whether, in that event, Jesus may still be regarded as a
member of the human species? (*God Was in Christ*, p. 92, New York: Charles Scribner's Sons, 1948). Is not Thornton sponsoring a modern Eutychianism?

what is true of us must be true of Him in just the same way, disclosed also the deeper assumption that Jesus Christ is "of no importance"[79] for Christianity. Of such inquiries—and it cannot be emphasized to what extent the Christology of the past two generations expended its effort in this kind of investigation—Brunner wrote bluntly: "Interest in a Jesus of this kind is all that is left when Jesus Christ has no longer any decisive message to give us."[80]

Barth pleads vigorously for a Trinitarian approach to the whole of dogmatics, against Roman Catholic dogmatics, much Protestant evangelical dogmatics, and the dogmatics of Liberalism. All these treatments move from questions of prolegomena to a discussion of the existence, nature and attributes of God, reserving until later the treatment of the doctrine of the Trinity, as if in ignorance of the fact that the self-revelation of God means that He has revealed Himself as Father, Son and Holy Spirit.[81] Hence Barth is the signal for trinitarian dogmatics, as against the liberal dogmatics especially which frequently began with a discussion of the reality and truth of religion generally, and also as against more orthodox traditions which, while championing Trinitarianism, obscured its centrality.

In the instance of Barth and Brunner, one finds an insistence on the supra-historical as well as the historical, on the infinite as well as the finite, on the unconditioned as well as the conditioned, in the person of Jesus Christ—and a glorying in the *paradox*. Both Barth and Brunner speak forth for the deity as well as humanity of Christ. Barth insists that the personality

---

79. Brunner, *The Mediator*, p. 72.
80. *Ibid.*, p. 73.
81. One can here make room for the wholesome element in this insistence—that it violates the genius of Biblical revelation to treat first the existence, nature and attributes of God, and then as sort of an appendage the doctrine of the Trinity, since it is the Trinity that is most distinctive in the Christian revelation of God—without endorsing the Barthian failure to provide an adequate doctrine of religious authority, in view of the attitude taken toward the Scriptures. Barth rightly insists that the *that* and *what* cannot be determined except on the presupposition of the *who* (*The Doctrine of the Word of God*, I, p. 345). Nor, on the other hand, need a Trinitarian dogmatics be opposed in the interest of a Christocentric dogmatics; a proper Christian statement will be both. But Barth's Trinitarianism has not gone unsuspected of modalism (cf. Leonard Hodgson's *The Doctrine of the Trinity*, p. 229). Nor have Brunner's protests against the "Roman Catholic view of the Trinity" created confidence in his formulations of the divine triunity.

of the Logos is divine; in common with Reformation thought, Jesus is granted a human nature, but no human person, in the incarnation of the Logos. The Logos constitutes the personality of the God-man. Hoyle reports that "Barth discards the *Kenosis* doctrine as implying a 'self-emptying' of deity,[82] citing the following passage from the *Dogmatik*: "The *Kenosis* consists not in a negation, but in the positive, that He took to Himself, to His own existence which is His own from everlasting to everlasting—He added to Himself, received in Himself, as the Eternal Word of the Father—He united with Himself human existence in time,"[83] and from *The Word and the Church*: ". . . Apart from the Logos there is not in general a 'person of Jesus'."[84] Likewise, Brunner declares than "Jesus Christ was no human person."[85]

Declares Karl Barth:

"The true God, without ceasing to be the true God, has become true man. This testimony would be misunderstood if an attempt were made to say less than than this on the one side or on the other. We must say both true God and true man, and both must be taken in all seriousness. God has so utterly humbled Himself, that he has submitted Himself to being in Jesus Christ what we are. And God has exalted man so highly, that the man Jesus Christ was no less than God Himself. . ."[86]

This coming of God in Christ is not merely a special instance of the divine indwelling of gifted men; rather, it is a truly unique event:

"This union (of the divine-human in Christ) according to its nature could not be general or manifold, but only once-for-all and not repeatable. Not general as mysticism and speculative idealism hold. Not manifold, for it would not occur more than once that God

---

82. R. Birch Hoyle, *The Teachings of Karl Barth*, p. 156. New York: Charles Scribner's Sons, 1930.
83. Barth, *Dogmatik*, p. 260.
84. Barth, *The Word and the Church*, p. 275.
85. Brunner, *The Mediator*, p. 283.
86. Barth, *The Knowledge of God*, p. 64. New York: Charles Scribner's Sons, 1939.

would come into such a relation with man. As truly as there is only one God, the conjunction with man could take place only once, unrepeatedly. There could be no second, third or fourth."[87]

The neo-supernaturalists, in view of their heightened emphasis on sin, give the Christological controversy a higher turn, seeking to safeguard Jesus from the consequences of original sin[*] by affirming that His personality is contributed by His deity. Thus, while "reinterpreting" the Biblical doctrine of the primal perfection of man, the Fall, and the implication of humanity in original sin, Barth and Brunner feel that the "myth of the Fall" is somehow crucial in its implications for Christology; hence a higher supernatural reference is required for Jesus than the lower views of the past generation, in view of a "fall" in which humanity is involved. Barth, however, insists on the virgin birth for the same reason, though Brunner does not go this far. But the deity of Christ must be obscured more than in the orthodox formulation of the doctrine of the two natures; Christ must not be as "evidently" God as man, as in the traditional view:

"But man cannot meet God as God; 'No man shall see me and live! Therefore He must meet man as man, and the deity as such must be hidden. The man in whom God's Word (as Person) discloses Himself must be entirely man... To meet man God must be entirely and really man and nothing else. And yet—such is the paradox in His revelation—God must be also entirely in His revelation. Hence the Son, as God, as the Word, becomes man."[88]

This emphasis on a God-man with a concealed divinity, a deity *incognito,* is found also in Brunner. "The doctrine of the Two

---

87. Barth, *Dogmatik,* vol. I, p. 244 (translated and quoted by William Emmett Powers in his dissertation, "The Barthian Movement," p. 45. Northern Baptist Theological Seminary library). Cf. Zerbe's *New Transcendentalism,* p. 135.

*And yet Brunner, like Niebuhr, does not seem to reconcile Christology and hamartiology: "We are sinners because we are human beings; the idea of a sinless historical life is from the Christian point of view an impossible idea" (*op. cit.,* p. 320).

88. *Op. cit.,* p. 345.

Natures itself is right," declares Brunner, but it must not be interpreted to mean that the *God*-man could be pereceived by all, for this would destroy the indirect character of the manifestation, would dispel the *incognito*, would rule out the decision of faith. Not only the perception of the deity of Christ had its spiritual conditions; the nature of the evidence, on Brunner's view, is such that the deity is never directly perceived.* To understand the emphasis on the hiddenness of Christ's deity, one must recall the difference of Lutheran and Reformed theologians on the relationship of the two natures. The Chalcedonian insistence on two unconfused natures united in one person is shared by both groups, but the Lutherans teach the *communicatio idiomatum* (attributes of divine nature are communicated to the human) whereas the Reformed theologians deny this. But the Neo-Supernaturalists give this denial a curious turn.

Brunner tells us that the humanity of Jesus "conceals the Divine Person quite as much as it reveals it".[89] This is apparent because, says Brunner, the God-man is not discerned as such during His earthly ministry except by an act of faith. His limitations as a human being, we are told, mean that he was "neither omniscient nor omnipotent",[90] though He is the God-Man, and this historical human being is God.[91] Brunner sug-

---

*One of the most vulnerable phases of neo-supernaturalist views is the insistence that the testimony of the Holy Spirit does not terminate upon the evidence, but that faith is a miraculous self-sustaining experience which moves on a different level. Given that emphasis, two far-reaching possibilities ensue. For one thing, it is not clear why the "myth of a God-man" might not serve as effectively as an actual historical incarnation. For another thing, the appeal to self-authenticating faith, without any necessity for the application of the criterion of coherence, would appear capable of doing service for any and every appeal to revelation by competitive religious traditions (Mohammedanism, Mormonism, etc.).

89. *Op. cit.*, p. 357. Brunner remarks elsewhere that "because this Word is an act of condescension, . . . a Presence in incognito, therefore this event of the Word points towards another event, one in which this indirect revelation becomes direct; . . . thus even in the Word of revelation, in the Word of the Person of Christ, the Coming of God has not been completely fulfilled. Decision is possible" (p. 392).

90. *Op. cit.*, p. 364.

91. *Op. cit.*, p. 392. Brunner declares that " Nothing is more foolish than to try to play off 'Theocentric' and 'Christocentric' standpoints against one another. . . . When the Christian message says with emphasis, 'Look to Christ,' it does not mean 'look away from God,' but 'look away to God where God really is,' for if God is contemplated apart from Christ, if Christ is ignored, then God is not seen as He really is . . . that which we are to see in Christ is absolutely nothing other than God, and indeed God's Eternal 'Being' " (*Op. cit.*, pp. 400f.).

gests that we may speak of the existence "of the divine-human 'Nature' of the Mediator without falling back into a metaphysic of being".[92] Brunner quotes approvingly a statement by Melanchthon which encourages the mood that "it does not matter how the divine and human Natures in Christ are united with each other, or how they can co-exist, but what does matter is what we have in this Christ; how Christ speaks to us, not what we think about Him, is the problem for faith."[93] We are then told that:

> "... how it comes to pass that an historical man is the Eternal Son, who has 'come', this is the secret of God. Those who know that this mystery is the Divine Intention will not feel inclined to try to probe into the mystery any further... Faith is not concerned with the Incarnation as a metaphysical problem".[94]

(1) *But Neo-Supernaturalist Christology Is Still Needlessly Obscure.*

What then shall we say about this neo-supernaturalistic Christology, which in the mid-twentieth century is absorbing the interest of many higher Protestant liberals now in revolt against the idealistic and even naturalistic categories which, at the beginning of the century, were authoritatively delivered by the German "liberal historical school" now in disrepute?

Rejoice one must in the insistence on a *once-for-allness,* an unapproximated *uniqueness,* for the Person who stands as the central fact of the Christian movement; both the Hegelian immanentism, and the continuity emphasis of the modern philosophy of science had precluded a true view of Jesus Christ.

Rejoice one must in the evident desire to single out a true divinity as that which is essentially unique about Christ Jesus.

---

92. *Op. cit.,* p. 405. He adds: "The duality of His being, the 'Two Natures,' means simply that the Eternal Word has come. . . . There is no surer method of thoroughly dampening the ardour of all speculative arrogance and metaphysical pretension than to look steadily at the message of the Being of the God-Man and at His dual Nature" (pp. 405ff.).

93. *Op. cit.,* p. 407.

94. *Op. cit.,* p. 411. The plea for a "reverent agnosticism" in Christology may grow out of a Kantian anti-metaphysical bias no less than a pious faith.

One cannot read Brunner without the feeling that, above all, the pre-existence of the Logos-nature of Christ must not be compromised, else we lose everything the Christian counts worthwhile.[95]

But there is also occasion for caution and hesitancy.

The first question to arise is whether the incognito of the God-man is occasioned only by the nature of the incarnation, or also by the sin-bent character of man. It is difficult to see what Barth and Brunner gain by the insistence that the incognito is due to the constitution of the God-man, as if in the very course of special revelation the divine self-disclosure is self-obscured.[96] Was the disclosure so concealed that unbelief was not a matter of sin? That is hardly the appraisal of Jesus! It is true that to behold the glory of the Only-Begotten there must have been exercised the act of faith, but faith transcended the limitations of a sin-bent insight rather than added to the incarnational revelation. But were the deity of Christ unper-

---

95. Brunner's reserve on the doctrine of the virgin birth of Jesus is based primarily on the contention that the insistence is "not part of the doctrine of the Apostles." It is not only that neither Paul nor John refer to it, says Brunner, but Paul's reference to the birth from the seed of David (Rom. 1) and from a woman (Gal. 4) seem to him hardly conciliable with the virgin birth idea—found only, says Brunner, in Mt. 1 and Lk. 1.

But exclusion of the virgin birth does not drive Brunner to an adoptionist view. The question of the pre-existence of Christ and His incarnation, it must be conceded, can be conceptually separated from the idea of the virgin birth. Greek theologians who denied the pre-existence of the Logos-Son nonetheless did not dispute the virgin birth. As Paul of Samosata believed in the virgin birth yet not in the divinity of Christ, so Brunner thinks (inconclusively to the mind of the writer) that Paul and John believed in the true divinity, including pre-existence of the Logos-Son, without holding to the idea of virgin birth. Brunner prefers, he has remarked, to "follow the line of Paul and John without mingling it with the idea of the virgin birth. At the same time one should leave the question open whether or not the idea of the virgin birth is a possible interpretation of the true divinity of Christ. I should neither negate nor affirm this question because it is no part of the apostles' doctrine."

To the writer's mind it is an unsatisfactory view of the Scriptures which makes it possible for Brunner to play off Paul and John against Matthew and Luke, when the two positions are not only reconcilable, but imply each other. Karl Barth does not stumble at the doctrine, viewing it as an essential part of the Christian creed, and Edwin Lewis embraces it as a "supreme acquiescence" (*A Philosophy of the Christian Revelation*, pp. 188ff.). A competent treatment of the problem here posed is found in J. Gresham Machen's *The Virgin Birth of Jesus* (New York: Harper and Brothers, 1930), despite Lewis' disparagement of the volume because of its high view of the Scriptures. O. Cullmann accepts the textual reading of John 1:13 which finds the virgin birth there.

96. Wilhelm Pauck observes that the emphasis upon the otherness of God, when applied to Barth's Christology, results in the occasional depiction of Jesus Christ "as the revealer of God's inaccessibility" (*Karl Barth*, p. 195. New York: Harper and Brothers, 1931).

ceivable within the sphere of history as such, what is the significance of the miracles as *signs?*[97]

If the humanity of Jesus in no way constituted the revelation,
as Barth and Brunner insist, one is tempted to suggest that the
incarnation is hardly central for Christianity. It is no doubt
true that, even in the incarnation, the divinity was transcendent
to the humanity; the Christian church resisted Eutychianism
for the Chalcedonian formula. But nonetheless the glory of
God was beheld in the face of Jesus Christ. The revelation
was there, wherever there was faith to perceive it; the hiddenness was not due exclusively to the nature of the incarnation,
but more so to the factor of sin and rebellion.*

---

97. The distinguishing fact about Biblical miracle, which differentiates it from the
miracle element in other movements, is the fact that the supernatural appears here not
as sheer *wonder* or *marvel,* but points beyond itself to a divine rationale or purpose,
that is, appears as a *sign.* And a sign is needed where faith is absent; when faith is
present, the sign is no longer necessary. Granted that without faith the miracles are
stumbling-blocks, the self-disclosure of Jesus nevertheless was not so obscured as to
make disbelief *natural; rather,* disbelief is an effect of sin, not of concealment of the
divine revelation. It is true that Luther stressed the incognito character of the Incarnation, but not without stressing also the distortion of revelation by man's sin-bent
character. Miner B. Stearns takes issue with the notion that the failure of many of
Jesus' contemporaries to recognize him as the Son of God means that He is not known
within historical categories. "There were incontrovertible historical evidences that Jesus
Christ was no mere man, even though the Pharisees would not let themselves admit
that He was God. . . . That there is much more in Christ than meets the eye of the
unbelieving critical student of history or of the unbelieving observer of Christ's own
day, we should not think for a moment of denying. That the operation of the Holy
Spirit, on the one hand, and of faith, on the other hand, are indispensable for a proper
appreciation of Christ is certainly true, and in that we agree with Barth. But there is
certainly a very subtle danger in such juggling with the word *history* as Barth has
permitted himself" (*Bibliotheca Sacra:* "Protestant Theology Since 1700," Vol. 105,
No. 417, Jan-Mar., 1948, p. 72).

*Faith, for Barth, does not terminate upon evidence (*The Doctrine of the Word of
God*, pp. 233ff.). No amount of inquiry on the historical level leads to faith; what
happens in history is always susceptible of another-than-revelatory meaning. This
position would seem to destroy the very sinfulness of unbelief. D. C. Macintosh comments: "Thus Barth agrees with Hume: the miracle of the Resurrection can only be
believed as a result of the miraculous bestowal of faith. Fundamentally, indeed, faith
is the only miracle" (*op. cit.,* p. 342). Now it is certainly true that no amount of
historical evidence constitutes faith, and that Barth does not intend to destroy the
historical evidence: "To deny (the) sign would mean to deny also the thing signified"
(Barth, *Credo,* pp. 63, 104. New York: Charles Scribner's Sons, 1936). But a faith
which is so indifferent to rational coherence, a faith which while supernatural is yet
so discontinuous with the historical appearances that it can afford to treat them with
considerable diffidence, hardly moves on the same sphere with faith as it shines forth
in the Biblical narratives. Barth confesses, averred Macintosh, "that in the end all
the miracle-stories may go, provided only that the miracle of a God-given faith (in
Christ as revelation) be allowed to stand" (*ibid.,* p. 346). Such a position not only
accepts the historico-critical method in Biblical study, with its usual doubt as to the
historicity of Bible miracles, but seems driven as well to its conclusions, which flow
from the same naturalistic premises.

This leads naturally to a second matter. Brunner, while carefully avoiding a repudiation of the doctrine of "two natures", thinks it ought not to be formulated metaphysically, for this destroys the incognito, materializes the deity, and turns a necessity for decision into a need for explanation.[98] And one who is alert to a Reformational mood will assuredly take a cautious attitude toward creeds, aware that while sometimes they precisely fix Biblical meanings, at other times they have been used in church history to add human invention to divine revelation; just as one who is alert to the Enlightenment mood will be aware that the revolt against creeds has often involved a revolt against revelation.[99] And it is assuredly true that the human mind, in its most precise formulations, will certainly not fully comprehend all that is involved in the miracle of the incarnation. But when all this is said, faith cannot escape the responsibility for orienting its convictions to competing contemporary philosophies: It must give, in relation to the metaphysical tensions of the day, a reason for the inner hope.[100]

If the Chalcedonian settlement of the person of our Lord is right in principle although encouraging certain malformations, faith can gain only by a clarification of the aspects which need rectification, and not by seeking refuge in a paradoxical mysticism.

98. *Op. cit.*, pp. 343ff. He remarks: "A relation produced by the authoritative personal Presence of the Word of God is turned into a magico-material substantial Presence. The doctrine of the Two Natures becomes the object of purely external, theoretical, semi-scientific discussion. . . . Faith becomes intellectualized, and it is henceforth possible to discuss the Deity of Christ in the same way that a physical phenomenon could be discussed. . . . Whereas in the earlier phase of Church history revelation tended to develop into metaphysics, in the later phase, revelation was reduced to ordinary human history. . . . Yet we owe a debt of frank gratitude to this antimetaphysical theology and to historical criticism for breaking through the rigidity of dogma, and it is to them we owe the fact that once more the question of the true Deity of the real Man, Jesus Christ, has become a living issue" (*Op. cit.*, pp. 344f.).

99. Brunner is alert to this danger (cf. *op. cit.*, p. 393).

100. Edwin Lewis declares: "The Incarnate Life, truly human as it was by virtue of the law of its experience, nevertheless was a Life whose subject possessed the metaphysical status that belonged only to God" (*A Christian Manifesto*, p. 187. New York: The Abingdon Press, 1934). This would seem to call for a defense, against modern modes of thought, of the two-nature doctrine. God is, writes Lewis, *the personal subject* of the life of Jesus Christ (*ibid.*, p. 177). While the Chalcedonian creed may not be beyond need of revision, he adds, the revisers ought not to say less than the creed says. But elsewhere Lewis speaks in a kenotic mood: "He is God 'emptied' of as much as he must empty himself of if he would become man and experience man's lot" (*The Faith We Declare*, p. 40. Nashville: The Cokesbury Press, 1939).

In Christology, the alternatives are a one-nature or a two-nature view. Contemporary philosophy had no room for Docetist emphasis on a completely divine Christ, so that a one-nature view in modern times has come always to mean a completely human Christ, differing from other men only in the degree of divine indwelling.

Nor has modern religious thought shown any partiality for the Eutychian notion of a mingled divine-human nature, a *tertium quid*. It avoided this alternative for the reason that it set up too much of a barrier between Jesus and other men, and compromised the integrity of His human nature (the divine also, though this was not a basic concern with liberal leftism).[101]

(2) *Kenosis Sympathies Create Insuperable Difficulty.*

The contemporary Christological mood is groping for some variant[102] of the two-nature theory, seeking a relationship somewhat other than the traditional view of Protestant Evangelicalism and Roman Catholicism. The newer atmosphere has a *kenosis* overcast. There is vigorous insistence on both the deity and the humanity of the God-man, but it is felt that the Chalcedonian view that the incarnate Christ retains full possession of His divine attributes needs revision. It is implied that the traditional view does not do justice to the *incognito* of the God-man, that it compromises the integrity of His humanity. Already Forsyth had suggested a new *kenosis* approach—that the God-man had set aside not certain of His attributes

101. Insistence on a single personality which is both divine and human was Sanday's forte. He considered this an improvement on the traditional two-nature doctrine, although in earlier days he had declared for the trinitarian view. On this approach, the one-natured Christ is supposedly God because of the paradox that "God is most God when He ceases to be God—when He becomes man," this being the supreme manifestation of His love. When Sanday finished his journey over his "new Christological path," he had a purely human Jesus who, to a higher degree merely than other human beings, was sustained and indwelled by Deity, whose life was directly continuous with that of God Himself as ours is, only more so. Here, starting out with a desire to show how God really became man, Sanday ended up with showing how man becomes God.

102. The modern mood is seeking not only a new Christology, but also a new Trinity path, a new revelation path, a new inspiration path, a new hamartiology path, a new atonement path, a new eschatology path. The implications of this are often lost sight of, when one segment of this mood is treated in isolated fashion.

(as older kenosis spokesmen were wont to say),[103] but rather that there was a self-reduction of the divine nature in the incarnation. In this mood Forsyth spoke, as we have seen, of a truly divine nature in potentiality, and H. R. Mackintosh of a modified yet fully divine nature. It is this mood which one senses in the newer Christology, though its ramifications are not yet fully clarified. Often, indeed, we hear of a renunciation of the ideal of a logically consistent Christology! The final word is not a self-consistent Christology, but paradox.[104] The *incognito* emphasis, would appear to lean more in this direction than in any other.

It is difficult to see how, in any real sense, a modified *kenosis** view, expresses a "two-nature" doctrine. Just as deity divested of all divine attributes, or even of some divine attributes, is no longer true deity, so also deity whose attributes are pared down, or are compromised to semi-divine proportions, can hardly be spoken of as real deity. Does not such a view destroy Christ's Godhood by compromising the divine attributes? Can it be said in any true sense that, if in the incarnate state the divine attributes are finitized—to whatever degree—the God-man nonetheless has in a real sense the nature of the infinite God? Does not the notion of a finitized divine nature in the incarnation suggest—however much the proponents of such a view would resist the thought—more of the Platonic Demiurge or the Christ of Arianism, somewhat more than man but nonetheless somewhat less than true God? Can Jesus really be called the God-man if in the incarnation He did not possess

---

103. As against the insistence of evangelical orthodoxy, that the God-Man in the incarnation temporarily surrendered not some aspect of His Godhood, but rather the independent exercise (or rather, as I would prefer to put it, the coordinate for the subordinate exercise) of His divine attributes.

104. A temporary advantage accrues to the Barth-Brunner movement by its inexplicitness in doctrine, for in a reaction upward from both Naturalism and immanental Idealism a movement which has not yet solidified is more attractive, and serves as a catch-all for discontent leftist liberals as well as evangelicals. But the danger is that the movement will crystallize in its vagueness and indecision. In the meantime, its judges are left to interpret the movement only from the partial definiteness which shines through its expositors.

* A discerning criticism of Kenoticism is given by D. M. Baillie, *op. cit.*, pp. 96-98.

divine (infinite) [105] attributes? What does the doctrine of the "two natures" come to mean in such a view, when it is granted to be "right in principle" but in actual interpretation the second nature is seen, after all, not to be in the only legitimate sense divine? In what sense does this God-Man, with less than infinite attributes, affirm of Himself: "Before Abraham was, I am" (John 8:58)? Can a "divine nature in potentiality or depotentiality"[106] ever be considered a truly divine nature?

(3) *Compromise of Early Creeds Involved in Rejection of Biblical Authority.*

Tensions of this kind should serve to warn us that, in addition to the failure of the newer Christology to find an adequate Biblical basis for its view, it is difficult to find how it provides a more satisfactory solution to the attendant problems than does the traditional theory. That there are problems

---

105. It may be suggested that one is on speculative rather than on New Testament ground by defining the attributes of Christ on the side of His deity, especially in view of Acts 1:7, where the risen Christ declares that "It is not for you to know the times or the seasons which the Father hath put in his own power." and Hebrews 5:7-10, where the writer declares that "Though he were a Son, yet learned he obedience by the things which he suffered." Can one who possesses the full attributes of unmitigated Deity be ignorant of the times or seasons of the kingdom's consummation, or learn through suffering? In reply, it may be remarked that (1) the total impression of the New Testament writings points to an unmitigated Deity, against a background of which such passages appear as exceptions; (2) it is unsafe to formulate an over-all theory based largely on the exceptions; (3) that over-all theory must not disregard the exceptions. It is to be noted that the difficult passages, an a Chalcedonian formulation, may find their cue in a pre-incarnation covenant, by which the Son sets aside in the incarnation the exercise of specific attributes apart from the concurrence of the entire Godhead. Such a hypothesis becomes artificial only when one has already precluded a trinitarian view. The distinction between possession and exercise of divine attributes, in the carrying out of the redemptive economy, may be the key to such passages. Modernism appealed to the passages which seemed to point against divine omniscience, and formulated a Christology which appealed basically to such references, rather than to the broader New Testament mood in which such passages appeared with an emphasis on their exceptional nature in view of the context. Thus Heb. 5:7-10 begins, *"Though he were a Son, yet . . . ,"* and Mk. 13:32 at worst would yield a Christology far higher than that for which Modernism enlisted the text: "But of that day or that hour knoweth *no one, not even the angels in heaven, neither the Son,* but the Father." J. Oliver Buswell has proposed the following translation of Heb. 2:5: "It is appropriate for Him on account of Whom everything (exists), and through Whose agency everything (was made), in leading many sons into glory, *to perfect (Himself as)* the Author of their salvation through suffering" (*The Bible Today,* Vol. XLI, No. 5, Feb., 1948, pp. 150f.). The early church councils had before them all such data and, free of the modern bias against the supernatural, felt driven by the records to acknowledge the essential deity of Christ as the starting-point, and then proceeded to reconcile the texts which produced tensions. On Mk. 13:32, see H. P. Liddon's *Our Lord's Divinity,* pp. 463ff.

106. The very notion is contrary to a Christian deity concept.

in the Chalcedonian formulation, no alert theologian doubts.[107] But the Chalcedonian settlement was an effort to do justice to the demand of the Scriptures in the formulation of the doctrine of the person of Christ. It did not begin with the problems, and endeavor to work back to a problemless theory. It began with revelation, and made no effort to gloss over or alleviate the problems, but was motivated by the conviction that the divine rationale doubtless breaks beyond the moulds of a human logic fashioned by familiarity in the area of general rather than special revelation.

That great Princeton theologian of a generation past, Benjamin B. Warfield, pithily remarked that:

> "The alternative of two natures is, of course, one nature: and this one nature must be conceived, naturally, either as Divine or as human."[108]

We affirm sympathy with the neo-supernaturalist desire to set forth a Mediator who is true God and true Man, but do we not have something less—a divinity in which the Hebrew-Christian tradition can find no delight—when once the attributes are modified? It is not sufficient at this point to say that the person of Christ does not lend itself to metaphysical definiteness, for when the true deity of our Lord is in the balances, the Christian message can gain not a whit from obscurity.

The mid-twentieth century Christ, however more supernatural than the humanistic Jesus of half century ago, can neither

---

107. Especially, of course, that of "an impersonal human nature"—though when one concentrates on an inpersonalized human nature the difficulty is lessened. This tension produced Nestorianism, with its two-ego mood. Speculatively there is no objection to both a divine and human personality provided they are so harmonized as to avoid a dual or split personality. But in that case, what is gained over the view of an *in*-personalized human nature, for the two egos then really merge in one—in an *in*person-alized humanity?

108. Benjamin B. Warfield, *Christology and Criticism*, p. 372. "The entire Christian tradition, from the beginning, whatever that may be worth, is a tradition of a two-natured Jesus, that is to say, of an incarnated God. Of a one-natured Jesus, Christian tradition knows nothing, and supplies no materials from which He may be inferred" (p. 298).

deliver contemporary culture from its crossroads,[109] nor modern man from his canker, unless He is the New Testament God-Man, who for us and our salvation was crucified and is risen again.

Were we to discard the guideposts furnished by the ecumenical creeds and to return to the sacred Scriptures alone for our estimate of the God-Man, it would not be long before once again we would be involved in church councils and find ourselves confronted by the problems which gave Nicea and Chalcedon no rest until they had affirmed the full deity and the full humanity of Christ.[110] Return to the sacred Scriptures— that is the battle-cry. Those who have broken in our times with some of the presuppositions of Harnack and Herrmann have not broken with enough. They stand yet with a destructive criticism of the Scriptures. They know that God is come once-for-all in Christ—to this extent they have the main trunk-line of clear Christological conviction which connects the Christian centuries—but they have only a fallible revelation, and hence their God-Man must always be, to some extent, a

---

109. In expressing this conviction, one cannot put out of mind how largely it was due to Barth's re-emphasis of the sovereignty of God and the crown-rights of Jesus Christ, King of Kings and Lord of Lords, that the issue was raised in Germany as between Antichrist (Nazis, Hitler and Rosenberg, etc.) and Christ (Niemoeller, Barth himself, and the Confessional Church)—as it is sometimes put. The overwhelming section of the non-conformist Baptists, Methodists, Free Evangelicals, Plymouth Brethren conformed in one way or another, or were silent. But this need not prove more than that the neo-supernaturalistic movement found at this moment more courage than Evangelicalism; it does not establish the orthodoxy of Barthianism, but it does unveil the lethargy of much contemporary Fundamentalism.

110. Norman Pittenger's *Christ and Christian Faith* presses the case for a Chalcedonian Christology, and emphasizes that the Biblical view requires the doctrine of the Trinity. Pittenger summarizes recent scholarship which seems "to show that the attempt to derive the doctrine (of the Trinity) from Neo-Platonic sources or from other sources not linked in proper chronology with the Jewish-Christian experience, has completely failed" (p. 134; New York: Round Table Press, Inc., 1941). Pittenger rejects the kenotic theory as suggesting "a mythology in which God can 'undeify' himself in some respects and yet remain fully God" (p. 20), for a view that the personality of Christ is resident on the side of His deity by his formula: "It is therefore not necessary to assume (when asserting the divinity of Jesus) that God was united with humanity, as it were by removing human psychology and inserting some divine psychology; God is united to the whole of a genuine humanity, including a genuine human psychology, and the result is not a supplanting of that psychology, nor the adding of a new consciousness (with the further result that there are now two similar consciousnesses brought into conflict or juxtaposition), but the total union of all of man with God, so that (as we shall see) the whole of the humanity is indwelt and informed by the divinity, without in any way removing the limitations which are part of humanity as such, though doubtless using them for great purposes—and in respect of 'unessential' human limitations speaking through them sufficiently clearly so that they do not 'count' in the pattern of the whole" (pp. 24f.).

revelation obscured as well as a revelation revealed, a *Deus absconditus* no less than *Deus revelatus*.[111] The mid-twentieth century has a diversity of higher Christologies. Is it not tragic indeed that God's supreme revelation should be thus obscured?[112]

4. *Tensions in Neo-Supernaturalistic Trinitarianism.*

Karl Barth's statement of the divine triunity (with which Emil Brunner disclosed his essential agreement during his last American tour) has gone to such extremes in the legitimate effort to avoid tritheism, that it has encouraged at the same time the suspicion of modalism.

The circumstance from which this trinitarian disagreement takes its rise is the widely conceded claim that the technical term *hypostasis* or *persona* in trinitarian doctrine does not mean precisely what is intended in modern speech by the word "person." In view of the fact that the term "personality" today suggests the attribute of self-consciousness, Barth contends that the concept of tri-personality necessarily suggests three distinct centers of divine consciousness, three self-conscious personal beings, in such a way as to require tritheism; therefore Barth prefers to speak of three "modes of being" in the Godhead.[113]

---

111. One can support the deep intention behind this formulation—that no one could discover in Jesus of Galilee the Christ except through divine enlightenment—without gaining from it the higher critical mood which expects on this account a fallible Word.

112. The Christological interrogations have moved along now to a moment in contemporary inquiry when the empirical study of the New Testament view of Jesus, carried out by Warfield in *The Lord of Glory*, will make relevant religious reading. In his later *Christology and Criticism*, Warfield set forth what seemed to him to be the only satisfactory conclusion: "The doctrine of the Two Natures supplies, in a word, the only possible solution of the enigmas of the life-manifestation of the historical Jesus. It presents itself to us, not as the creator, but as the solvent of difficulties—in this, performing the same service to thought which is performed by all the Christian doctrines. If we look upon it merely as a hypothesis, it commands our attention by the multiplicity of phenomena which it reduces to order and unifies, and on this lower ground, too, commends itself to our acceptance. But it does not come to us merely as a hypothesis. It is the assertion concerning their Lord of all the primary witnesses of the Christian faith. It is, indeed, the self-testimony of our Lord Himself, disclosing to us the mystery of His being. It is, to put it briefly, the simplest statement of 'the fact of Jesus,' as that fact is revealed to us in His whole manifestation. We may reject it if we will, but in rejecting it we reject the only real Jesus in favor of another Jesus—who is not another, but is the creature of pure fantasy. The alternatives which we are really face to face with are, Either the two-natured Christ of history, or—a strong delusion" (*op. cit.*, pp. 309f. Used by permission of The Presbyterian and Reformed Publishing Co.).

113. Barth, *The Doctrine of the Word of God*, pp. 403ff.

But in employing such terminology, Barth at the same time repudiates Sabellian modalism, and insists that the three "modes of being" are eternal distinctions, and are not foreign to the Godness of God. Barth's emphasis on "modes of being," he stresses, is intended merely to return to the patristic sense of *persona*, thus safeguarding that concept from a modern notion of personality which would involve tritheism; in the modern sense of the term, Barth suggests, it would be more proper to speak of God as one person than three.

That the neo-supernaturalist statement[114] of divine triunity, in its caution to avoid tritheism, veers too far in the modalistic direction, is a complaint which has been voiced vigorously in several circles, but especially among Anglican theologians. Using the "social analogy" of the Cappadocian fathers in the patristic age, according to which the social relationships of the Trinity were stressed in such a way as to emphasize the personal rather than modal distinctions within the divine essence, these theologians appeal to Clement C. J. Webb for authority for the essential continuity of the ancient and modern notions of personality.[115] Webb sought to justify the doctrine of the Trinity along the lines of philosophical idealism, and it has frequently been pointed out that, in principle, he did not rise above a philosophic necessity for binitarianism. But his emphasis on the continuity of the meaning of *persona* has been used by theologians who have shaped their systems more in

---

114. While Edwin Lewis does not give the notion of dialectical paradox quite the same prominence as Brunner, there remain modes of statement which need clarification in terms of a satisfactory Christology in relation to the divine triunity. It is not so much that Lewis hesitates to affirm a trinitarian view, for we are told that the Trinity is "the inevitable corollary, humanly speaking, and the inevitable postulate, *sub specie aeternitatis*, of the Christian history and experience" (*ibid.*, p. 190). The doctrine of the Trinity, like that of the Virgin Birth and of the Resurrection, is vindicated by Lewis not on the ground of Biblical authority, but as a congruous context for the Gospel Figure. The subjectivistic danger in such an approach is quite evident. Again, we are told that "The Christianity of the New Testament leads directly to the Trinity, or at least to that view of the complexity of the nature of God which the doctrine is designed to express. You may criticize the doctrine *as formulated;* you cannot deny that what is *aimed at* is essential to maintaining the Christian view of life and the world and God" (*ibid.*, pp. 194f.). But how is one to reconcile, with evangelical statements of the divine triunity, such statements as that Jesus "has his roots in God"? (*The Faith We Declare*, pp. 91f.).

115. Clement C. J. Webb, *God and Personality* (Gifford Lectures) (New York: The Macmillan Co., 1919).

accord with the Biblical view of a triune disclose in the divine saving revelation. The writings of Leonard Hodgson,[116] L. S. Thornton,[117] and Charles W. Lowry,[118] disclose a resistance to the Barthian formulation of the divine triunity, and indicate that not alone in the area of Christology but in its statement of the Trinitarian view the Neo-Supernaturalism so vigorously urged by continental theologians will face serious resistance from those who wish to honor the higher elements of Biblical theology.

116. Leonard Hodgson complains that Barth appears to sacrifice an ontological Trinity to modalism "in flat contradiction to the biblical evidence" (*The Doctrine of the Trinity*, p. 229. New York: Charles Scribner's Sons, 1944).

117. L. S. Thornton in *Essays Catholic and Critical*. One of the best statements for the distinction between the Holy Spirit and the Risen Christ, on the basis of New Testament teaching, is found in Thornton's *The Incarnate Lord*.

118. Charles W. Lowry, *The Trinity and Christian Devotion*.

THE PROTESTANT HORIZON

V

The Protestant Horizon

THE outlook for a vigorous Protestantism in the immediate future is proportionate to the extent to which the Christian message is proclaimed with New Testament purity. If Protestantism presses ahead, through the modern denials and reductions, to the unique *gospel* of the Biblical disclosure, it may properly lay claim to that distinguishing spiritual power which has characterized the Hebrew-Christian tradition in centuries past. If Protestantism fails to eliminate from its religious affirmations those tensions and uncertainties which devoid any adequate interpretation of existence of the spiritual vigor, intellectual power, and compelling assurance necessary for an influential voice in the world in which we live, its future is hardly secure.

The question of the future of Protestantism is not the same as that of the future of the church. Concerning the true church, we have the assurance of its living Lord that hell's gates cannot prevail against it. The future of the true church is assured, for its assurance is its living, triumphant and exalted Head. Nor need an uncertainty about the future of Protestantism encourage the exorbitant Roman Catholic claims, that it is the fold of Rome alone which is the true church of Christ. For the church against which the Reformation protested, in view of its dilution of the essential New Testament message, and its political and spiritual corruption, is not a movement to which those who are interested in a purer Christianity are eager to return.

What is at stake is the role of Protestantism in the mid-twentieth century crisis. Whether the downfall of Renaissance ideals spells at the same time a spiritual opportunity for a new and higher cultural expression, just as the downfall of Graeco-Roman civilization meant the rise of medieval culture, and just as the corruption of medieval Romanism meant the opportunity for Reformation in northern Europe, depends upon the purity and power of contemporary Protestantism, in its message and life. And we have been concerned, in this volume, to indicate those inner contradictions which have accrued to Protestantism by virtue of its concessions to non-Biblical philosophies, as a result of which the academic life-stream of Protestantism largely yielded to Liberalism.

A. *Present Problems and Protestantism's Future*

The modern man is heir to a distinctive set of religious and philosophical problems and, as is the case with most inheritances, the bequest involves some disturbing, and often apparently excessive, exactions. Heirship in philosophical no less than in family life requires the establishment of one's legitimate dependency and it is at this point, of insisting on an ideological kinship with the religious philosophy of the recent past, that mid-century Protestant thought involves itself in an internecine conflict.

1. *Liberalism and the Problem of Authority*

The chief problem of mid-century thought is the problem of authority. The problem is posed by a multiple inheritance: the Hebrew-Christian tradition, with its uncompromising claim to special revelation; the Graeco-Roman classic philosophy and modern idealism, with their case for the supernatural divorced from the miraculous; ancient naturalism, Renaissance and contemporary empiricism, and modern scientific positivism, with their reduction of man to complex animality and of all reality to nature.

There can be little doubt that the rationalistic tradition, in severance from the revelational assurance of the Biblical mood, has not waged a wholly successful war on naturalistic metaphysics. The world in which Christianity has existed has been unable to turn back positivism with anything like the success of Plato and Aristotle in the world into which Christianity had not yet come. The weakening of Biblical convictions —in the sense of what is most distinctive about the Hebrew-Christian outlook (creation, providence, special revelation, redemption, regeneration) has meant, in our times, the weakening of the whole case for theism. The plea for an autonomous, rather than a theonomous, solution to the persistent problems of philosophy, has issued in a theism which has had to fight vigorously for any right to the notion of a personal deity, man's essential super-animality, objective moral norms, and the meaningfulness of history—because, if it has appeared to its proponents as a purer philosophy, it has often appeared to their hearers as an emasculated theism the main outlines of which answer equally to naturalistic premises. Having made extensive concessions to Hume, or presuming to answer him largely in the spirit of Kant or Hegel, it is not surprising that the theisms of recent decades have lacked some of the richness and inner content which appeared first only in the revelational tradition and which, as long as rationality is defined so as to exclude revelation, can hardly be retained in a coherent way.

While the philosophic arena has its ardent and able champions of emasculated theisms, a vital theism—which calls men in great numbers to dedicate themselves to a life of missionary or pulpit or teaching service, and which issues in the establishment of pioneer churches and in the reaching of the "lost" with a message of "eternal life"—depends for its vigor not only upon the prior conviction that God is conceived as a rational and moral will, but also on the assurance that He has clearly revealed Himself to be such. And it is at this important threshold—the certainty and nature of divine disclosure—that mid-century theology is now poised.

Can the concept of divine disclosure be formulated in a way that will not sacrifice the modern demand for an inner and spiritual, as against an outer authoritarian view? Does the desire for such a formulation itself assume man to be in a relationship to God which the Biblical view of revelation itself disputes? Is God under such antecedent obligation to humanity in its present state that, if He discloses Himself at all, it must be along the lines of general or universal revelation, so that the notion of special revelation is to be ruled out *a priori?* Can it be shown that in dealing with creatures whom He regards as sinners, a just God would have no dealings with special revelation, beginning with a particular people chosen for that purpose to be a witness to the world? Does the notion of a rational revelation require the surrender of human reason as an instrument, so that the appeal to revelation can be made only by a setting aside of rational coherence?

These are some of the problems involved in the larger problem of authority as the concept of revelation comes in for a greater centrality in mid-century theological thought. The most striking advance, beyond the liberalism of the generation past, is the conviction that the Hebrew-Christian tradition cannot be explained apart from an appeal to *special* revelation. The complication posed by this is apparent. If by *special* revelation is meant simply a higher degree of what is afforded elsewhere universally, then in principle there is no reason why another special revelation may not supersede it. Such an explanation comes in the end to a denial of its eternal significance. But the cost of avoiding such a notion is the affirmation of a special revelation which is unique, is once-for-all, is normative, is final and supreme. The scandal of Christianity from the very outset—and it is a scandal in which it gloried—is its claim that God has done here something which He has done nowhere else.

The problem of authority centers in the query, do we have an authoritative revelation of God and, if so, is it rightly conceived as a word of God in the traditional sense? If it is not rightly conceived in these terms, how could those to whom any actual revelation came have so misunderstood its inner content? If they were wrong about the nature of revelation, can they be trusted as to the actuality of revelation? But is it as apparent as some modern religious philosophers would have us believe that they were wrong in their statement of the nature of revelation? Is not the Hebrew-Christian tradition at one, in the insistence of the records, that God has disclosed Himself intelligibly, so that the Biblical mood proclaimed in clear terms that inner content of that supernatural realm which other men worshipped unknowingly?

Only by the removal of those elements which place the insistence on divine disclosure at the mercy of non-revelational philosophy can the newer insistence of revelation retain its significance. The champions of special revelation who have taken higher ground, as against the Liberalism of a generation ago, halt far short of an adequate view. They have brought back the Biblical terminology of original sin, of substitutionary atonement, of the wrath of God, but they assure us in the next moment that these are not to be taken literally, but have a symbolic, or parabolic, or figurative reality. It is not too far afield to ask how, on such an approach, one can avoid the question whether revelation itself may not be merely a symbolic notion.

Either the concept of special divine revelation means something far more than the mid-century higher Liberal mood— means indeed that God has given a rational revelation which, without setting aside human reason as an instrument, is corrective of the distorted and inadequate views which man has by virtue of his moral revolt, and aims at the full surrender of human life to the divine in a redemptive relationship—or it does not matter so much that it marks an advance upon the older view which looked more in a naturalistic than in a supernaturalistic direction. If God has spoken, everything turns upon what He has said and done, and His activity gains meaning for us by His interpretation of it.

2. *Liberalism and the Problem of Man.*

The problem of man is but that of authority, viewed in another way. It inquires whether human nature and human destiny is such that it requires a divine reference for its source and meaning. What is the human predicament, and what, if any, is the resolution of it?

It is a curious fact that modern philosophers of religion have followed the wearisome pattern of first appropriating an influential non-Biblical view of man, and then struggled to retain as much Biblical significance for him as appeared possible—and that often by generous inconsistencies. Hume's *A Treatise on Human Nature* by the reduction of man's mentality to sense percepts and memory images waved aside the essential difference between human and animal psychic activity. Hume could hardly be appropriated piece-meal, because his basic premise, conditioning all else, is naturalistic. To appropriate Hume piece-meal was already to give the naturalistic camp an advantage from which it could take new ground. If, as Kant himself reports, Hume awakened him from his dogmatic slumbers, it is precisely by Kant's concession to Hume of the limitation of the content of human knowledge to sense experience, that one is encouraged to wonder whether the Koenigsberger was fully awake in the projection of his masterful *Critique*. For man is not by Kant distinguished from the animals on the *knowledge* level; his categories of thought do not extend to the transcendental, and he has no more conceptual awareness of the supernatural than the animals. Kant argued fervently, of course, that the moral nature of man marks him off from sheer animality; the conscience demands the postulate of God. But the human predicament was no longer that of a rational creature in revolt against a holy God, the Creator of man and the source of all meaning. Man's predicament now was his "creatureliness"—a creature who risks the belief that reality is objectively intelligible when he cannot be sure, whose cognitive processes reduce an unordered sense world to order, whose intelligibility struggles, indeed, to champion values and meaning in a natural world of determinism and unintelligibility. It is clear in all of this how much man parades in a heroic role—the savior of meaningfulness, the moral link to divinity, the incarnation of the voice of duty.

But where in all of this is the *sinner* of Biblical narrative, whom we are able to recognize in ourselves in the dark night of soul agony? Where is the creature made in God's image, whose predicament is an abnormal rather than natural dilemma, and who can plead no ultimate necessity of human nature, but must acknowledge his implication in a voluntary moral revolt?

He is gone. In his stead stands man the creature whose predicament is that he is *man,* not that he is sinner; a creature for whom to be man means at the same time to be sinner—in other words, a creature who is conceived as no longer human nor immoral in the Biblical sense. Instead of that primal Adam, whose spiritual rebellion had disastrous repercussions for himself and his posterity, arose Hegel's primal man, whose first sense of guilt was a "happy day" in the moral progress of the universe, and Darwin's "missing link," whose guilty conscience marked the dawn of the ascendency of the spiritual over the animal side of man's being. The pageant of human moral progress stands here in the forefront; man is God's "hope," as it were, for the introduction of values into the created world; heaven delights in, more than it disapproves of him—and man is necessary to God, for the ultimate triumph of value in the universe.

But, again, what has become of the *sinner,* of the man who knows that deity is not truly understood apart from God's distinguishing holiness.[1] It is one of the tragic curiosities of mod-

---

1. D. M. Baillie comments: "Has the typical decent 'modern' man after all a sense of sin? No, I do not think that he has. But I should like to suggest that he has a kind of *moralistic substitute* for the sense of sin, and that this much less wholesome substitute is the chief cause of that perennial *malaise* which surely underlies the superficial complacency of the modern mind. . . . A great many persons in the world today have something like a repressed 'moral inferiority complex' or 'moral-failure complex.' They do not confess their sins to God or man, but they have an uneasy dissatisfaction with themselves and with what they have made of their moral opportunity" (*God Was in Christ,* p. 162f.).

ern thought that, as man denied his essential sinfulness and affirmed his essential godliness, he moved directly in the animalistic direction. From the Biblical viewpoint, this is quite understandable. Man was created for fellowship with God, and stands always in personal relationship with Him. Man is man only in this personal relationship with God, whether in the way of acceptability or in the way of spiritual revolt. Man knows himself in his present state as man—as the distinctive creature that he is—only by an awareness of his personal relationship to God, that is, by an awareness of his sinfulness. Deny that man is sinner, and man destroys the awareness of His relationship with God. Deny that man is sinner, and he makes himself not a god, but an animal. Deny that man is sinner, and it is not man crowned with glory and honor, but man steeped rather in brutality, in egoism, that we behold, despite all efforts at idealism and altruism. Schooled to believe that physico-chemical and biological factors disclose no such reality as sin, and asked as the price of his modernity, to believe that sensatio-inductionism gives an exhaustive interpretation of man, he knows little of a guilt complex—except that it is a psychic abnormality which the psychiatrists assure him he must disregard for a serene and happy life.

But the modern man has come to view the sociological events of the past generation with genuine horror, through interpretative lenses of a new sort. That the sense of guilt has cosmic significance is more readily admitted. That human behavior can hardly be equated with the translation of divine ideals into reality is more evident. That history is hardly to be explained adequately as the transcript of deity is clear to the generation of two world wars.

But can the higher moods, such as Neo-Supernaturalism, which emphasize the transcendental significance of guilt and the relevance of redemptive religion, safeguard their reverence for the view of man as sinner and of God as redeemer, while at the same time beginning with a view of man in which sin is conceived—as in all modern non-Biblical theologies—as an inevitability of man's original or essential nature? Is guilt possible in the Biblical sense, when the offender is no longer the Biblical man, but rather a Darwinian man with Humean or Kantian or Hegelian features?

This is the second key problem of mid-twentieth century Protestantism. Having by the Liberal concessions to evolutionary science lost the Biblical man, it is sensing how difficult it is to retain the Biblical view of man's predicament and of the resolution of that predicament. But it has not yet raised seriously, in the higher Liberal mood, the question of the incompatability of a return in part to the Biblical definitions of man's predicament and its resolution, without a clearer treatment of how these are relevant to a man whose origin can hardly be fitted into the Biblical story, without allowing almost everything else to be accommodated on the same principle. The problem of authority has its implications also for the problem of man.

3. *Liberalism and the Problem of Christ.*

The difficulties inherent in Liberal theology are not relieved, but rather are multiplied, by the new centrality given Jesus Christ.

In a sense, Jesus has always been central, as the supreme example of the Christian way of life, in Liberal theology. This factor, more than any other, has distinguished Liberalism from Humanism, which required no exclusive point of reference for the achievement of an integrated personality.

The movement away from the Bible as spiritually authoritative, to the authority of Jesus Christ, characterizes the most vocal theology of recent decades,[2] and this insistence is retained in Neo-Supernaturalism, along with its insistence on a higher view of Christ.

Once Christ as against the Bible is made the final appeal, it really is not as significant as higher Liberalism thinks, that He

---

2. A. B. Bruce noted: "To the burning question, who or what is the seat of ultimate authority in religion? the most recent apologetic answers, Christ: Christ, not other religious masters, not the individual reason, not the Church, not even the Bible" (*Apologetics*, pp. 492f. New York: Charles Scribner's Sons, 1892).

is, in the higher contemporary statements, given an essentially transcendent rather than strictly humanitarian reference. If the higher view of Christ is not able to sustain itself from declension into lower views, its advantage is but temporary and illusive.

It is true, of course, that a major turning point of Christological inquiry is the ascription of essential deity to Christ, so that His humanity is conceived as superadded to His divinity, rather than the divinity superadded to His humanity. And, from this viewpoint, the insistences of Neo-Supernaturalism that the older Liberalism misconstrued the uniqueness of Christ by discovering it within the highest potentialities of human nature, and that He can be adequately understood only in terms of the entrance of a divine being into the conditions of human existence, assuredly mark a great advance.

But is the advance as secure from modification as may at first appear? What is the relation of this transcendent Christ to the Scriptures, in which we learn of him? Is it possible to sustain His authority over us, apart from the authority of the Scriptures, any more than the case for Biblical authority can be properly stated if it is put in competition with the authority of the Living Word? Is it not the authority of the Living Word through the Written Word over the lives of men that alone offers a self-sustaining view of both Christ and the Scriptures, as well as an adequate spiritual authority?

That Liberalism was unable to arrive at any single picture of the historical Jesus, once the trustworthiness of the Gospel narratives was disputed, is no longer a secret. The competing Jesuses sustained by equally competent authorities, all sharing the Liberal compromise of the Biblical portrait in greater or lesser degree, led finally to the distintegration of Liberalism by the road of Christological chaos.

But now, what is to be gained by the case for a transcendent Jesus which, because of a refusal to break sufficiently with higher criticism, holds that the Gospel picture of Jesus is a

matter of indifference for faith?[3] It may be true that believing
faith exists only in conjunction with response to a divine witness which is not reducible to written words, or to flesh and
blood; the revelation of Christ's deity is an insight which is
supernaturally given. But the divine witness terminates upon
evidence, and in this connection it is all-important just what
the Gospels narrate of God's manifestation in the flesh. The
mood of the evangelists was not that the Gospel records are
a matter of indifference for faith, but that, in the words of one
of them, "These things are written, that ye may believe that
Jesus is the Christ, the Son of God, and that believing ye may
have life in his name" (John 20:31). It might have afforded
considerable surprise to the writer of these words, to have suggested to him that his effort was quite superfluous.

It may be a significant apologetic gain that Biblical theology
shall have recovered the essential deity of Christ. For, if church
history discloses anything, it is that the compromise of the deity
of Christ involves itself in inner contradictions which can hardly
escape, in the long run, a Christological agnosticism.[4] But how
the view of the essential deity of Christ can itself be sustained,
while the trustworthiness of the Biblical records is jeopardized,
or is accepted only where it suits the predilections of the theologian for constructive or destructive purposes, is hardly apparent. The case for the deity of Christ loses its full vigor apart
from a view of the Biblical records which places them beyond
their reduction at this point or that in deference to non-Biblical
assumptions. Why Brunner, for example, should be permitted
to champion the deity of Christ while maintaining a reserve
about His virgin birth, and yet protest that others champion
the sinlessness of Christ while maintaining a reserve about His

---

3. D. M. Baillie protests against disinterest in the historical Jesus on the ground that
the loss of knowledge of Jesus as He actually was in His earthly ministry involves the
loss of any convincing basis for belief in the Incarnation (*op. cit.*, pp 52ff). This
is firm ground. Baillie goes on to argue that the Jesus of history commits us to dogma,
to a Christology of incarnation.

4. See James Orr's treatment of this in *The Christian View of God and the World.*
The denial of the deity of Christ works itself around to the denial of almost everything
else that can be affirmed of Him.

essential deity, is not quite clear. A higher view of Christ which can sustain itself only by taking a wholly indifferent attitude toward the Gospel narratives appears, in the final analysis, a sort of gnosis far different from first century faith which took its rise from the claim which God made upon men in the incarnate Christ.

B. *Recovery of Biblical Theology the Key*

If current Protestantism is in quest of the Biblical message undiluted in its main outlines by competing non-Biblical philosophies, its sure *word* of God remains the Hebrew-Christian Scriptures.

Is it asking too much of a Liberal tradition, which has so long gloried in its championing of open-mindedness in the search for causes, that it shall once again return to the Scriptures in a frank study of the Biblical record on its own assumptions? Is it possible for Liberalism, increasingly aware of unresolved tensions and inherent contradictions in its present formulation, to inquire whether, in its inadequate views of revelation, of the predicament of man, and of Christ, the failure to arrive at a fully Biblical view does not derive from the inheritance of modern philosophical positions which are already compromised in part by the Liberal movement to higher ground? If, indeed, the movement to higher ground can be justified, why may not a fuller movement be permitted? If the higher, traditional view is precluded, do not the modern assumptions which preclude it actually prevent the sub-Biblical views to which higher Liberalism now aspires?

If Biblical theology is to be taken seriously, as Protestantism formulates its constructive thrust in the mid-twentieth century, it will be able to rally contemporary civilization from the dregs of the disintegration of a culture to higher ground only by sounding a message essentially distinct from that which permitted the collapse of modern values and ideals. And it is just possible that, in the full proclamation of that message, it will come to a more critical evaluation of those modern values and ideals themselves, and sense how much the higher meaning of the culture of our times has derived from a Biblical view of God and the world which contemporary humanity had been gradually weaned to dismiss as unreal. The dilemma of Protestantism, no less than any other dilemma of human history, cannot hope for an abiding solution, unless it comes to terms with that word which, while couched in the words of men, has been for prophets and apostles, and for the Christian community, the *word of God.*

APPENDIX

Appendix

NOTE A: *Calvin on the Word and the Spirit*

Calvin's attitude toward the Scriptures is too transparent to make it profitable to invoke him in the interest of any novel view of revelation and inspiration, as Brunner well sees.

". . . Since it is only in the Scriptures that the Lord hath been pleased to preserve his truth in personal remembrance," writes Calvin, "it obtains the same complete credit and authority with believers, when they are satisfied of its divine origin, as if they heard the very words pronounced by God himself" (*The Institutes of the Christian Religion*, I, 1, ch. 7, sec. 1. Philadelphia: Presbyterian Board of Christian Education, 1936).

Nor can one take the phrase "when they are satisfied of its divine origin" in a subjectivistic sense. For while Calvin stresses that the testimony of the Spirit is superior to all testimony of enlightened reason, and that "that alone is true faith which the Spirit of God seals in our hearts" (I, 1, ch. 7, sec. 5), and that "the word itself has not much certainty with us, unless when confirmed by the testimony of the Spirit" (I, 1, ch. 9, sec. 3), yet he leaves no doubt that he is not exalting the Spirit at the expense of the trustworthiness of the written word. For he inquires of those who disparage the written word, "what spirit that is, by whose inspiration they are elevated to such a sublimity, as to dare to despise the doctrine of the Scripture, as puerile and mean. For, if they answer that it is the Spirit of Christ, how ridiculous is such an assurance! for that the apostles of Christ, and other believers in the primitive Church, were illuminated by no other Spirit, I think they will concede. But not one of them learned, from his teaching, to condemn the Divine word; they were rather filled with high reverence for it, as their writings abundantly testify" (I, 1, ch. 9, sec. 1). Again, he shows the inner connection between the written word and the testimony of the Spirit: "For as God alone is the sufficient witness of himself in his own word, so also the word will never gain credit in the hearts of men, till it be confirmed by the internal testimony of the Spirit. It is necessary, therefore, that the same Spirit, who spake by the mouths of the prophets, should penetrate into our hearts, to convince us that they faithfully delivered the oracles which were divinely intrusted to them . . . Let it be considered, then, as an undeniable truth, that they who have been inwardly taught by the Spirit, feel an entire acquiesence in the Scripture, and that it is self-authenticated, carrying with it its own evidence, and ought not to be made the subject of demonstration and arguments from reason; but it obtains the credit which it deserves with us by the testimony of the Spirit. For though it conciliate our reverence by its internal majesty, it never seriously affects us till it is confirmed by the Spirit in our hearts" (I, 1, ch. 7, secs. 4, 5). And again, "For the Lord hath established a kind of mutual connection between the certainty of his word and of his Spirit; so that our minds are filled with a solid reverence for the word, when by the light of the Spirit we are enabled therein to behold the Divine countenance; and, on the other hand, without the least fear of mistake, we gladly receive the Spirit, when we recognize him in his image, that is, in the word . . . he (Paul) does not lead them to empty speculations independent of the word; for he immediately adds, 'despise not prophesyings'; clearly intimating, that the light of the Spirit is extinguished when prophecies fall into contempt . . . A very different sobriety becomes the children of God; who, while they are sensible, that, exclusively of the Spirit of God, they are utterly destitute of the light of truth, yet are not ignorant that the word is the instrument, by which the Lord dispenses to believers the illumination of his Spirit. For they know no other Spirit than who dwelt in and spake by the apostles; by whose oracles they are continually called to the hearing of the word" (I, 1, ch. 9, sec. 3). Once again, "God did not produce his word before men for the sake of sudden display, intending to abolish it the moment the Spirit should arrive; but he employed the same Spirit, by whose agency he had administered the word, to complete his work by the efficacious confirmation of the word" (I, 1, ch. 9, sec. 3).

As to Calvin's attitude toward Biblical inerrancy, it will be sufficient to convey the judgment of Benjamin B. Warfield, in *Calvin and Calvinism* (New York: Oxford Univ. Press., 1931): "Calvin not only asserts the freedom of the Scripture as given by God from all error, but never in his detailed dealing with Scripture allows that such errors exist in it" (p. 65). Warfield thus summarizes Calvin's formula of the word and the Spirit: "Only in the conjunction of the two can an effective revelation be made to the sin-darkened mind of man. The Word supplies the objective factor; the Spirit the subjective factor; and only in the union of the objective and subjective factors is the result accomplished. The whole objective revelation of God lies, thus, in the Word. But the whole subjective capacitating for the reception of this revelation lies in the will of the Spirit. Either, by itself, is wholly ineffective to the result aimed at—the production of knowledge in the human mind. But when they unite, knowledge is not only rendered possible to man: it is rendered certain" (*op.cit.,* pp. 82f).

NOTE B: *Luther on the Word and the Spirit*

This footnote on Luther's formulation of the written word's relationship to the Spirit is appropriately prefaced by a comment on the distinction between the Lutheran and Reformed over-all attitudes toward the means of grace, a distinction to which Warfield draws attention: " 'By His Word and Spirit'—therein is expressed already the fundamental formula of the Calvinistic doctrine of the 'means of grace.' In that doctrine the Spirit is not, with the Lutherans, conceived as in the Word, conveyed and applied wherever the Word goes: nor is the Word, with the mystics, conceived as in the Spirit always essentially present wherever He is present in His power as a Spirit of revelation and truth"(*Calvin and Calvinism,* p. 83).

And yet, whatever Luther's questions may have been about the canonicity of certain books (see the comments, pages 62, 71), he had no question whatever about the authority and inerrancy of the books viewed as canonical. "I have learned to ascribe this honor (namely, infallibility) only to books which are termed canonical," declares Luther, "so that I confidently believe that not one of their authors erred" (M. Reu, *Luther and the Scriptures,* p. 24. Columbus: Wartburg Press, 1944; quoting Luther's *Werke,* p. 56, II, 626). And, whatever differences between the Lutheran and Reformed views over the impartation of the divine in, with and under the human, does not in the least provide encouragement for an emphasis on the testimony of the Spirit which at the same time makes room for errors in the Scripture.

As to the essentiality of the testimony of the Spirit, Luther leaves no doubt, any more than Calvin. "Surely a person can preach the word to me, but no one is able to put it into my heart except God alone, who must speak to the heart, or all is vain; for when he is silent, the Word is not spoken" (Hugh Thomson Kerr, *Compend of Luther's Works,* pp. 11 f., citing from "*Gospel Sermon, Eighth Sunday After Trinity*). It seems clear that this is the spirit in which we are to interpret such statements as: "How can we know what is God's Word, and what is right or wrong? . . . You must determine this matter yourself, for your very life depends upon it. Therefore God must speak to your heart: This is God's Word; otherwise you are undecided" (*op. cit.,* p. 12) ; and, "Every man must believe only because it is God's Word, and because he is convinced in his heart that it is true, although an angel from heaven and all the world preached the contrary" (*op. cit.,* p. 14, citing "That Doctrines of Men Are To Be Rejected").

But the Spirit is not to be disjoined from the written word. "The Holy Spirit is the plainest writer and speaker in heaven and earth, and therefore His words cannot have more than one, and that the very simplest, sense, which we call the literal, ordinary, natural sense" (*op. cit.*, pp. 18f., quoting from "Answer to the Super-christian, Superspiritual, and Superlearned Book of Goat Emser"). Again, "The Holy Ghost is sent by the word into the hearts of the believers . . . without any visible appearance; to wit, when by the hearing of the external word, we receive an inward fervency and light, whereby we are changed and become new creatures; whereby also we receive a new judgment, and new feeling, a new moving. This change, and this judgment is no work of reason, or of the power of man, but is the gift and operation of the Holy Ghost, which cometh with the word preached . . . " (*Luther's Works*, Lenker Ed., vol. VIII, pp. 11ff.).

Moreover, the objective authority is in the written word, apart from which the Spirit conveys no knowledge: "These are the speeches of the Holy Ghost taken from Moses (Gen. 1, God said, 'let there be light') that can be comprehended by no human reason or wisdom, not even the highest. Therefore we should not ask our reason but give the honor to the Holy Ghost that what he says is divine truth, and believe his Word, blind, even putting out the eyes of our reason" (Reu, *op. cit.*, p. 11, . . . quoting Luther's Epistle Sermon, Second Sunday in Advent)

"Not only the words, but also the diction used by the Holy Ghost and the Scripture is divine" (Rue, *op. cit.*, p. 58) . . . " . . . You should so deal with Scripture that you believe that God Himself is speaking" (*ibid.*, p. 92) . . . " . . . We refer all of Scripture to the Holy Ghost" (*ibid.*, p. 63) . . . "God's will is completely contained therein, so that we must constantly go back to them. Nothing should be presented which is not confirmed by the authority of both Testaments and agrees with them. It cannot be otherwise, for the Scriptures are divine; in them God speaks and they are His Word" (*ibid.*, p. 17) . . . "A faithful Christian cannot be forced beyond the Holy Scriptures which are really the divine law unless a new and authentic revelation is added; indeed, we are prohibited by divine law from believing something that is not proved by the divine Writing or clear revelation" (*ibid.*, p. 23) . . . "The saints were subject to error in their writings and to sin in their lives; Scripture cannot err" (*ibid.*, p. 35). Julius Kostlin, in *The Theology of Luther* (translated by Charles E. Gray), tells us that "The Scriptures at large Luther calls directly 'The Spirit's own writing—in contrast with writings of the Fathers' " (II, p. 252. Philadelphia: Lutheran Publication Society.)

Note C: *The New Testament on the Word of God*

It is oversimplification to narrow the identification of the written word with the word of God to the Old Testament prophets. An examination of the New Testament discloses no reluctance to identify the two, to the full extent of the written word.

In passages like 2 Peter 3:5 ("For this they willingly are ignorant of, that by the word of God the heavens were of old, and the earth standing out of the water and in the water") and 3:7 ("But the heavens and the earth, which are now, by the same word are kept in store, reserved unto fire against the day of judgment and perdition of ungodly men") the tension with the written word is not in view.

The opening verses of the apocalypse, especially Rev. 1:1-2 (". . . unto his servant John: Who bare record of the word of God, and of the testimony of Jesus Christ, and of all things that he saw") and 1:9 ("I John . . . was in the isle that is called Patmos, for the word of God, and for the testimony of Jesus Christ") suggest no distinction.

There are indeed passages which point to the Spirit's enlivement of the preached or written word, as I Th. 1:5 ("For our gospel came not unto you in word only, but also in power, and in the Holy Ghost, and in much assurance . . ."); or to the fruitlessness of the preached word when unmixed with faith on the hearer's part, as Heb. 4:2 ("For unto us was the gospel preached, as well as unto them: but the word preached did not profit them, not being mixed with faith in them that heard it"), with which one might compare I Co. 4:20, ("For the kingdom of God is not in word, but in power"); or to its fruitfulness in believing hearts, as 1 Th. 2:13 ("For this cause also thank we God without ceasing, because, when ye received the word of God which ye heard of us, ye received it not as the word of men, but, as it is in truth, the word of God, which effectually worketh also in you that believe"). Other passages stress the vitality of the Word, as Heb. 4:12 ("For the word of God is quick, and powerful, and sharper than any two-edged sword, piercing even to the dividing asunder of soul and spirit, and of the joints and marrow, and is a discerner of the thoughts and intents of the heart") and 1 Pet. 1: 23-25 ("Being born again, not of corruptible seed, but of incorruptible, by the word of God, which liveth and abideth for ever . . . But the word of the Lord endureth for ever. And this is the word which by the gospel is preached unto you").

This last verse, in which the apostle does not hesitate to identify the apostolic preached word as the lifegiving and abiding word of God, forms an apt transition to those many verses in the New Testament, in which one looks in vain for a distinction of content between the word of God and the preached or written word of the Saviour and His apostles, or between the written word and the testimony of the

Spirit. The testimony of the written word on this subject is not justly
treated until one has evaluated verses like the following: Mt. 24:35
("Heaven and earth shall pass away, but my *words* shall not pass
away") ; Mk. 16:20 ("And they went forth, and *preached* every where,
the Lord working with them, and confirming the *word* with signs following") ; Lk. 24:44 ("And he said unto them, These are the *words*
which I spake unto you, while I was yet with you, that all things
must be fulfilled, which were *written* in the law of Moses, and in the
prophets, and in the psalms, concerning me") ; Jn. 2:22 ("When
therefore he was risen from the dead, his disciples remembered that
he had said this unto them; and they believed the *Scripture,* and the
word which Jesus had said") ; Jn. 5:24 ("Verily, verily, I say unto
you, He that heareth my *word,* and believeth on him that sent me,
hath everlasting life, and shall not come into condemnation; but is
passed from death unto life") ; Jn. 8:31 ("Then said Jesus to those
Jews which believed on him, If ye continue in my *word,* then are ye
my disciples indeed") ; Jn. 10:35 ("If he called them gods, *unto whom
the word of God came, and the Scripture cannot be broken*") ; Jn.
12:48 ("He that rejecteth me, and receiveth not *my words,* hath one
that judgeth him; *the word that I have spoken,* the same shall judge
him in the last day") ; Jn. 14:23-24 ("Jesus answered and said unto
him, If a man love me, he will keep my *words*: and my Father will
love him, and we will come unto him, and make our abode with him.
He that loveth me not keepeth not my *sayings*: and *the word which ye
hear is not mine, but the Father's which sent me*") ; Jn. 15:25 ("But
this cometh to pass, that the *word* might be fulfilled *that is written in
their law,* They hated me without a cause") ; Jn. 17:8 ("For I have
given unto them the *words which thou gavest me; and they have received them,* and have known surely that I came out from thee, and
they have believed that thou didst send me") ; Acts 4:4 ("Howbeit
many of them which *heard the word* believed . . .") ; Acts 4:31 (". . .
"And they were all filled with the Holy Ghost, and they *spake the
word of God* with boldness") ; Acts 6:2 (". . . It is not reason that we
should *leave the word of God,* and serve tables") ; Acts 6:7 ("And
the word of God increased . . .") ; Acts 8:25 ("And they, when they
had testified and *preached the word of the Lord,* returned to Jerusalem, and *preached the gospel* in many villages of the Samaritans") ;
Acts 12:24 ("But the word of God grew and multiplied") ; 'Acts
13:46 ("Then Paul and Barnabas waxed bold, and said, It was
necessary that the *word of God* should first have been *spoken* to
you . . .") ; Acts 13:49 ("And the *word* of the Lord was published
throughout all the region") ; Acts 17:11 ("These were more noble
than those in Thessalonica, in that they *received the word* with all
readiness of mind, *and searched the Scriptures daily, whether those
things were so*") ; Acts 19:20 ("So mightily grew the word of God

and prevailed"); Acts 20:35 (". . . Remember the words of the Lord Jesus . . .") ; 2 Co. 2:17 ("For we are not as many, which corrupt the word of God: but as of sincerity, but as of God, in the sight of God speak we in Christ") ; 2 Co. 5:19 (". . . God was in Christ, reconciling the world unto himself, not imputing their trespasses unto them; and hath *committed unto us the word of reconciliation*").

When there is found a single verse which indisputably teaches that the written word is not to be treated as authoritative in some places, then it will be time enough to afford a hearing to those who would "try the written word" rather than "try the spirits," whether they be of God.

NOTE D: *Subjective and Objective Authority*

In *The Infallible Word* (Philadelphia: Presbyterian Guardian Pub. Corp., 1946), a symposium by members of the faculty of Westminster Theological Seminary, John Murray remarks:

"The thesis maintained . . . in our examination of the objective witness is that Scripture is authoritative by reason of the character it possesses as the infallible Word of God and that this divine quality belongs to Scripture because it is the product of God's creative breath through the mode of plenary inspiration by the Holy Spirit. The rejection of such a position has appeared to many to involve no impairment of the divine authority of the Bible, because, even though the infallibility of Scripture has to be abandoned, there still remains the ever abiding and active witness of the Holy Spirit, and so infallible authority is fully conserved in the internal testimony of the Holy Spirit. Scripture is authoritative, it is said, because it is borne home to the man of faith by the internal testimony of the Spirit.

". . . The Barthian view is that Scripture is authoritative because it witnesses to the Word of God; it is the vessel or vehicle of the Word of God to us. In that respect Scripture is said to be unique and in that sense it is called the Word of God. But what makes Scripture really authoritative, on this view, is the ever-recurring act of God, the divine decision, whereby, through the mediacy of Scripture, the witness of Scripture to the Word of God is borne home to us with ruling and compelling power. The Scripture is not authoritative antecedently and objectively. It is only authoritative as here and now, to this man and to no other, in a concrete crisis and confirmation, God reveals himself through the medium of Scripture. Only as there is the ever-recurring human crisis and divine decision does the Bible become the Word of God.

"It is apparent, therefore, that for the Barthian the authority-imparting factor is not Scripture as an existing corpus of truth given by God to man by a process of revelation and inspiration in past history, not the divine quality and character which Scripture inherently posesses, but something else that must be distinguished from any past action and from any resident quality. The issue must not be obscured. Barth does not hold and cannot hold that Scripture possesses binding and ruling authority by reason of what it is objectively, inherently and qualitatively.

". . . it may be argued, the factor arising from past events and activities enters into the whole complex of factors that combine and converge to invest Scripture with that unique character which makes it the fit medium for the ever-recurring act of divine revelation. It is not then an either or but a both and.

". . . it does not eliminate the issue . . . there still remains the fact, that, on Barthian presuppositions, it is not the divine quality inherent in Scripture nor the divine activity by which that quality has been imparted to it that makes Scripture authoritative. That past activity and the resultant quality may constitute the prerequisites for the authority by which it becomes ever and anon invested, but they do not constitute that authority. It is rather the ever-recurring act of God that is the authority-constituting fact. This ever-recurring activity of God may be conceived of as the internal testimony of the Spirit and so it is this testimony that constitutes Scripture authoritative.[1]

". . . It is, however, by 'the inward word of the Holy Spirit bearing witness by and with the Word in our hearts' that we become convinced of that authority. The authority of Scripture is an objective and permanent fact residing in the quality of inspiration; the conviction on our part has to wait for that inward testimony by which the antecedent facts of divinity and authority are borne in upon our minds and consciences. It is to confuse the most important and eloquent of distinctions to represent the former as consisting in the latter" (*op. cit.*, pp. 48ff.).

NOTE E: *W. M. Horton's Christology*

Critical reading will convince the reader of nothing so much as the fact that Horton's Christology has missed the heart of Nicaea and Chalcedon, and finds more affinity with the thought to which those councils opposed themselves. For Horton affirms that "the life of Jesus shades off into mystery, whether we consider its ultimate source or its ultimate outcome" (p. 14). He declares that "the salvation which Jesus has brought us did not absolutely begin with him" (p. 87), but he does not expand this. He remarks that "we find Christ in the Church, and not only in Jesus" (p. 20). Jewish literature had "recognized in God's creative, prophetic Word of Wisdom an eternal

---

1. Cf. Karl Barth, *Die Kirchliche Dogmatik, Die Lehre vom Wort Gottes,* Erster Halbband (Munchen, 1932), pp. 189ff. English Translation (Edinburgh, 1936), pp. 207ff.

'Son of God' i.e., a power coming forth from God into the world), but . . . Paul and John saw God's eternal Word more evidently present in the Man Jesus . . ." (pp. 130f). And he insists that "it is not necessary to despoil all peoples of their characteristic virtues and values, and load those excellencies upon the figure of Jesus; nor is it necessary to deny that outside of him we have real access to God by many avenues. No more necessary than this: that his human character should be such as to make it conceivable that the central line in God's redemptive process should pass through such a one as he" (pp. 22f).

While Horton is prepared to say only to Jesus, 'I am your man. I belong to you, body and soul,' yet "that is not to say that I would never argue with him about his teachings, or what purport to be his teachings. It would be idolatrous for me to render absolute allegiance to anything in him that is not eternally true; and there is much in his teachings that is temporal and transient. What claims me is not just his teachings, but . . . his central *meaning* or *intention*, his central self, which is one with the Will of God and makes the Will of God concretely real for me" (pp. 55f). "To us and our children's children, we are confident, Jesus will always remain the Prophet of Prophets, God's own Wisdom made powerfully manifest in a human life" (p.60). Horton declares that God came "in humble human guise into the world He had created, as the 'Suffering and Sacrificial God' who 'shares the bitter destiny of the world and of man' in order to win them back to unity with himself." But immediately he adds that "Such an act on the part of God demands as its counterpart the freely surrendered will of a human being. Jesus was such a human being as God needed to find free entrance into humanity" (p.108). "Through a willing and prepared human being, chosen from a chosen people, God enters into humanity while still remaining above humanity. In Jesus of Nazareth, God's creative, prophetic, redemptive Word 'was made flesh and dwelt among us, and we beheld His glory, glory as of the only begotten of the Father, full of grace and truth." (p. 129).

Horton finds ambiguities in the Scriptural teaching concerning the person of Christ. The Pauline Christology (Phil. 2:5-11, Col. 1:13-20) "is not unambiguously clear whether the celestial being . . . was only the 'first-born of every creature' (as Arius long afterward insisted) or 'of one substance with the Father' (as Athanasius and the Council of Nicaea declared). The Gospel of John's statement of the Incarnation . . . makes clear that the Word which became flesh in Jesus . . . essentially '*was* God' pp. 131f). But aside from the prologue, remarks Horton, the Fourth Gospel "represents the Man Jesus as wearing and exercising the divine attributes of omniscience and omnipotence that were his before his birth," which prompts Horton's declaration that in that case "the human limitations that he wore were a mere garb; in short, his life was not a genuine *incarnation* at all, in spite of what the prologue says, but only a *theophany* . . ." (p. 132). Horton then declares that he stands with Knox in holding that whenever the complete humanity of Jesus has been qualified, Christian thought has receded from its high-water mark. "The only fully Christian idea of the Incarnation is that in Jesus *God Himself* (as the prologue to the Fourth Gospel says) *became fully human remaining 'God over all, blessed forever.'* " (p. 133). "In and through a true and willing human servant, God accomplished His eternal design and called His children back into fellowship with Himself." (p. 137). "In its practical meaning, it (the issue of the relationship of the two natures in Christ) is essentially the issue as to *the kind of relationship between God and man which obtains in the new redeemed SOCIETY OF THE SONS of God. . .*" (p. 137). "The relationship between God and man in him is the type and pattern of what it ought to be and may be in us. The question is whether our communion with God is definable in terms of ethical *oneness* with God's will, or whether it involves a more intimate and *mystical* oneness, that transforms our very *being*. What was at stake in this great ancient controversy was something exceedingly practical; the nature of the Christian life" (p. 137). "The answer surely is that the Christian life at its best is always *both ethical and mystical;* both *obedience to God's commands* and *trust in His redeeming grace*" (p. 138)

"Of course, the Church has never completely identified the new divine-humanity which she finds in her own life with the divine-humanity of her Lord and Head. Concerning him, the classic is that he was tempted in all points in like manner as we are, yet without sin." It is clear that his Sonship is meant to be the type and pattern of our sonship, and the ardent expectation of the primitive Church was that through union with him we might become absolutely sinless; but the sober judgment of the centuries has been that this does not follow." (p. 138). "The union of God and man which is embryonic in them (the redeemed) is full-fledged in him." (p. 139).

"New Testament criticism has done a great service in making it perfectly clear that Jesus' psychology as well as his physiology was fully human. In countless ways he shared the imperfect knowledge of his time; and he faced the mystery of the future with the same lack of detailed knowledge which makes us feel the solemnity of each New Year's Day" (p. 139). Horton concurs with Pittenger (*Christ and Christian Faith*, p. 19) in Bishop Gore's declaration that the limitation of Jesus' human knowledge is definitely clinched by His "mistaken acceptance of the Davidic authorship of Psalm 110."

Horton writes of Jesus as "the One who became the Living Christ." (p. 142). He writes that Jesus "survived his Crucifixion" and became "by his Spirit, a living Presence at the heart of the Church." There is no mention of bodily resurrection. That Horton has no use for the essential deity and eternality of Christ, and hence for the doctrine of the Trinity, is seen in his statement that "It is not necessary to distinguish too sharply between the idea of the Living Christ and the idea of the Holy Spirit." (p. 143). "Whether we describe this inward Presence of God in the Church as the Holy Spirit, or as the Living Christ, it proceeds from Jesus, and is an extension of his life." (p. 144). He tells us that it is "Jesuolatry" to load every conceivable divine attribute upon his human shoulders. (p. 144).

INDEX

Index of Subjects

Index of Persons